Michael Anthony

V is for Vegetables

Michael Anthony

WITH DOROTHY KALINS

V is for Vegetables

INSPIRED RECIPES & TECHNIQUES FOR HOME COOKS FROM ARTICHOKES TO ZUCCHINI

PHOTOGRAPHS BY MAURA McEVOY
DESIGN BY DON MORRIS DESIGN

(L)(B)

LITTLE, BROWN AND COMPANY
New York Boston London

ALSO BY MICHAEL ANTHONY

The Gramercy Tavern Cookbook

Little, Brown and Company
Hachette Book Group
1290 Avenue of the Americas, New York, NY 10104
littlebrown.com

First Edition: October 2015

Little, Brown and Company is a division of Hachette Book Group, Inc.
The Little, Brown name and logo are trademarks of Hachette Book Group, Inc.

The publisher is not responsible for websites (or their content) that are not owned by the publisher.

The Hachette Speakers Bureau provides a wide range of authors for speaking events. To find out more, go to hachettespeakersbureau.com or call (866) 376-6591.

Produced by **Dorothy Kalins Ink**

Photographs by **Maura McEvoy**

Design by **Don Morris Design**

Recipe editor, **Kathleen Brennan**

Endpapers and line drawings by **Mindy Dubin**

Archival color lithographs, A to Z, sourced, page 356

ISBN 978-0-316-37335-7
LCCN 2015931409

10 9 8 7 6 5 4 3 2 1

IMAGO

Printed in China

"This ABC is the way I wrote it. There is room between its lines, and even its words, for each man to write his own gastronomical beliefs, call forth his own remembered feastings, and taste once more upon his mind's tongue the wine and the clear rock-water of cups uncountable." –M.F.K. Fisher, *An Alphabet for Gourmets*, 1949

DEDICATION

This book is dedicated to cooks of all kinds who incessantly search to create vibrant, healthy, and memorable meals every day.

Contents

INTRODUCTION 1

A

ARTICHOKES 10
Prepping Globe Artichokes 11
Stuffing Artichokes 13
Whole Stuffed Baked Artichokes 14
Lemon Vinaigrette 14
Prepping Artichoke Hearts 16
Artichoke Hearts with
Crab & Tomato Sauce 17
Prepping Baby Artichokes 18
Braised Baby Artichokes with
Oyster Mushrooms 18

ASPARAGUS 20
Asparagus with
Preserved Ginger Relish 21
Pan-Roasted Asparagus with
Sunny-Side-Up Eggs 22
Salad of Shaved Asparagus &
Beluga Lentils 25
Blanching 25

AVOCADO 26
Avocado Yogurt with Lime Mash 26
Cutting an Avocado 27
Avocado & Blood Orange Salad
with Quinoa 28
Segmenting Citrus 28

B

BEANS 32
String Beans with Sesame Sauce 33
Cranberry Beans with Smoky Bacon &
Collards 34

Black Beans with
Tomatoes & Mussels 36
Sweating It 36

BEETS 38
Roasting Beets 39
Roasted Beets with
Pickled Eggs & Mustard Seeds 40
Roasted Beet with Rose Ricotta 41
Michael's Borscht 42
Beet Tartare 45

BOK CHOY 46
Stir-Fried Bok Choy 46

BROCCOLI 48
Broccoli Bruschetta 49
Bribery Pasta 50
Broccoli Stems 50

BRUSSELS SPROUTS 52
Roasted Brussels Sprouts
with Maple Syrup 53
Using Brussels Sprout Leaves 53

C

CABBAGE 56
Cabbage Cooked Quickly 56
Goldie's Cole Slaw 58
Warm Red Cabbage Salad
with Sweet Potatoes 60
Kimchi-Style Fermented
Cabbage 61
Cabbage & Pork Dumplings with
Dipping Sauce 63

CARROTS 64
Setting Up a Workstation 65
Basic Pickling Recipe 66
Pickled Baby Carrots 66
Carrot Juice Cocktail 66
Simple Syrup 66
Carrot Soup with Coconut Milk 69

Shaving Carrot Ribbons 69
Roasted Carrots with Spiced Nuts (or
King Tut's Carrots) 70
Carrots & Farro 72

CAULIFLOWER 73
Cauliflower Curry in a Bowl 74
Caramelized Cauliflower with
Peppers & Onions 76
Chowchow Relish 77

CELERY 78
Two-Celery Salad 78
Chicken Soup with Celery & Dill 80

CELERY ROOT 82
Celery Root & Apple Puree 83
Celery Root & Chestnut Soup 84
Grapeseed Oil 84

CHICKPEAS 86
Chickpea Puree 86

COLLARD GREENS 88
Collard Greens Frittata 88

CORN 90
Cooking with Water 92
Corn Stock 92
Chilled Corn Soup with
Coconut Milk 93
Corn on the Cob with Basil 95
Sweet Corn, Tomato &
Cranberry Bean Salad 96
Corn Pancakes 97

CUCUMBERS 98
Chilled Cucumber Soup 98
Japanese-Style Salt-Cured
Cucumbers 100
Cucumber-Yogurt Sauce 101

D

DAIKON 104
Classic Grated Daikon
on Pan-Roasted Fish 104

Daikon Kinpira 107
Cutting Matchsticks 108
Making Dashi 109

E

EGGPLANT 112
Caponata 113
Grilled Eggplant with Miso Glaze 114
Roasted Japanese Eggplant 114
Gramma Anthony's
Pickled Eggplant 116
Baked Eggplant Casserole 119

ESCAROLE 120
Escarole Salad with
Fennel & Pears 120

F

FAVA BEANS 124
Favas with Sea Salt & Olive Oil 124
Fava Bean Salad 125

FENNEL 126
Braised Fennel with Saffron &
Orange Juice 126
Fennel Tabbouleh 128

G

GARLIC 132
Garlic Confit 133
Mincing Garlic 133
Garlic Green & Black 134
Omelet of Garlic Scapes 134

GINGER 136
Ginger Tea 136
Pickled Ginger 137
Peeling Ginger 137

H

HERBS 140
Parsley with
Brown Butter Croutons 140
Using Croutons 141
All-Herb Salad with Couscous 143
Preserving Lemons 143
Chimichurri on Steak 144
Chive Matzoh Brei 147
Blanching Herbs 147

HORSERADISH 148
Root Vegetable Stew in
Horseradish Beef Broth 148
Horseradish Compound Butter with
Roasted Sweet Potatoes 150

I

ICEBERG LETTUCE 154
Grilled Iceberg Lettuce with
Marinated Tomatoes 154
Lemon Zest Confit 155

J

JERUSALEM ARTICHOKES 158
Sliced Raw Jerusalem
Artichoke Salad 158

Roasted Jerusalem Artichokes &
Brussels Sprout Leaves 161
Prepping Jerusalem Artichokes 161
Jerusalem Artichoke Chowder
with Monkfish 162

K

KALE 166
Kale Salad with Kale Chips &
Soy Dressing 166
Kale Soup with Potatoes & Leeks 169
Kale Cooked Quickly 169

KOHLRABI 170
Crunchy Salad of Kohlrabi & Toasted
Walnuts 170
Unlocking Kohlrabi 172
Roasted Quartered Kohlrabi 173

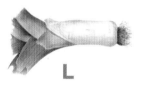

L

LEEKS 176
Braised Leeks & Yellow Lentils with
Anchovy Dressing 176
Roasted Whole Leeks with
Tangerine Vinaigrette 179
Cutting & Washing Leeks 179
Leek Quiche 180
Tart Dough 182

M

MUSHROOMS 186
Sautéed Mushrooms on Flatbread with
Braised Greens 186
Mushroom Crepes 188

Contents

Mushroom Broth 191

Mushroom Hot Pot with
Beef & Daikon 192

N

NETTLES 196
Nettle Puree 196
Nettle Custard 197
Handling Nettles 197

NUTS 198
Toasted & Spiced Almonds 198
Peel & Eat Chestnuts 199
Walnut Mashed Potatoes 200

O

OKRA 204
Pickled Okra 204
Cornmeal-Fried Okra 205
Okra Stew with Tomatoes 207

ONIONS 208
Onion Puree 208
Slicing Onions 209
Onion & Bacon Tart 211
Caramelizing Onions 211
A Real Onion Soup 212
Pickled Onions & Lentil Salad 215
Shrimp & Cipollini Stew
with Onion Puree 216
Shrimp Stock 216

P

PARSNIPS 220
Parsnip Chips 220
Parsnip & Kale Gratin 223
Roasted Parsnips with
Hazelnut Pesto 224

PEAS 226
Bowl of Peas, Rice &
Pickled Onions 227
Peeling Sugar Snaps 228
Sugar Snap Salad with Quinoa 228
Warm Wilted Pea Shoots 230
Fresh Peas with Braised Morels 231
Warm Salad of Snow Peas,
Cherries & Baby Chard 232

PEPPERS 234
Making Hot Pepper Oil 235
Drying Seasoning Peppers 236
Pickled Peppers 236
Pepper Stew 237
Stuffed Peppers with
Chorizo & Wild Rice 239

POTATOES 240
Pan-Roasted Fingerlings 241
Potato Pancake 242
Potato & Cheese Croquettes 245
Granmaw Hartle's
Potato Dumplings 246
My Potato Salad 248

Q

QUINCE 252
Quince Mostarda 252

R

RADISHES 256
Salted Radish Salad with
Black Bass 257
Slicing Radishes 258
Braised Radishes with
Honey & Black Pepper 260

RAMPS 262
Pickled Ramps 263
Ramps & Spaghetti 264

RHUBARB 265
Sweet & Sour Rhubarb Sauce 266

RUTABAGA 268
Prepping Rutabaga 268
Rutabaga Gratin 269

S

SALSIFY 272
Glazed Salsify & Carrots 272

SCALLIONS 274
Scallion Pancakes 274
Steamed Clams with
Scallion & Tarragon Sauce 277

SHALLOTS 278
Sweet & Sour Shallots 278
Frying Oysters 279

SPINACH 280

Washing Greens 281

Spinach & Garlic Puree
with Scallops 282

Garlic Puree 282

Spinach Egg Crepes 284

SWISS CHARD 286

Chard Shakshouka 286

Sautéed Chard Arancini 289

T

TATSOI 292

Sautéed Tatsoi with
Matchstick Radishes 292

TOMATILLO 294

Roasted Tomatillo &
Pepper Salsa 294

TOMATOES 296

Tomato Water Cocktail 297

Tomato Sashimi 299

Oven-Dried Plum Tomatoes 299

My Tomato Sauce 300

*From Barely Touched to
Completely Transformed* 302

Tomato & Roasted Peach Salad 303

Tomato & Shrimp Pasta 304

TURNIPS 306

Turnip & Squash Stew
with Chicken 306

Glazed Hakurei Turnips with
Turnip & Mustard Greens 309

Japanese Fermented Turnips 310

U

UPLAND CRESS 314

Upland Cress Salad
with Carrot Dressing 314

Cooked Carrot Dressing 315

V

VIDALIA ONIONS 318

Charred Vidalia Onions with
Peas & Beans 318

W

WATERMELON
RADISH 322

Watermelon Radish Salad with
Ginger Vinaigrette 322

WINTER SQUASH 324

Winter Squash Stuffing 325

Cutting Winter Squash 325

Roasting Squash with Wild Rice 326

Roasted Spaghetti Squash
with Country Ham 329

Lacy Winter Squash Tempura 330

X

EXTRA-VIRGIN
OLIVE OIL 334

Olive Oil–Poached Squid 334

Olive Oil–Braised Vegetables 336

Y

YAMS 340

Baked Sweet Potato Fries 340

Z

ZUCCHINI 344

Warm Zucchini Salad 345

Ratatouille 347

Sautéed Summer Squash with
Fried Zucchini Blossoms 348

Stuffed Zucchini Blossoms
with Sun Gold Tomato Sauce 350

Sun Gold Tomato Sauce 351

Open "Ravioli" of Summer Squash 352

ACKNOWLEDGMENTS
354

INDEX 358

Introduction

ON COOKING VEGETABLES

THERE ARE PLENTY OF OTHER PLACES TO GO for botanical classification of vegetables and for information about how to grow them. This is a book about cooking. My cooking. And here's what I believe: I celebrate local foods grown close to home; I like to share the backstory of the foods I cook, the people who grew them, where they're grown, and how they got to our kitchens. I cook with a particular point of view. Nature leads, but a cook's job is to create delicious flavors and healthy meals. That's what my recipes are all about.

When you look at a basket of just-picked, garden-fresh vegetables, it's sometimes hard to imagine dinner. You may look at a piglet and see bacon, but it's less natural to envision how fresh vegetables can become a meal, or many meals. I want you to look at that market basket and see crispy composed salads, fresh herb sauces, satisfying warm gratins, thick pureed soups, sautéed greens over a bowl of grains. Yet this book is emphatically not a call to vegetarianism. I do not cook that way, I do not eat that way, and I do not want to suggest that you should. Rather, this book is a celebration of vegetables in their greatest glory. Often that glory is not immediately obvious; you need a bit of technique, a little knowledge, and a whole lot of courageous exploration.

EATING WELL, LIVING WELL

WHAT'S REALLY IMPORTANT TO ME is this new, exciting, and sensible way of eating that puts vegetables in the spotlight and consciously reconsiders the role that proteins play. I do not want to give up fish or meat, and you'll find recipes that include them here. To have a healthy farm, you need a healthy cycle of elements that includes livestock. It is only in meat-centric America that we think loving vegetables inevitably means hating meat. But I like eating well, I like living well, and I do not believe in a cuisine of deprivation. I believe in finding a better balance. For me, cooking with vegetables is not a political act; it's an enlightened way of thinking.

I support farmers who are committed to rebuilding their soil and who think holistically about pest management but somehow cannot manage the long process necessary to become certified organic. Generally, in the argument of local vs. organic, I look for what's growing close to where I'm cooking, rather than what's simply labeled organic.

This book is the next step in the evolution of American food. These recipes are directional. They suggest a more healthy and luxurious way of eating: intense vegetable purees stirred into flavorful broths, the bright surprise of a carrot pickle, how roasting brings out the delicious caramelization of root vegetables, the fun of a dish where shaved raw vegetables appear with their cooked version. I'm thrilled to help you master ways to make veggies shine. I really want you to feel excited about cooking vegetables; I want to share techniques so you can translate that excitement into finished dishes of your own.

NAME IT & TAME IT

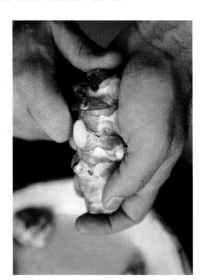

FIRST, IDENTIFY that vegetable. Look it up in a book (such as this one!). Is it a turnip or a radish, kale or Swiss chard? Our photographs will help you with that. Then, I'll help you figure out what to do with it: how to clean it and peel it and chop it. Next, I'll help you make it taste wonderful. I promise this book won't suggest you slip the skin off each English pea. Being a cook is a discipline though. It's like playing music. It doesn't have to be difficult; you just have to want to hear it.

People in the farmers' market ask me all the time, "How do I know which vegetable is good?" I answer, "You can't make a mistake!" It's pretty simple: Just

VEGETABLES A TO Z

THIS BOOK IS ABOUT VEGETABLES in the most generous sense; that is, neither animal nor mineral. My choices are personal, sometimes fanciful. Spend a moment leafing through my alphabet and you'll discover the idiosyncrasies. Yes, I know that avocados, tomatoes, nuts, and mushrooms are not vegetables in the strict botanical sense. But

what matters more is how delicious and healthy they are and the distinctive flavors they bring to our meals. Yes, quince is a fruit, but I do love to cook with it in savory dishes, and, well, we needed a Q. U for "upland cress"? V for "Vidalia onion"? Sure! Just turn to those pages for my rationale. If you think X for "extra-virgin olive oil" is a stretch, that's exactly what this book is for—to stretch our imaginations, to stimulate fresh ideas for exciting eating. I've been holding forth on why I only cook with extra-virgin olive oil since we began developing recipes, but it was only when our editor suggested we use X for that spot that I realized it gave me an eXcuse (sorry) to explain my conviction that pure extra-virgin olive oil is the *only* olive oil to use. And Y reveals why all yams sold in this country happen to be sweet potatoes.

get yourself to the market and you'll be fine. Trust your senses, and follow your hunger. You've got to taste it to know it. There's nothing wrong with asking a neighbor, or the farmer. Even if you are not sure what it is (a luscious head of tatsoi, a gnarly Jerusalem artichoke, left) or what to do with it, be unafraid.

I started a program at a local elementary school where I've experienced the wonder of handing a first-grader a whole head of cauliflower.

When they get their hands on it, they see cauliflower as important and new, something magnificent, a wonderful sculpture, a piece of art. That thing could be a Martian's brain! I want to convey their sense of innocence and discovery. Without being pretentious about it, I want you to see vegetables as important. You do not have to be a food historian or a botanist or a health food nut to appreciate the magic of vegetables. All you have to be is hungry!

VEGETABLES UNZIPPED

PEOPLE MISTAKENLY ASSUME chefs have special powers: For us, garlic automatically falls into cloves, then peels itself; onions wriggle out of their skins, willingly submit to a chef's knife, almost dice themselves. Carrots, parsnips, celery root—these vegetables do not need to be peeled by professionals. But I assure you, chefs do the same things home cooks do in the kitchen. (Okay, we do have prep cooks, but not at home!) What's different is that we do not look for a way to get out of it or around it. I guess I've adopted an almost Zen-like focus, a reverence for the lemon I'm about to reduce into segments, an appreciation for the quirkiness of a Jerusalem artichoke. And a deep acceptance of what must be done to unlock the secrets of each vegetable. We may peel a bit faster, cut a bit straighter, but we still have to do it. Just accept that prepping is a necessity and give yourself over to it. There's magic in the monotony of the repeated task.

Sharp knives and handheld mandolines open a beautiful world of preparing vegetables. But unlike the brigades in a classic French kitchen, I am not obsessed with knife skills, reducing cooking to so many piles of geometrically cut bits: haché, brunoise, or julienne. That defeats the purpose of anchoring you to the natural imperfection of the vegetable itself. Just as halving a single carrot lengthwise can draw attention to its unique shape, there are simple gestures a cook can use to unlock the potential of every vegetable. It's about looking at every part of a plant with fresh eyes, seeing its edible possibilities, like broccoli stems and leaves. Discovering not just something that you *can* eat, but something you *want* to eat.

All good cooking shares an ancient ideal—a combination of thrift and innovation—that is essential to me. I believe we're obliged to use every last bit of these plants that someone has put so much effort into growing from tiny seeds; these plants that can nourish us and bring us such pleasure. I've decided to spend my life focusing on making those things taste good. This book is about hoping you'll do the same.

A SENSE OF PLACE

ONE OF THE THRILLS about cooking vegetables is that each of those bright, colorful ingredients can say something distinctive about the flavor of the *place* where we're cooking them. Incorporating a sense of place in your cooking connects you with the people, the culture, the nature of where you are. It's the polar opposite of the homogenized world we live in, where most of the time you could be, well, anywhere, like in some science fiction movie, or a strip mall in Any City, U.S.A.

Our American dream of consolidating a huge nation has made us yearn for the regional, the specific, the almost-lost flavors of where we live. There are still places in this country known for their distinctive flavors, and those are the ones I want to preserve. I'm thrilled when I cook something from here, wherever I am; it makes the meal special.

At home, whatever fresh vegetables arrive in my weekly CSA box from Norwich Meadows Farm in central New York are just the things I want to cook that week. At my parents' house in Ohio, I'm hungry for fresh asparagus from the farm next door. If I were on Michigan's Upper Peninsula, I'd be going crazy for cherries; and in Charleston, I'd be sure to get my hands on Carolina Gold rice. I am far more interested in telling a local story than in importing ingredients from anywhere. For me it's a living truth, overwhelmingly exciting. You might get to the point where you grow all your own food, or you may just want to cook a simple dinner for friends. However you get there from here, it's amazing. Celebrate that.

A MEAL IN A BOWL

I OFTEN THINK THAT if we reimagined the all-American meal in a bowl instead of on a plate, we'd create meals differently than we do now. A bowl demands another way of eating. You can't cut a big steak in a bowl. Instead, a bowl of rice or grains can become the stage for so many delicious vegetables: stews of beans, piles of greens, roasted roots, sparked by zingy pickles and relishes. How satisfying! For the way I like to eat, vegetables often work better in bowls. Many recipes in this book provide imaginative ideas for eating that way.

TEAM VEGGIE

OUR UNIQUE PROCESS of producing *V is for Vegetables* meant that our little editorial team of producer, photographer, recipe editor, and sous chef shopped for, cooked, tasted, tested, photographed, wrote, and critiqued each recipe—all in real time. I cooked every dish in a home kitchen, not in a photography studio. And although I had to put up with no small amount of back talk from the peanut gallery, it gave our process a bit of a reality check: If one of us found a component of a recipe too fussy, or an ingredient unrealistic for the home cook, I really listened, and that made our working together fun. Our photo shoots became a happy,

real-world laboratory where we used the very process of producing recipes to test new ideas as we tasted our way through the book. Sometimes I reinterpreted tried-and-true classics; other times I invented exciting ways to discover and enjoy each vegetable.

A RECIPE IS A SKETCH, NOT A BLUEPRINT

IF A RECIPE CALLS FOR something green, find
something green. If you have no kale for that Kale
Soup with Potatoes & Leeks (page 169), use
zucchini, or collards, or Swiss chard. You want to
make a salad? Use mustard or young radish tops;
almost any combination of leafy greens will work.
Turnip & Squash Stew with Chicken (page 306)
will be great with any root vegetable. This is the
time to discover wonderful artisanal ingredients
like oil-cured anchovies (page 14); a pristine,
sustainable seafood like squid; pickled ginger
(page 137); or yellow lentils (page 176), which
can completely change a dish. Sweet potatoes
with red cabbage? Imagine! Use your intuition.
Experiments can lead to happy solutions. As cooks
we are part foragers and part magicians. But this
book doesn't celebrate those rare varieties that
only grow deep in the forest or on the top of some
mountain, hard to find, impossible to get your
hands on. Garden variety is thrilling to me.

One of the challenges in writing this book was
to find a way into the home cook's imagination;
to express the sincere appreciation that comes from tasting complex flavors, being
seduced by color and texture, falling in love with vegetables. Because in our lifetimes,
many of us have rarely known the vegetable as a star; it can be difficult to imagine menus
where that is the case. I may improvise a recipe, but I'm not just making it up out of the
blue. My recipes are not tricky or unapproachable; I've developed them to share, not to
show off. I lean on my love of the vegetable first, then on my culinary foundation. And
always, it is about the best way to make that thing taste good. Sometimes I follow rules;
sometimes I break them. Knowing when to do which is what makes a cook. I'm hoping to
pass that knowledge along to you.

"*The artichoke above all is the vegetable expression*

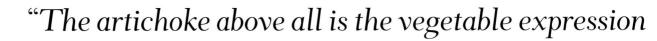

Artichokes
10

Asparagus
20

Avocado
26

of civilized living." — JANE GRIGSON, *Jane Grigson's Vegetable Book*, 1978

A

ARTICHOKES

ARTICHOKES, FOR ME, were always elusive. Kind of dangerous. Really beautiful. But I didn't understand what people loved about eating a prickly thistle; I never got their seductive quality. Even though as a chef I had dutifully learned how to "turn" artichokes, it took spending an Easter with my daughters in Rome (where artichokes are prized and prepared with great style) to truly become enamored of this vegetable. Artichokes—fried whole *(alla giudia),* braised with fava beans in spring *vignarola,* sliced raw with anchovies and lots of lemon, and baked on pizza—were a real discovery for me as an eater. As I travelled to other places where artichokes are grown and appreciated, I began to experience the nostalgia around the tradition of eating them, and I really fell in love. I felt inspired to dream about these delicious ways of preparing them.

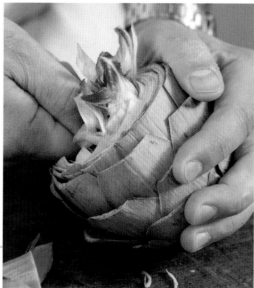

Prepping Globe Artichokes

This book is full of inspiration, of course, but I also want to make sure to share with you the techniques you need to unlock these delicious vegetables. Each artichoke recipe asks for a different approach—not difficult, different! To stuff a big globe artichoke, there's some trimming to do, plus removing the choke. Getting to the prized artichoke hearts take some serious cutting.

Stuffing Artichokes

Once the artichokes are trimmed and hollowed out with a spoon, use a paring knife to flatten the bottoms so they'll sit upright in a deep baking dish. Season the hollowed-out artichokes with salt, pepper, butter, olive oil, and lemon juice. Combine the stuffing ingredients—clockwise from top, coppa or pancetta, bread crumbs, oregano, garlic, capers, anchovies, black and green olives—in a small bowl and mix well. Spoon the stuffing into each prepared artichoke, filling generously.

WHOLE STUFFED BAKED ARTICHOKES
SERVES 4

THIS IS MY INTERPRETATION of an iconic
Italian-American classic. All the great flavors
of that irresistible culture are baked into
the hollowed-out vegetable itself. Olives,
anchovies, capers, coppa, oregano—the stuffing
shares its bold, nostalgic flavors with the soft
artichoke heart as it bakes. As you pull apart
the leaves, the aromatic seasonings penetrate
the entire artichoke. I like to spoon Lemon
Vinaigrette over the artichokes.

½ cup diced coppa or pancetta
¼ cup chopped pitted green olives
¼ cup chopped pitted black olives
2 anchovy fillets, chopped
1 clove garlic, minced
2 tablespoons fresh lemon juice
1 tablespoon chopped fresh flat-leaf parsley
1 tablespoon capers, chopped
1 teaspoon dried oregano
½ teaspoon crushed red pepper flakes
3 tablespoons bread crumbs
2 tablespoons butter
4 tablespoons olive oil
    Salt and pepper
4 large artichokes, trimmed, chokes removed
    (page 16), and submerged in lemon water
½ cup dry white wine

Preheat the oven to 375°F. Combine the coppa or
pancetta, green and black olives, anchovies, garlic,
lemon juice, parsley, capers, oregano, red pepper
flakes, 1 tablespoon of the bread crumbs, butter,
2 tablespoons of the oil, salt, and pepper in a
large bowl.

Gently pack about one-quarter of the mixture into
the cavity of each artichoke. Put the stuffed
artichokes in a baking dish. Sprinkle with the
remaining 2 tablespoons bread crumbs, followed by
the remaining 2 tablespoons oil. Pour the wine into
the baking dish, cover with aluminum foil, and bake
until the artichokes are tender, about 45 minutes.
Remove the foil and bake until the bread crumbs are
deep brown, about 10 minutes more.

LEMON VINAIGRETTE
MAKES ABOUT ¾ CUP

IN A SMALL BOWL, mix 1 tablespoon Dijon mustard
with 2 tablespoons fresh lemon juice and a dash
of salt and pepper. Slowly whisk in ½ cup olive oil.
Serve on the side for dipping.

Prepping Artichoke Hearts

To "turn" an artichoke means to hold it upside down in one hand and trim away the green outer leaves with a sharp knife. Sculpt the bottoms into a rounded shape, keeping as much of the delicious hearts as you can. Dip the hearts in lemon water so they don't turn brown. Use a spoon to scrape out the chokes. Submerge the artichokes in water in a large saucepan to cook evenly. Parchment paper cut into a circle can help this.

ARTICHOKE HEARTS WITH CRAB & TOMATO SAUCE

SERVES 6

IF YOU'RE GOING TO MAKE A DIP, I say make one that's over the top! This combination brings together some of the richest, most decadent American flavors. I leave the artichokes in chunks so you can really savor their texture with the crab.

- 6 artichoke hearts, trimmed, chokes removed (left), and submerged in lemon water
- 1 tablespoon olive oil
- 2 tablespoons butter
- 1 clove garlic, smashed
  Salt and pepper
- ¼ cup Garlic Puree (page 282)
- 1½ cups My Tomato Sauce (page 300) or other good tomato sauce
- ½ pound lump crabmeat, picked over

  Tabasco sauce
  Fresh lemon juice

- ½ tablespoon minced fresh chives
  Toasted pita or sliced baguette

Put the artichoke hearts in a medium saucepan, cover with water by about 2 inches, and simmer, with parchment paper on top or cover with a lid, until just tender, 20 to 25 minutes. Drain the artichokes, let cool slightly, pat dry, and quarter. Heat the oil and 1 tablespoon of the butter in a medium saucepan over medium-high heat. Sweat the artichoke quarters with the garlic, salt, and pepper for about 4 minutes.

Add the garlic puree, tomato sauce, and remaining tablespoon butter, stir to combine, then bring to a simmer. Stir in the crabmeat and turn off the heat. Add a few dashes of Tabasco, a squeeze of lemon juice, salt, and pepper. Transfer to a serving dish, sprinkle with the chives, and serve with toasted pita or baguette.

A

BRAISED BABY ARTICHOKES WITH OYSTER MUSHROOMS

SERVES 4

A SLOW BRAISE RENDERS baby artichokes soft, tender, and succulent. Cooking them in white wine and vinegar preserves their bright color and adds mouthwatering acidity. Cooking the mushrooms in the same pan with the other vegetables creates a flavor that is so much greater than the sum of the parts. This dish can be enjoyed warm or at room temperature.

- 5 tablespoons olive oil
- ¾ pound oyster mushrooms, separated into petals
  Salt and pepper
- 12 baby artichokes, trimmed, halved lengthwise, and submerged in lemon water
- 8 cipollini onions
- 8 small carrots
- 2 teaspoons coriander seeds
- 1 bay leaf
- 2 cups dry white wine
- ¼ cup white wine vinegar

Heat 2 tablespoons of the oil in a large skillet over high heat. Brown the mushrooms with salt and pepper, about 5 minutes. Transfer to a bowl.

Heat the remaining 3 tablespoons oil in the same skillet over medium-high heat. Add the artichokes flat-side down, onions, carrots, salt, and pepper and cook until the artichokes are lightly browned, about 6 minutes. Add the coriander seeds, bay leaf, wine, and vinegar, bring to a simmer, and reduce for about 2 minutes. Add about 1 cup water to almost cover the vegetables. Simmer until the vegetables are just tender, about 12 minutes. Return the cooked mushrooms to the skillet and heat through.

Prepping Baby Artichokes

Trimming baby artichokes is similar to the technique shown on page 11. I leave the stems intact, peel them, and since there are no chokes, I just pull off the hard outer leaves; don't be surprised at how many of them you must discard. Keep the trimmed hearts in lemon water until ready to use.

ASPARAGUS

HARVESTING ASPARAGUS feels to me more like the act of foraging, discovering an edible plant in the wild, than gardening. After all, asparagus are the springtime shoots of plants that live underground for years and years, and in some places grow completely wild. Each spring, the plant throws off tender green shoots in an attempt at propagation. When we show up at just the right time, it's so easy to snip them off in a celebration of that magic moment when spring arrives at last. Asparagus have become such a ubiquitous commercial commodity—uniform spears trapped as they inevitably are in a wide rubber band, more often than not imported.

It's a totally different experience to crouch down in an asparagus field looking for the earliest green stems that poke through the refuse of last year's crop, just waiting to send their tender shoots to reach up toward the sun. Older plants produce thicker stems, but they are not necessarily better. No matter where you get your asparagus, always look for spears that are still moist, with no sign of drying where the stalks are cut.

ASPARAGUS WITH PRESERVED GINGER RELISH

SERVES 4

I FIRST SERVED A SIMILAR tomato condiment at an impromptu lunch at my parents' house to highlight the room-temperature asparagus we'd just cut from the neighbor's field. Ginger, tomato, and sesame have a great relationship together and happen to love asparagus. This condiment is so tasty and versatile that you can use it on grilled vegetables, fish, or meat. It will keep, refrigerated, for about 3 days.

1 tablespoon sesame oil
¼ cup sliced spring onions or scallions
1 clove garlic, minced
1 tablespoon chopped Pickled Ginger (page 137), plus 1 tablespoon pickling liquid
Pinch crushed red pepper flakes
5 tomatoes, roughly chopped
½ tablespoon sugar
Salt and pepper

½ tablespoon soy sauce
1 teaspoon sesame seeds
1 pound asparagus spears, blanched (page 25)
2 tablespoons thinly sliced scallion greens or chopped fresh herbs

Heat the oil in a medium saucepan over medium heat. Add the spring onions or scallions, garlic, pickled ginger, and red pepper flakes and cook until the garlic turns golden, about 2 minutes. Add the tomatoes, sugar, salt, and pepper and simmer, stirring often, until the tomatoes start to break down, about 6 minutes.

Stir in the pickling liquid, soy sauce, and sesame seeds. Let the mixture cool to room temperature, then spoon over the asparagus and top with the scallions or chopped herbs.

PAN-ROASTED ASPARAGUS WITH SUNNY-SIDE-UP EGGS

SERVES 4

THIS DISH REVELS in the simplicity of only three ingredients: just-cut asparagus, the freshest country egg, and a few young spinach leaves. Sautéing the asparagus spears in a pan— not boiling them—concentrates their flavor and adds a little browning, too.

3 tablespoons olive oil

16 asparagus spears

1 clove garlic, smashed

Salt and pepper

1 cup packed spinach (stems removed)

Zest from ¼ lemon

4 eggs

Parmigiano for shaving

Heat 2 tablespoons of the oil in a large skillet over medium-high heat. Add the asparagus, garlic, salt, and pepper and cook, turning the asparagus occasionally, until it's lightly browned and tender, about 4 minutes. Add the spinach and lemon zest and wilt, about a minute more. Remove the vegetables from the pan and set aside.

Heat the remaining tablespoon oil in the skillet over medium heat. Crack the eggs into the skillet, sprinkle with salt and pepper, and cook until the whites are set but the yolks are still runny, about 4 minutes. Slide the eggs onto 4 plates and top with the asparagus and spinach. Shave the cheese over the top.

SALAD OF SHAVED ASPARAGUS & BELUGA LENTILS
SERVES 4

I USE THE MANDOLINE as a tool to transform so many vegetables—even long, thin asparagus spears—into crunchy salad. Slicing vegetables thinly makes them accessible and, in the process, increases their surface for seasonings. Holding the slices in ice water helps keep them crisp, and the long asparagus shavings curl beautifully in the cold water.

I love lentils of every kind, eating them in every way you might imagine: firm and cold with an acidic vinaigrette, as in this recipe, or warm and creamy in soups and stews, such as Braised Leeks & Yellow Lentils with Anchovy Dressing (page 176). Or cooked to a satisfying mush, mixed with crispy fried shallots and garam masala—my favorite sandwich. Beluga lentils, with their wonderful inky color, are named for the caviar they resemble. Any kind of lentil will work here.

> 3   tablespoons olive oil
> 16 asparagus spears, 8 shaved lengthwise and held in ice water, 8 halved
> 1   clove garlic, smashed
>   Salt and pepper
> 1⅓ cups cooked beluga lentils
> 2   large handfuls salad greens
>   Juice from ¼ lemon

Heat 1 tablespoon of the oil in a large skillet over medium-high heat. Add the 8 halved asparagus pieces, garlic, salt, and pepper and cook, turning the asparagus occasionally, until lightly browned and tender, about 4 minutes. Remove from the heat and set aside.

Toss the lentils in a small bowl with 1 tablespoon of the oil, salt, and pepper, then spoon onto 4 plates and top with the cooked asparagus. Drain the shaved asparagus and toss with the greens in a bowl with the remaining tablespoon oil, lemon juice, salt, and pepper, then scatter on the cooked asparagus. (Or just toss all the ingredients together in a big bowl.)

Blanching

I promise not to use sometimes confusing professional culinary jargon in this book, but blanching is one method that is fundamental to cooking vegetables. When I call for blanching, I mean briefly cooking a vegetable in salted boiling water, and then shocking it quickly in a bowl of very cold water with ice cubes. Blanching preserves bright color and fresh flavor, both of which cooked vegetables need.

AVOCADO

LOOK, I KNOW that avocado is really a fruit, and so do you. But let's not get distracted by that distinction. Because the rich flesh of an avocado isn't naturally sweet, I treat it as I would a vegetable: as the building block of so many great dishes, or simply sliced over a bowl of grains.

AVOCADO YOGURT WITH LIME MASH

MAKES ABOUT 2 CUPS

HERE IS A SLIGHTLY DIFFERENT WAY to look at avocados, amplifying their smoothness with yogurt and their nuttiness with toasted pumpkin seeds, and adding bright contrast with spicy red pepper flakes. It's as luscious as a spoonful of caviar! This combination is a favorite at my local midtown Manhattan café, Little Collins. I make the toasts small enough that two bites is enough to delight and keep your attention.

1 baguette, sliced
  Olive oil
1 clove garlic, halved
2 avocados, pitted and peeled
⅓ cup Greek-style yogurt
¼ cup fresh lime juice
  Salt

  Large handful toasted pumpkin seeds
  Crushed red pepper flakes
2 tablespoons thinly sliced fresh chives
  Pumpkin seed oil or olive oil
  Sea salt

Toast both sides of the baguette slices and rub with olive oil and the garlic. Process the avocados, yogurt, and lime juice in a blender until just smooth (a little texture is good) and add salt. Heap a spoonful of the mixture onto each toast, and top with pumpkin seeds, red pepper flakes, chives, pumpkin seed oil or olive oil, and sea salt.

Cutting an Avocado

Ripe avocados can get messy, but here's a trick to opening them that's clean and fast: Squeeze gently to assure that the avocado has just a little give (that's how you know it's ripe). Cut around the circumference until you feel the pit with your knife. Using both hands, one on top and one on the bottom, twist and open the avocado. Holding the side with the pit up, and your chef's knife in the other hand, tap gently on the pit with the blade, then twist and remove the pit. Use a large spoon to scoop out the meat. Done.

AVOCADO & BLOOD ORANGE SALAD WITH QUINOA

SERVES 4

THIS LUSH SALAD is a wintertime favorite. The sweet tartness of blood oranges acts like tomatoes would in combination with the rich avocado. Quinoa holds the flavorful vinaigrette well, making this salad so satisfying to eat.

½ cup quinoa
  Salt
3 blood oranges, segmented (below), juices squeezed from the membranes and reserved (you'll need about ½ cup; add orange juice if needed)
1 teaspoon sherry vinegar
3 tablespoons olive oil
  Pepper
½ small red onion, sliced into thin rings
1 avocado, pitted, peeled, and cut into chunks
  Tiny pinch crushed red pepper flakes
  Large handful bite-size salad greens
  Fresh lemon juice

Put the quinoa in a small saucepan and add 1½ cups water and a pinch of salt. Bring to a simmer, then cover and cook until soft, about 15 minutes. (Red quinoa will take a bit longer to cook.) Turn off the heat and let sit for about 10 minutes.

Meanwhile, put the ½ cup blood orange juice in a very small saucepan and simmer until reduced by about half. Let cool for a few minutes, then whisk in the vinegar and 2 tablespoons of the oil, salt, and pepper.

Fluff the quinoa with a fork, add salt and pepper, then spoon onto a platter. Combine the orange segments, onions, avocado, and red pepper flakes in a small bowl, toss with the orange vinaigrette, and arrange the mixture over the quinoa. Season the greens with salt, lemon juice, and olive oil and scatter the salad greens over the platter.

Segmenting Citrus

Here's the way to turn just about any citrus fruit into perfect bites. Cut the top and bottom off the fruit and set on a cutting board. Starting from the top, use a paring knife to remove the peel from top to bottom, sculpting the flesh so as not to waste any precious fruit. Remove all the white pith. Free the segments by cutting down along the membrane on both sides. Work your way around the fruit. The remaining membrane holds lots of delicious juice, so squeeze it over a bowl to capture it.

"*Beet's ... jewel-like color is both its joy and its downfall.*"

Beans
32

Beets
38

Bok Choy
46

Broccoli
48

*Brussels
Sprouts*
52

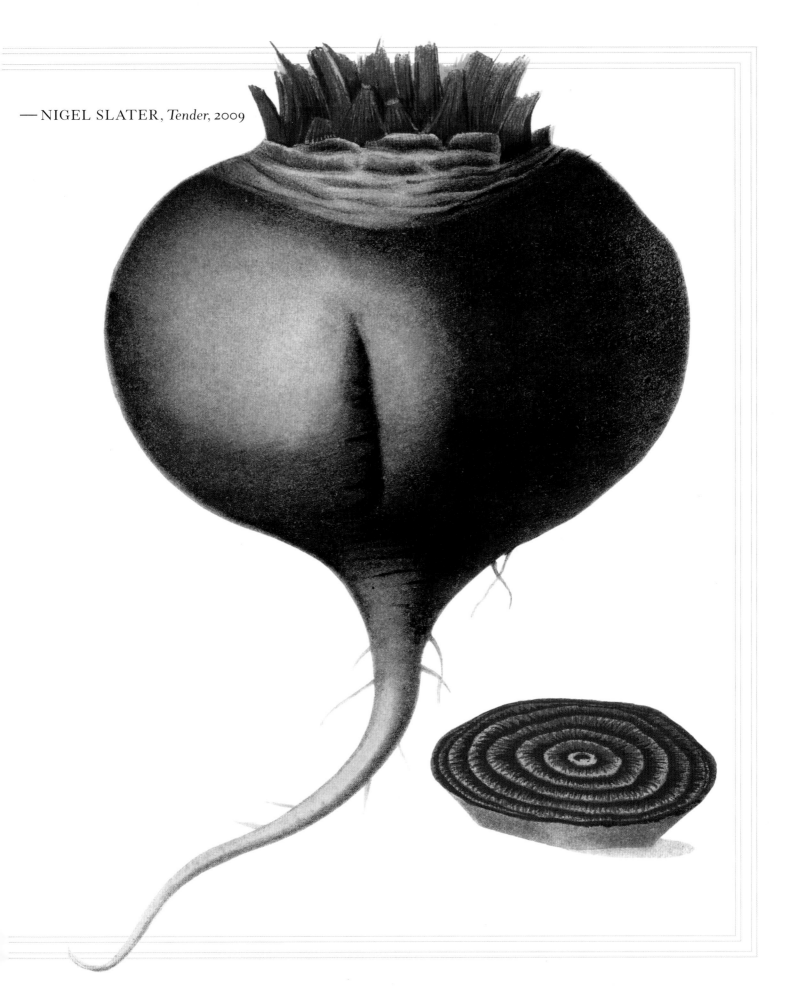

— NIGEL SLATER, *Tender*, 2009

BEANS

BEANS ARE LIVING HISTORY.
Behind every variety there's a colorful, striped, and dotted story that gets passed on from gardener to gardener, cook to cook, diner to diner. Planting beans is the first momentous step. Eating them perpetuates our direct connection to their place and their past. My Gramma Anthony preserved an Italian-American tradition of eating what she called "lu-beans," the modest lupini beans, and only on New Year's Eve. She'd spend a week soaking the dried beans in a crock, changing the water daily, softening and plumping them to their impressive size, then seasoning them with olive oil, salt, and pepper.

My favorite part was to pop those beans out of their skins and into our mouths. When I asked John Corkendahl, head gardener of Blackberry Farm, in Walland, Tennessee, about the heirloom beans that grow well in his garden, he shared a creamy white cowpea called Whippoorwill, which dates back to 1868. You have to grow these beans to perpetuate the seeds, so I gave some of John's Whippoorwill bean seeds to Zaid Kurdieh of Norwich Meadows Farm in central New York and asked him to grow them. It's more important than ever to support small farmers, the Seed Savers Exchange, and heirloom varieties, because in this commercial world, it is hardly a given that they will be there tomorrow.

STRING BEANS WITH SESAME SAUCE

SERVES 4

I DISCOVERED THIS WAY of cooking string beans in a friend's home kitchen outside Tokyo. In Japan, nutty, sesame sauce is often served with beans and other fresh vegetables at room temperature, such as spinach, broccoli, and asparagus—a practice I continue. This simple preparation appears often in bento boxes as well as on the menus of small, casual neighborhood restaurants in Japan.

Crush the sesame seeds in a mortar and pestle. Do not worry about grinding every last seed. Add the mirin, white soy sauce or shiro dashi, sesame oil, lemon juice, sugar, and a teaspoon of water and stir until combined. The sauce should be the consistency of loose peanut butter. Thin with a little water if needed. Put the string beans in a bowl, drizzle with the sauce, and top with the scallions.

- 2 tablespoons toasted white sesame seeds
- 1 tablespoon mirin (sweet rice wine)
- 2 teaspoons white soy sauce or shiro dashi
- 1 teaspoon sesame oil
- 1 teaspoon fresh lemon juice
- 1 teaspoon sugar
- 1 pound string beans, tips trimmed and blanched until crisp-tender
- 3 scallions (green parts), thinly sliced

CRANBERRY BEANS WITH SMOKY BACON & COLLARDS

SERVES 4

WE CAN ALWAYS COUNT ON dried beans as a staple, but the fresh versions of those beans are a fleeting seasonal delicacy. Their creamy texture is the true luxury of fresh beans. Of course, there's the shelling, but the glorious color of fresh cranberry beans makes it an easy pleasure. I like to share the task with my daughters: Many little hands make light work.

I use cranberry beans in this recipe, but there are so many other kinds of fresh shell beans to discover, from tiny Southern cowpeas to tender, chubby lima beans. It's a great dish to make a day or two in advance. Cooked beans benefit from an overnight spent in the refrigerator, soaking up the liquid. To keep the flavors vibrant, I like to add the greens and freshen up the seasonings just before serving.

- 1 tablespoon olive oil
- 2 ounces smoky bacon, diced
- ½ small onion, minced
- 1 small carrot, diced
- 1 clove garlic, smashed
- 2 cups shelled fresh cranberry beans
- 8 scallions (white parts)
   Pinch crushed red pepper flakes
- 2 large handfuls baby collard greens
   Salt and pepper
   Red wine vinegar
   Olive oil for drizzling

Heat the tablespoon of olive oil in a medium saucepan over medium heat. Add the bacon and cook until it renders its fat, about 3 minutes. The smell of the bacon sizzling is the first sign that

something delicious is on its way. Add the onions, carrots, and garlic and cook until softened, about 6 minutes. Add the beans, scallions, and red pepper flakes and stir for a minute or two.

Add 3 cups water and simmer until the beans are tender, 10 to 15 minutes. To serve right away, add the collards and cook until the beans are completely soft (the skins unbroken), another 10 to 15 minutes. There should still be plenty of liquid in the pan; if not, add more water—we want soupy beans! Add salt, pepper, and a splash of vinegar, and drizzle with olive oil.

BLACK BEANS WITH TOMATOES & MUSSELS

SERVES 4

THIS BASIC RECIPE for cooking dried beans is worth doubling because you can do so many things with the cooked beans. On Day 1, serve them with some grilled bread; Day 2, add more water or stock and blend to make a soup; Day 3, add seasonings such as red pepper flakes or ground cumin and serve on fish or as a dip for vegetables. When you add mussels to the cooked beans, along with their cooking liquid and tomatoes, you're giving the beans new layers of complex flavor. The beans and mussels become a real meal in a bowl.

- 1½ cups dried black beans, soaked overnight in water, drained, and rinsed
- 1½ tablespoons minced garlic
- 1 carrot, diced
- ½ onion, minced
- 1 sprig flat-leaf parsley
- 2 (2-inch) sprigs rosemary
- 2 sprigs thyme
  Salt and pepper
- 2 tablespoons olive oil
- 3 tablespoons minced shallots
- 1 cup dry white wine
- 2 pounds mussels, cleaned
- 1 tablespoon minced jalapeño
- 4 tomatoes, diced
  Pinch smoked paprika

  Olive oil for drizzling

Combine the beans, ½ tablespoon of the garlic, carrots, onions, parsley, a rosemary sprig, and a thyme sprig in a medium saucepan. Add enough water to cover by 2 to 3 inches, and simmer for

Sweating It

My goal is to make this book easy to follow, so I consciously avoid professional jargon, but some words are so intrinsic to the way I cook that I must include them. Take the concept of sweating. Nothing is more important as a way to build flavor into your cooking. *Sweating* means cooking vegetables such as onions, garlic, celery, or carrots in a little fat over medium heat until they are soft, without browning or adding other liquids. Sweating is the first step to making any complex sauce, soup, braise—so many recipes. It ensures that all the flavor is there at the beginning. Okay. Now that we've established that, I'm using this term throughout the book!

30 minutes. Add salt and pepper and simmer until the beans are just tender, about 20 minutes more. Drain, saving about 1½ cups of liquid, and discard the herb sprigs. If you're not using the beans right away, cool them in their liquid, which will make them even more flavorful, then refrigerate. They'll keep in the liquid for up to 3 days.

Stir in the reduced mussel liquid and simmer for a couple more minutes. Discard the rosemary sprig, then add the mussels, beans, and 1 cup of the reserved bean liquid. Add more liquid if you like it soupier. Serve in bowls and drizzle with olive oil.

Steam the mussels. Heat a tablespoon of the oil in a large pot over medium-low heat. Add ½ tablespoon of the garlic and a tablespoon of the shallots and cook until softened, about 3 minutes. Raise the heat to high, pour in the wine and a cup of water, and bring to a boil. Add the mussels, cover, and steam for about 3 minutes, shaking the pot to open the mussels. Transfer the open mussels to a bowl with a slotted spoon, leaving the mussel broth in the pot. Simmer until it reduces to about ⅓ cup and then set aside. Meanwhile, pull most of the mussels from their shells, discarding those that have not opened and reserving a few for serving.

Heat the remaining tablespoon oil in a saucepan over medium-low heat. Add the remaining minced garlic and shallots and cook until almost softened, about 2 minutes. Add the jalapeño and cook about a minute more. Add the tomatoes, smoked paprika, remaining rosemary sprig, and the leaves picked from the remaining thyme sprig. Add salt and pepper and simmer, stirring occasionally, until the tomatoes are softened but still hold their shape and the liquid is almost evaporated, about 5 minutes.

BEETS

I HAVE A GREAT CHILDHOOD MEMORY of eating beets. Our neighbors in rural Ohio would pull huge beets from their garden, wrap them in aluminum foil with lots of salt, and toss them in a campfire. For hours. Our parents would unwrap the beets, rub the skin off, slice them an inch thick, tuck them in napkins, and hand those roasted beets to us kids to eat, just like that. I still remember our candy-red smiles. More recently, the Argentine chef Francis Mallmann cooked at our Autumn Harvest Dinner at Gramercy Tavern, burying beets in the hot coals of a grill we set up right on 20th Street. Hours later, when those beets were done, Francis served them to our guests by crushing them in the palm of his hand, placing them ceremoniously on a plate, and drizzling them with a generous pour of Argentine olive oil and salt.

In both cases, these cooks treated beets like the most precious ingredient you could imagine. The smooth and silky slices of my childhood were worlds away from Mallmann's passionately earthy crushed beets. Both were memorable. Three things make beets interesting to eat: first, the way you value them; that is, are they pedestrian or precious? Clearly I'm in the latter camp. Second, the way you cook them (obviously I prefer roasting). Third, the way they're grown. This vegetable is the purest expression of the ground they're grown in. Rich, earthy, well-cared-for soil makes delicious beets. It's as simple as that.

Roasting Beets

I love to roast large beets because I like the meaty texture when I bite into them. Roasting always takes a lot longer than you think it should—a solid 1½ to 2 hours. Just rub the beets with olive oil, sprinkle with salt, wrap in aluminum foil, and roast at 375ºF. When they're soft, peel the beets with a paper towel. I like to put a piece of parchment paper on the cutting board before I cut the beets to keep the board from getting stained. I always roast more beets than I need and keep them in the refrigerator for salads, Roasted Beet with Rose Ricotta (page 41), or for Beet Tartare (page 45) or Michael's Borscht (page 42).

ROASTED BEETS WITH PICKLED EGGS & MUSTARD SEEDS

SERVES 4

MY GRANDMOTHER IN INDIANA always made pickled eggs, and I grew up thinking that was her special magic. The pickling liquid is what I use to make thinly sliced beet pickles, too. I like to pickle the mustard seeds separately, in a bit of the same pickling liquid without the beet, so they won't turn red. They'll stay fresh for months, refrigerated in the pickling liquid.

For the eggs, hard-boil and peel 2 eggs and place in a wide bowl. Make a red pickling liquid: Chop 1 raw beet. Combine with ¾ cup rice wine vinegar, ¼ cup water, ¼ cup sugar, and 1 tablespoon kosher salt in a small saucepan. Bring to a boil over high heat, stirring until the sugar and salt are dissolved. Strain the pickling liquid over the eggs and cover

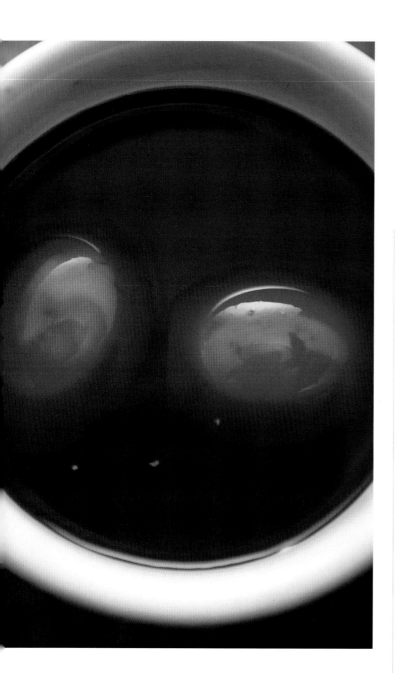

ROASTED BEET WITH ROSE RICOTTA

SERVES 4

I SEE ROASTED BEETS as a wonderful vessel for any number of imaginative toppings, as a lovely first course, or as one of a few vegetable plates on the table. Here are just a few ideas: Seasoned ricotta is a luscious topping with just salt and pepper, or vinegar, or lemon zest. Or use something special: dried rose petals.

⅓ cup fresh ricotta
1 tablespoon olive oil
1 teaspoon sherry vinegar
Salt and pepper
1 large beet, roasted and peeled
2 tablespoons dried rose petals

Stir together the ricotta, oil, and vinegar in a small bowl, then add salt and pepper. Thickly slice the beet, lay the slices on plates, and top each with a dollop of seasoned ricotta and a few rose petals.

with a plate so they stay submerged. After the mixture cools to room temperature, cover the bowl with plastic wrap and refrigerate for at least 6 hours, or overnight. Transfer the eggs and liquid to a container, cover, and refrigerate. To serve, thickly slice the roasted beet, halve the eggs, and top both with the separately pickled mustard seeds.

B |

MICHAEL'S BORSCHT

SERVES 6

BORSCHT IS OFTEN MADE with beef for body, but you can build delicious, complex, and satisfying flavor by caramelizing lots of onions and red cabbage as a base, and topping the beet soup with lightly sautéed green cabbage. A good borscht is a balancing act of savory ingredients, bright vinegar, and sweet beets. This ancient soup is based on combining and cooking whatever root vegetables were available. I always add flavor with different toppings: In winter I'll choose roasted Jerusalem artichokes, sautéed cabbage, and yogurt; in summer I'll use raw tomatoes and radishes. This soup is delicious served cold.

- 3 tablespoons olive oil
- 1 red onion, thinly sliced
- 1 white onion, thinly sliced
- 1 shallot, thinly sliced
- 3 cloves garlic, minced
- 2 potatoes, diced
- 2 carrots, diced
- ½ head red cabbage, thinly sliced
- 5 beets, roasted (page 39), peeled, and chopped
- 5 tablespoons red wine vinegar
  Salt and pepper
  Olive oil for drizzling

- 5 Jerusalem artichokes, peeled, roasted (page 161), and diced
- ¼ head green cabbage, thinly sliced and sautéed (page 56)
  Greek-style yogurt

Heat the 3 tablespoons oil in a heavy pot over medium heat. Add the red and white onions, shallots, and garlic and cook until softened and lightly caramelized, about 15 minutes.

Add the potatoes, carrots, and red cabbage, and cook until the cabbage is tender, about 15 minutes. Add the roasted beets and cook for a few minutes more. Add 4 tablespoons of the vinegar, salt, and pepper, and cook until the vinegar is evaporated, about 3 minutes.

Add 4 cups water, cover the pot, and gently simmer for about 30 minutes. Remove from the heat and stir in the remaining tablespoon vinegar and a drizzle of olive oil. Add salt and pepper. Serve in bowls topped with the Jerusalem artichokes, green cabbage, and a spoonful of yogurt.

BEET TARTARE

SERVES 4

I CALL THIS DISH TARTARE not because I want a substitute for beef, but because the name helps people understand the play of textures I'm after. The beets are roasted, not raw, and are enhanced by the crunch of toasted nuts. I like to serve it as part of an assortment of dishes l ike Kimchi-Style Fermented Cabbage (page 61), Japanese-Style Salt-Cured Cucumbers (page 100), and Roasted Quartered Kohlrabi (page 173).

- 4 small beets, roasted, peeled (page 39), and roughly chopped
- 3 tablespoons olive oil
- 1 tablespoon red wine vinegar
- ½ teaspoon minced onion
- ⅛ teaspoon minced garlic
  Salt and pepper
  Fresh lemon juice

- 3 tablespoons toasted pine nuts
- 1 tablespoon minced fresh chives

Put the beets, oil, vinegar, and 1 tablespoon water in a food processor. Pulse until finely chopped, but not pureed. Transfer the mixture to a bowl, add the onions, garlic, salt, pepper, and lemon juice, and stir to combine. Serve the tartare topped with the pine nuts and chives.

BOK CHOY

BOK CHOY IS DELICIOUS at every stage of its life, from micro leaf to 2 feet tall. You can eat every bit of it: its hearty, moisture-filled stems, its slightly bitter leaves, and even its flowers when the plant matures. It's so versatile, fast-growing both indoors and outdoors, available in every season; it's an amazingly healthy renewable food source. And despite its heartiness, bok choy (and its many relatives) cooks quickly, with little peeling or trimming. It's the best kind of instant food!

STIR-FRIED BOK CHOY

SERVES 4

I LOVE BOK CHOY for its robust stems and leaves: Even when cooked tender, the heads hold their beautiful shape. This aromatic combination of ingredients is common throughout Asia and a staple in my house. I love to serve this stir-fry over rice.

2 tablespoons sesame oil
1 tablespoon minced garlic
1 tablespoon minced shallots
1 tablespoon minced fresh ginger
3 heads bok choy, leaves separated
2 tablespoons soy sauce
  Fresh lime juice
  Salt and pepper

Heat the oil in a large skillet over medium heat. Add the garlic, shallots, and ginger and cook until softened, about 2 minutes. Add the bok choy and cook, tossing it until just wilted, about 3 minutes. Add ¼ cup water and the soy sauce.

Cook until the bok choy is just tender, about 2 minutes more, then add lime juice, salt, and pepper. Serve the bok choy with its pan juices.

BROCCOLI

BRASSICAS LIKE BROCCOLI (and Brussels sprouts, cauliflower, cabbage, and kale) get a bad rap because when they're boiled, their smell is off-putting. Or they're perceived as just plain boring. The common negative stereotype of broccoli is as a flavorless commodity veg, at its very best on a catered platter of crudités that become edible only when dunked in gobs of blue cheese dip. Many people undercook broccoli, worrying unnecessarily about preserving its bright green appeal or rightfully about preserving its nutritional value. But I think broccoli shows off its best qualities and tastes really delicious when it's cooked a bit longer, until it is just tender. Life's too short and broccoli is way too good to perpetuate bad stereotypes.

There's a world of difference between the pedestrian version of a vegetable and growing it yourself or buying it from a local grower. What excites me is exploring just how extraordinary broccoli can be when it's fresh, and how delicious it can become when paired with a couple of key ingredients. One of my favorite ways to use bright, fresh broccoli is in a puree. It's surprisingly easy to blanch broccoli and blend it with some olive oil into satiny smoothness to serve under a piece of fish or meat.

BROCCOLI BRUSCHETTA

SERVES 4

HERE'S A WAY TO MAKE eating broccoli irresistible. *Irresistibility* and *broccoli* are rarely found in the same sentence. Nor, for that matter, are anchovies. But Broccoli Bruschetta is a revelation for both ingredients. This topping on grilled bread becomes a delightful appetizer or party snack. Imagine that delicious time before dinner when people come together and drink something light and sparkly. This could be your go-to recipe!

2   handfuls fresh flat-leaf parsley
3   cloves garlic, minced
1½ anchovy fillets, minced
1   tablespoon capers, chopped
    Crushed red pepper flakes
6   tablespoons olive oil
    Small pinch dried oregano
1   small head broccoli, separated into small pieces, blanched until soft
    Salt and pepper

4   thick slices country bread, grilled
3   olives (green or black), pitted and sliced
2   anchovy fillets, halved lengthwise
1   small hot pickled pepper, seeded, skinned, and quartered
    Pecorino for shaving

In a mortar, combine the parsley, two-thirds of the garlic, half the anchovies and capers, and a small pinch of red pepper flakes. Smash into a coarse paste while drizzling in 4 tablespoons of the oil, then set the green sauce aside.

Heat the remaining 2 tablespoons oil in a medium skillet over medium heat. Add the remaining garlic, anchovies, and capers, a small pinch of red pepper flakes, and the oregano. Cook until the garlic turns golden, about 2 minutes. Add the broccoli and heat through, mashing a bit, then add salt and pepper.

Spread the green sauce on the grilled bread, then the broccoli mixture. Top with olives, anchovies, peppers, and shavings of Pecorino.

B

BRIBERY PASTA

SERVES 4

MY GRANDMOTHER MADE A VERSION of this dish that I loved: pasta with broccoli and oregano. I call it Bribery Pasta because being a professional chef does not give me a free pass to getting my kids to eat their veggies. Even the small amount of pasta in the dish is a big attraction. My grandmother used orzo. I like it with trofie, cooked ahead of time (the Italian pasta police won't come after you), then reheated in a skillet with the broccoli.

3   tablespoons olive oil
½   small onion, halved and thinly sliced
2   cloves garlic, thinly sliced
4   scallions, white and pale green parts left whole, greens thinly sliced
½   pound Swiss chard, stems halved lengthwise, center ribs removed, and leaves cut crosswise into thin ribbons
    Pinch crushed red pepper flakes
    Big pinch dried oregano
1   small head broccoli, stems thinly sliced crosswise, florets cut into bite-size pieces and briefly blanched
    Salt and pepper
    Scant ½ pound short pasta, such as orzo, rotini, or trofie, cooked, tossed with a little olive oil, and cooled
    Handful fresh flat-leaf parsley, chopped
    Olive oil for drizzling
    Parmesan for grating

Heat the oil in a large skillet over medium heat. Add the onions and garlic and stir for a minute. Add the scallions and Swiss chard stems, red pepper flakes, and oregano and sweat for about 3 minutes.

Raise the heat to medium-high, add the broccoli florets, and cook for a minute. Add the chard leaves, ½ cup water, salt, and pepper, and cook until the chard is wilted, about 3 minutes. This beautiful, tasty tangle of greens is your "sauce." Add the cold pasta and toss until it's heated through, then stir in the raw broccoli stems, parsley, and a drizzle of oil. Serve in bowls topped with grated cheese.

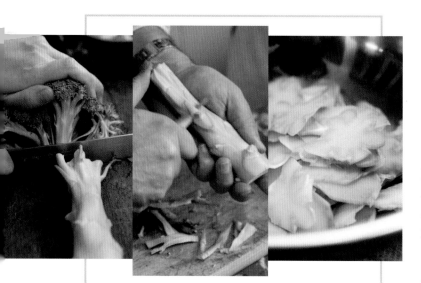

Broccoli Stems

I think of broccoli stems as a found vegetable. You bought the bunch of broccoli, so why not use the whole thing? Of course, freshness matters. Peel the thick outside skin from the stem to reveal its tender core. Sliced thinly crosswise, broccoli stems can be eaten raw, used to scoop Cucumber-Yogurt Sauce (page 101), or steamed or sautéed on their own.

B

BRUSSELS SPROUTS

BRUSSELS SPROUTS ARE AMAZINGLY HARDY PLANTS, a symbol of the end of the growing season. Long after everything in the garden has wilted or disappeared, these sturdy stalks stand guard over the frozen ground, their tight, compact leaves seeming to fight off the late-harvest cold. No wonder the flavor of Brussels sprouts is so distinctive and defiant. I like to cook them dry—roasting or pan-roasting—as opposed to boiling them in water, which emphasizes their undesirable cabbage-y aspects. Their compact leaves carry flavor in an amazing way: I season Brussels sprouts with soy sauce or steep them in pan juices from a roast chicken.

ROASTED BRUSSELS SPROUTS WITH MAPLE SYRUP

SERVES 4

HERE I COMPLEMENT the browning of both the Brussels sprouts and the garlic with a generous amount of salt and a drizzle of maple syrup added at the end. I'm not trying to make a sticky glaze, just a light contrast of flavors. Irresistible!

3 tablespoons olive oil
1 pound Brussels sprouts, trimmed and halved
  Salt and pepper
1 tablespoon minced onion
1 small clove garlic, minced
2 tablespoons maple syrup
  Fresh lemon juice
  Olive oil for drizzling

Preheat the oven to 375°F. Heat the oil in a large ovenproof skillet over medium heat, add the Brussels sprouts cut-side down, salt, and pepper, and cook until golden, about 5 minutes. Transfer the skillet to the oven and roast until the Brussels sprouts are tender, about 15 minutes.

Return the skillet to the burner over medium heat. Scatter the onions and garlic over the Brussels sprouts, drizzle with the maple syrup, then turn the sprouts over and let the syrup bubble and caramelize a little. Remove from the heat and drizzle with lemon juice and oil.

Using Brussels Sprout Leaves

There's a special way to treat Brussels sprouts that makes them even more delicious. Separating the heads into individual leaves (by cutting off the base of the stem and pulling the leaves apart with your fingertips) gives you a pile of individual leaves just begging to be quickly sautéed, browning only the tips of the leaves. I like to toss the sautéed leaves with minced shallots, onions, garlic, and herbs and add a squeeze of lemon juice. Or mix them with a soft grain like emmer wheat or barley for dinner in a bowl.

"*Cabbage is the Rodney Dangerfield of vegetables:*

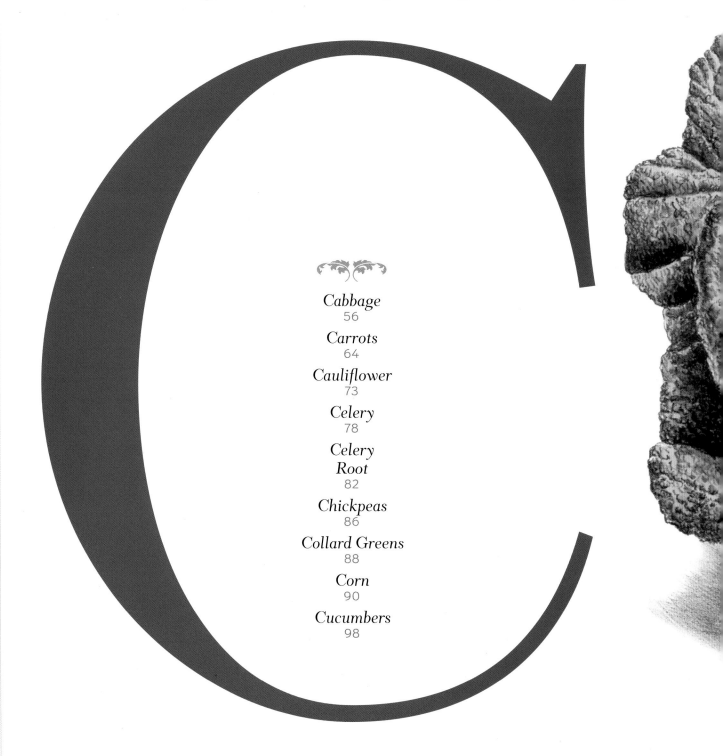

Cabbage
56

Carrots
64

Cauliflower
73

Celery
78

*Celery
Root*
82

Chickpeas
86

Collard Greens
88

Corn
90

Cucumbers
98

inexpensive, nutritious, delicious. But it gets no respect."

—BRIAN HALWEIL, *Edible East End*, 2014

CABBAGE

CABBAGE HAS THE ADVANTAGE of being available almost year-round because it grows in cool weather and stores really well. But that very ubiquity has made us somewhat indifferent to its charms. While many cabbage recipes conjure nostalgia (yes, we have a recipe for Goldie's Cole Slaw, on page 58), other preparations are inspired by travel. Generally I avoid boiling cabbage, the source of much of its bad press. Instead, I highlight its fresh and crunchy qualities, seasoning napa, savoy, red, and green cabbage in exciting ways. I especially love the varietals of cabbage that my local farmers (and yours, too) grow. I can guarantee that *any* cabbage at a farmers' market will have more flavor than old cabbages on grocery shelves.

So many other vegetables need to be unzipped—peeled, trimmed, understood—in order to enjoy them, but cabbage is ready to go. Nothing to do but chop and cook. It's sometimes hard to imagine building a meal around a vegetable, but cabbage has substance. Look at cabbage with fresh eyes. I was stunned to discover in the markets and fields of Strasbourg, France, a variety of tightly packed white cabbage called

CABBAGE COOKED QUICKLY

SERVES 4

I MAKE THIS SAUTÉED CABBAGE as a crunchy topping for Michael's Borscht (page 42), but it's delicious on its own. Combined with other fresh, thin-cut vegetables like broccoli, cauliflower, or fennel, and served over rice, it's a complete meal. The secret, as with all cabbage, is to not overcook it. Keep your eyes open for new varieties of cabbage, because all cabbage is good sautéed and each has its unique flavor.

Quintal d'Alsace that can weigh as much as 7 kilos (almost 15 pounds!), which is used to make the famed choucroute garnie. There, the identity of an entire region is based on cabbage. No wonder cabbage is at the heart of so many cuisines: You can ferment it into sauerkraut for your Reuben sandwich, or prepare it Kimchi-Style (page 61); you can braise it with chestnuts for Christmas dinner; you can have it stewed with your Peking duck in Chinatown; you can stuff it with wild rice and sausage or chop it up into endless varieties (and colors) of slaw. A pretty great range for one simple vegetable.

3 tablespoons olive oil 1 clove garlic, smashed ½ teaspoon caraway seeds 1 small head cabbage, thinly sliced crosswise Salt 1 tablespoon white balsamic vinegar Fresh lime juice Pepper Handful fresh flat-leaf parsley, chopped	Heat 2 tablespoons of the oil in a large skillet over medium-high heat. Add the garlic and caraway seeds and cook until fragrant, about a minute. Add the cabbage and a sprinkle of salt and cook, stirring, until wilted and the edges are starting to brown, about 5 minutes. Add the vinegar and cook until evaporated. Then add the remaining tablespoon olive oil, lime juice, salt, and pepper, and stir in the parsley.

GOLDIE'S COLE SLAW
SERVES 8

COLE SLAW IS AWESOME because it's one of the few salads that works in every season. This version is based on my wife's grandmother's specialty. Cole slaw is a way to use all those hard-to-love root vegetables, like red or black radish or kohlrabi, or just delicious carrots. I make mine with homemade mayo (which only takes a few minutes, and believe me, it's worth the trouble). Use the mayonnaise again as a dip for vegetables; make aioli for grilled fish by adding minced garlic; or add a little ketchup, brandy, and pickles for Thousand Island dressing. Cutting the cabbage (and other vegetables) very thinly matters here.

FOR THE MAYONNAISE
- 2 egg yolks
- ½ tablespoon Dijon mustard
  Salt and pepper
- ½ cup olive oil
- ¼ cup peanut or grapeseed oil
- 2 tablespoons red wine vinegar
  Fresh lemon juice

FOR THE SLAW
- 1 medium head cabbage, quartered and thinly sliced
- 3 carrots, thinly sliced
- 1 small onion, thinly sliced
- 1 clove garlic, minced
  Handful fresh flat-leaf parsley, chopped
- 1 tablespoon red wine vinegar
  Fresh lemon juice
  Salt and pepper

To make the mayonnaise, secure a medium bowl by placing it in a towel-lined heavy pot just big enough to hold it firmly. Combine the yolks and mustard in the bowl, add salt and pepper, and whisk until smooth. Add the olive oil drop by drop while whisking continuously; as the oil incorporates, it forms a nice emulsified mayonnaise. After you've whisked in all the olive oil, slowly whisk in the peanut or grapeseed oil, then add the vinegar and a squeeze of lemon juice. You can make the mayonnaise in a food processor, but I like to do it by hand for control, especially for a small amount.

Combine the cabbage, carrots, onions, garlic, and parsley in a large bowl. Add the mayonnaise little by little until the slaw is as creamy as you like it. Season with the vinegar and lemon juice, and add salt and pepper.

WARM RED CABBAGE SALAD WITH SWEET POTATOES

SERVES 6

RED CABBAGE IS BOTH denser and sweeter than green cabbage, and I like it both cooked and raw. It's great in Cabbage Cooked Quickly (page 56). Looking for something soft and equally colorful to combine with red cabbage for a winter composed salad, I decided on sweet potatoes simmered with sweet raisins and pine nuts. An easy way to shred red cabbage is to quarter it, remove the core, then cut crosswise into ¼-inch ribbons.

- 1 large sweet potato, peeled and diced
- 1 tablespoon butter
  Pinch brown sugar
  Salt and pepper
  Handful raisins
- 2 tablespoons toasted pine nuts
- 4 tablespoons olive oil
- 1 teaspoon red wine vinegar
  Large handful fresh flat-leaf parsley, chopped
  Fresh lemon juice
- ½ medium head red cabbage, quartered and shredded
- 2 cloves garlic, smashed

Combine the sweet potatoes, butter, brown sugar, and 1½ cups water in a small saucepan, and add salt and pepper. Simmer until the potatoes are tender and there's almost no water left, about 12 minutes. Add the raisins, pine nuts, 2 tablespoons of the oil, vinegar, parsley, and a squeeze of lemon juice and cook until the liquid is evaporated, a few minutes more.

Heat the remaining 2 tablespoons oil in a large skillet over high heat. Add the cabbage, garlic, salt, and pepper, and stir until the cabbage begins to wilt, about 5 minutes. Remove the garlic cloves. Put the cabbage in a large bowl and spoon the sweet potato mixture on top.

KIMCHI-STYLE FERMENTED CABBAGE

MAKES ABOUT 3 CUPS

THE INFLUX AND INFLUENCE of Korean cooks and prominence of their cuisine has prompted new interest in preparations like kimchi, which, in turn, inspires the way we cook and eat. I love to serve my own variety of small vegetable plates on the table at once, the way Koreans do. Kimchi taps into fermentation, the natural method of preserving foods. It's a mysterious and fascinating process and a wonderful way to make food delicious. And of course, as we're learning every day, fermented foods are beneficial to our digestion and overall health. I like this rather mild and very basic kimchi with just about any meal: Eat it as a dish on its own, or mix it with other vegetables for a complex salad, or serve as a condiment to enhance just about anything!

4	tablespoons salt
1	head napa cabbage, quartered
1	onion, minced
½	cup minced garlic
3	inches fresh ginger, peeled and minced
¼	cup Korean chile powder
1	tablespoon sugar

Rub a tablespoon of the salt between the cabbage leaves and put the cabbage in a large bowl. Mix the remaining salt with a quart of water, pour over the cabbage, cover with plastic wrap, and weight down the cabbage so that it is totally submerged. Leave at room temperature overnight.

Drain the cabbage and rinse thoroughly with fresh water. Squeeze out every last bit of water and pat dry.

In a small bowl, mix the onions, garlic, and ginger with the chile powder and sugar. Rub the mixture evenly between the leaves of the cabbage. Transfer to a bowl and cover. Leave it on the counter for 3 to 4 days to allow fermentation to take place. Refrigerate. Kimchi will keep for 2 weeks.

CABBAGE & PORK DUMPLINGS WITH DIPPING SAUCE

MAKES ABOUT 48

THESE TRADITIONAL DUMPLINGS are called gyoza in Japan. When I cooked in Tokyo at the beginning of my career, I fell in love with eating them at my neighborhood ramen shop, where I'd go on my Sunday nights off. Making the dumplings might seem daunting, but you can buy the wonton skins in a package and, as you see here, folding them is really easy. They're fun to do with a group, and they cook quickly. I make a whole bunch and freeze any extras, uncooked.

4½ tablespoons sesame oil, plus more for sautéing
2 small cloves garlic, minced
1 tablespoon minced fresh ginger
4 scallions, very thinly sliced
3 cups very thinly sliced cabbage
Salt
1 tablespoon soy sauce
Pinch crushed red pepper flakes
½ pound ground pork
1 package round dumpling wrappers (about 48)

Cabbage leaves for lining serving platter (optional)
Dipping Sauce (recipe follows)

Heat 2 tablespoons of the oil in a large skillet over medium heat. Add the garlic, ginger, and scallions and cook until softened, about 3 minutes. Add the cabbage and a sprinkle of salt and cook, stirring, until just tender, about 5 minutes. Stir in the soy sauce and red pepper flakes, then transfer the cabbage mixture to a large bowl and let cool slightly. Add the pork and ½ tablespoon oil to the cabbage, and stir to combine.

To seal the dumplings, have a small bowl of cold water within reach. Dip your finger in the water, then run it around the edge of a dumpling wrapper. This is enough to make a good seal. Put about ½ tablespoon of the cabbage-pork filling in the center of the wrapper. Then pleat the wrapper as shown, moving from one side to the other, pushing the air out. Pinch firmly to seal.

Heat 2 tablespoons sesame oil in a large skillet over medium-high heat. Add as many dumplings as can comfortably fit and cook until the bottoms are golden brown, about 4 minutes. Add about ¼ cup water to the skillet, cover, and let steam until the pork is cooked through, about 5 minutes more. Transfer the dumplings to a serving platter lined with cabbage leaves, if you like. Serve with the dipping sauce.

DIPPING SAUCE

MAKES ABOUT ⅓ CUP

I LIKE THIS SAUCE with the dumplings, because it's a traditional way to eat them, but you might want to add some spice (like a teaspoon of sriracha), which tastes great, too. In a small bowl, stir together 2 tablespoons soy sauce, 2 tablespoons fresh lime juice, 1 tablespoon sake or dry white wine, 1 tablespoon sugar, and 2 thinly sliced scallions.

CARROTS

THE CARROT IS AN AMAZING VEGETABLE. Just think about how the energy of the entire plant is directed to that super root. Starting from a fibrous, functional root system whose only job is to support their lacy (and edible) foliage, carrots have benefited from years of hybridization by folks who imagined just what a carrot could become. Our farmers now produce carrots in a multitude of colors, degrees of sweetness, and mineral content. It's insane that one plant has the capacity to capture so much strength from the soil and so much energy from the sun. Like clay for a sculptor, the meat of the carrot gives us cooks a foundational raw material to build flavor from. We know carrots from childhood: Bunnies eat them!

I had a magical moment when Patty Gentry, a farmer on eastern Long Island, took our then three-year-old daughter Addie into the fields at her Early Girl Farm to harvest a carrot. Instantly, Addie realized that a carrot was not a rock or a stone. It was something alive that she could pull from the ground. It even had a name: Scarlet Nantes. And it could be eaten. In this case, by a large Kunekune pig called Cynthia. Forgive me for thinking Addie discovered a small eternal truth: The pig was excited to eat the carrot; a carrot was desirable. In that moment, for Addie, a carrot went from being a plant to being food.

See Cooked Carrot Dressing (page 315).

Setting Up a Workstation

Even in my small home kitchen, I like to set up my kitchen counter like a professional workstation because it's efficient, clean, and safe. I like a big cutting board, about 24 by 18 inches. It makes working easier and saves a lot of time. It's important to steady the cutting board with a wet towel beneath it so it doesn't slide around or rock. I like to peel vegetables over a bowl next to the cutting board. It's not a great habit to peel dirty vegetables on the clean cutting board you'll be chopping on. And I never peel vegetables over the garbage can, because inevitably, trust me, the vegetables will fall in. When slicing, if you're right-handed, stack the peeled vegetable slices in small piles on the left side of your cutting board, use the middle of the board to cut, and, as you go, move the cut slices to the right. If you're left-handed, start out with the veggies on the right of the cutting board.

BASIC PICKLING RECIPE

MAKES ABOUT 1 PINT

THE PICKLES WILL KEEP, refrigerated, for about 3 weeks. I constantly reach for them when I'm cooking at home. You'll find references to many kinds of pickles throughout the book.

¾ cup rice wine vinegar
¼ cup water
¼ cup sugar
1 tablespoon kosher salt
2 cups trimmed vegetables, such as cauliflower, kohlrabi, okra, or turnips

Bring the vinegar, water, sugar, and salt to a simmer in a small saucepan. Put the vegetables in a bowl or small jar and pour the liquid over them. Let cool to room temperature, cover, and refrigerate.

VARIATION: PICKLED BABY CARROTS

Follow the Basic Pickling Recipe, adding a pinch of coriander seed. If you do not have baby carrots, cut large carrots into matchsticks.

CARROT JUICE COCKTAIL

SERVES 1

WE SERVE THIS as an amuse-bouche/cocktail at Gramercy Tavern. The sweetness from the orange juice and the tartness from the carrots and vinegar really wake up your palate. If you have a juicer, make the carrot juice yourself; if not, just buy it.

½ cup carrot juice
¼ cup Simple Syrup (below)
1 tablespoon orange juice
1 teaspoon rice wine vinegar
1 teaspoon egg white
  Salt

Combine the carrot juice, simple syrup, orange juice, vinegar, egg white, and a pinch of salt in a cocktail shaker and shake vigorously for about a minute. Pour the liquid into a tall glass, top with the foam, and serve right away.

Simple Syrup

Simple syrup is simply equal parts sugar and water boiled until the sugar dissolves. Make extra and use it to sweeten iced tea or coffee, or in a cocktail. It keeps indefinitely. Combine 1 cup water and 1 cup sugar in a small saucepan and boil until the sugar is dissolved. Cool and refrigerate. Makes about 1½ cups.

CARROT SOUP WITH COCONUT MILK

SERVES 4

WHEN FRIENDS AND FAMILY visit me in New York, they're always interested in tasting lively, exotic flavors. Here's a soup I love to serve them. The combination of coconut, orange, and fennel makes it aromatic and fun and puts the carrot in a whole different neighborhood.

- 4 tablespoons olive oil
- 1 small onion, halved and diced
- ½ small fennel bulb, halved and thinly sliced
- 1 clove garlic, minced
- 1½ pounds carrots, sliced
- 3 cups vegetable stock or water
- 1 cup orange juice
- ½ cup coconut milk
  Salt and pepper

- ¼ cup minced radishes

Heat 2 tablespoons of the oil in a medium saucepan over medium heat. Add the onions, fennel, and garlic and cook until softened, about 5 minutes. Add the carrots and cook for about 5 minutes. If the aromatics start to brown, lower the heat a bit. Add the stock and orange juice and simmer until the carrots are just tender, about 10 minutes. Add the coconut milk, salt, and pepper, and simmer for another 10 minutes.

Transfer the soup to a blender and process until satiny smooth. Drizzle with the remaining oil and check the seasonings. Serve hot or cold and top with the radishes.

Shaving Carrot Ribbons

An indispensable (and inexpensive) tool in my kitchen for shaving vegetables paper-thin is a handheld mandoline. I use it with a surprising number of vegetables to add texture to many dishes.

Finishing a dish with a delicate, raw slice of radish, carrot, turnip, cucumber, or other vegetable adds a welcome layer of crunch and flavor. For an echoing effect, I love to scatter slices of a raw vegetable over the cooked version of itself.

ROASTED CARROTS WITH SPICED NUTS (OR KING TUT'S CARROTS)

SERVES 4

I INVENTED THIS WAY of serving carrots for a dinner to celebrate the centenary of *Vanity Fair* magazine. The conceit was to reference historical moments in the past hundred years. I chose to mark the worldwide furor created in 1922 by the opening of the tomb of King Tutankhamun in Egypt. I focused on the jewel-like quality of glazed pistachios and almonds, the exotic husk cherries, and the surprise of roasted carrots, which are brown and shriveled outside but, when cut, reveal a gloriously gemlike interior. I called the dish King Tut's Carrots.

2 tablespoons olive oil
8 medium carrots
   Salt and pepper
1 teaspoon white sesame seeds
1 teaspoon black sesame seeds
1 teaspoon cumin seeds
1 teaspoon mustard seeds
2 tablespoons pistachios
2 tablespoons chopped almonds
1 tablespoon honey
1 tablespoon sherry vinegar

Large handful husk cherries, or olives, halved

Preheat the oven to 375°F. Heat the oil in a large ovenproof skillet over high heat. Add the carrots, salt, and pepper, then toss to coat with the oil. Pop the skillet into the oven and roast until the carrots are tender, tossing them every 10 minutes or so, about 45 minutes in all. Can you smell them cooking? Roasting brings out the sweetness in carrots.

Combine the white and black sesame seeds, cumin seeds, mustard seeds, pistachios, and almonds in a small skillet. Turn the heat to medium and cook, tossing occasionally, until lightly toasted, about 2 minutes. Add the honey, bring to a boil, then stir in the vinegar. Remove from the heat. Cut the carrots in half lengthwise, arrange on plates, and spoon the hot glazed nuts and seeds over the carrots. Top with the husk cherries or olives.

CARROTS & FARRO

SERVES 4

THIS DISH IS THE POSTER CHILD for a central idea of this book: that combinations of vegetables and grains—here, carrots, Swiss chard, and farro—can make a satisfying main course.

Another core idea is to create complex dishes that use all parts of the vegetable—soft leaves, crunchy stems, satisfying bites of the root, and even juice—to set up contrasting flavors and textures. Each distinctive component is served in a bowl, which blends the flavors in an interesting way. The last bite is as moist and delicious as the first.

- 4 tablespoons olive oil
- ½ small onion, minced
- 1 clove garlic, minced
- 1 cup farro, rinsed
- ¾ cup carrot juice
  Salt and pepper
- 1 tablespoon butter
- 2 carrots, thickly sliced on the diagonal
- 2 cloves garlic, smashed
- ½ tablespoon honey
- 1 bunch Swiss chard (about 1 pound), stems reserved, center ribs removed
  Pinch crushed red pepper flakes

Heat a tablespoon of the oil in a medium saucepan over medium heat. Add the onions and minced garlic and stir for about 2 minutes. Add the farro and toast for about a minute. This step adds a nice nutty note. Pour in 2 cups water and the carrot juice, add salt and pepper, and simmer, stirring, until the farro is tender and a little soupy, about 30 minutes. (It's delicious to eat at this point!)

Meanwhile, in another small saucepan, heat another tablespoon of the oil and the butter over medium heat. Add the carrots, 1 of the smashed garlic cloves, salt, and pepper, and stir for about a minute. Add a cup of water and the honey and simmer, stirring occasionally. The liquid will evaporate as the carrots cook. By the time they are just tender, after about 12 minutes, the liquid will reduce to a glaze. Shake the saucepan to evenly coat the carrots.

While the carrots are cooking, trim leafy bits and fibrous strings from the Swiss chard stems. Heat another tablespoon oil in a medium saucepan over medium-high heat. Add the remaining smashed garlic clove and the chard stems and cook for a couple of minutes. Add the chard leaves and cook until they wilt, about 5 minutes. Add ½ cup water and the red pepper flakes, salt, and pepper, and continue to cook until tender, another 5 minutes or so. The chard should be moist but not wet. If there's too much liquid in the saucepan, raise the heat and let it evaporate. Stir in the remaining tablespoon of oil.

Spoon the farro into bowls, top with the chard leaves, then add the glazed carrots and chard stems.

CAULIFLOWER

AS A CULINARY STUDENT in France, I fell in love with the classic cauliflower creamed soup called *crème du Barry* and all sorts of creamy, cheesy cauliflower preparations. I still love my grandmother's flavorful fried cauliflower, too, but the world doesn't really need another recipe for those dishes. Meanwhile, I've grown fonder of lighter preparations and faster cooking times, like briefly sautéing cauliflower in olive oil and adding it to beans and grains for deeper flavor. Cauliflower, these days, comes in an amazing array of colors: purple, orange, and green, as well as white; the flavors are similar, and they're all equally nutritious.

Historically, cauliflower was one of the cash crops of Long Island that, with potatoes and broccoli, fed New York City. It was shipped on a specially built railroad line called the Scoot. Today, in the spirit of eating ingredients from our area, I've become fascinated by this hearty vegetable. I even served a slab of cauliflower as a "steak" at Gramercy Tavern. Another idea came from the early days of Ferran Adrià at El Bulli in Spain. He would finely grate the tips of cauliflower florets to the consistency of couscous. Now used worldwide, this is a delicious and practical way to use cauliflower, especially at home.

CAULIFLOWER CURRY IN A BOWL

SERVES 4 TO 6

HERE IS A HEARTY, soul-satisfying way to serve cauliflower. Browning the cauliflower first builds flavor and hides undesirable cabbage-y qualities. Any kind of pickled pepper is good, but I'm looking for a little heat here.

  3   tablespoons olive oil
      Florets from ½ head cauliflower
  1   small butternut squash, peeled and cubed
  ¼   cup raisins (golden and black)
  ¼   cup minced shallots
  2   cloves garlic, minced
  2   thick slices fresh ginger, minced
  2   small hot pickled peppers, like jalapeño, seeded, skinned, and chopped
1½   teaspoons ground turmeric
  ½   teaspoon mild curry powder
      Pinch crushed red pepper flakes
      Salt and pepper
  1   (14-ounce) can coconut milk
  1   cup cooked chickpeas (page 86)
      Fresh lime juice
      Handful fresh flat-leaf parsley, finely chopped

Heat the oil in a large pot over medium-high heat. Add the cauliflower and cook until golden brown in places, about 5 minutes. Transfer the cauliflower to a bowl, add the squash to the pot, and cook for a few minutes. Add the raisins, shallots, garlic, ginger, pickled peppers, turmeric, curry powder, red pepper flakes, salt, and pepper, and cook until the garlic and shallots are softened.

Add the coconut milk and 1 cup water, bring to a simmer, cover, and cook about 10 minutes. Add the cauliflower and chickpeas and simmer, covered, for another 10 minutes. Add lime juice and parsley.

CARAMELIZED CAULIFLOWER WITH PEPPERS & ONIONS

SERVES 4

HERE'S A QUICK AND EASY WAY to celebrate the vegetable—just chop it and you're ready to go. The smaller pieces create more surface for browning, which is where the magic is when you're cooking cauliflower without liquid. That's why I like to pop the pan into the oven to roast the cauliflower for a few minutes; it tastes best when it holds its shape. Peppers and onions are a natural pairing that enhances the cauliflower experience, especially eaten with a bowl of quinoa—now that's a meal.

3 tablespoons olive oil
1 small head cauliflower, chopped
1 small head Romanesco, chopped
Salt and pepper
1 tablespoon butter
½ bell pepper, quartered, seeded, and sliced
½ small onion, halved crosswise and sliced
A few gratings nutmeg
Handful fresh flat-leaf parsley, roughly chopped

Preheat the oven to 350°F. Heat the oil in a large ovenproof skillet over medium-high heat. Add the cauliflower and Romanesco and cook until well browned in places, about 4 minutes, then add salt and pepper. Put the skillet in the oven and roast until tender, about 6 minutes.

Return the skillet to the stove, turn the heat to high, and add the butter, peppers, onions, and a little nutmeg. Add salt and pepper and cook until the peppers and onions are softened and lightly browned, about 5 minutes, then stir in the parsley.

CHOWCHOW RELISH

MAKES ABOUT 1 QUART

THERE ARE FASCINATING THEORIES as to the origins of this vegetable relish. None is conclusive, but I tend to buy the idea that its origins are Indian or Persian, because of the turmeric and other spices. The preparation has become an American classic, made from end-of-harvest vegetables that almost always include cauliflower. Chowchow, today, is a superb salsa to be scooped up with crackers, pita, or pappadums (lentil chips).

- 3 carrots, halved and roughly chopped
- 3 stalks celery, roughly chopped
  Florets from ½ head cauliflower, roughly chopped
- 2 bell peppers, seeded and roughly chopped
- 3 cups rice wine vinegar
- 1 slice fresh ginger
- 1 clove garlic, smashed
- 6 tablespoons sugar
- 2 tablespoons salt
- 1 teaspoon ground turmeric
- 1 teaspoon coriander seeds
- ½ teaspoon mustard seeds
- 1 bay leaf
  Pinch crushed red pepper flakes

Put the carrots and celery in a food processor and process until finely chopped. Add the cauliflower and peppers and pulse briefly.

In a medium saucepan, combine 1 cup water, the vinegar, ginger, garlic, sugar, salt, turmeric, coriander seeds, mustard seeds, bay leaf, and red pepper flakes and bring to a simmer. Once the sugar has dissolved, add the chopped vegetables and return to a simmer, stirring occasionally so all the pieces pick up the color from the turmeric. Immediately transfer the contents of the pan to a large bowl and let cool to room temperature.

Using a slotted spoon, transfer the vegetables to a covered container and add enough liquid to cover the vegetables. The Chowchow will keep, covered in the refrigerator, for about a month.

CELERY

CELERY FROM A GARDEN or farmers' market is almost a different vegetable from the supermarket variety—the flavor is that much more intense. If you've never tasted the real thing, you have a delicious surprise ahead. Fresh from the garden, celery's abundant leaves and crisp stalks remind you why we cultivated it in the first place—for its herbaceous qualities. The one good thing about our store-bought celery, however, is its generous size and seductive crunch. Once you strip off the tough outer stalks (and save them for vegetable stock), the hefty branches carry the flavor of the sauce they're served in. And the heart is a tender replica of the entire plant, sweet yellow leaves and all. Of all vegetables, celery's tendency to retain the qualities of the soil it's grown in makes a strong case for choosing an organically grown variety.

TWO-CELERY SALAD

SERVES 6

I LOVE THE IDEA OF COMBINING these two varieties of celery, one bred for its green stalk, the other for its mellow white root. While celery remoulade is a classic salad, adding the stalks really celebrates the vegetable. It may seem old-fashioned, but the hard-boiled egg and the caper mayonnaise ensure that the result is far greater than the sum of its parts.

6 stalks celery, peeled and very thinly sliced on the diagonal
2 teaspoons white balsamic vinegar
1 tablespoon olive oil
　 Fresh lemon juice
　 Salt and pepper
1 celery root, cut into matchsticks and blanched
½ recipe Mayonnaise (page 58)
2 tablespoons finely chopped fresh flat-leaf parsley

1 tablespoon finely chopped fresh dill

1 heaping tablespoon capers, chopped

2 hard-boiled eggs (optional), whites and yolks each pushed through a fine-mesh strainer with a rubber spatula or bench scraper and kept separate

Blanch half the sliced celery stalks and keep the other half raw. After blanching both of the celeries, be sure to pat them dry so that water will not dilute the mayonnaise. Combine the raw and blanched sliced celery stalks, vinegar, and oil in a medium bowl, then add lemon juice, salt, and pepper. In another bowl, combine the celery root with the mayonnaise, parsley, dill, capers, salt, and pepper. Arrange the celery root on a platter, sprinkle with the egg yolks and whites, then scatter the raw and blanched celery stalks on top.

CHICKEN SOUP WITH CELERY & DILL

SERVES 8

THIS RECIPE FOR CHICKEN SOUP begins and ends with celery, which really needs the richness of chicken to enhance its aromatic quality. When I buy a whole chicken, I know that I can plan at least three different meals: The breast and thighs can each be prepared in any number of ways, but most of all, I look forward to the soup I'll make from the wings, neck, and carcass. Browning the bones in the soup pot with the celery and other aromatics is a great way to build flavor. I add more celery at the end for its crunchy texture.

2   tablespoons olive oil
3   pounds chicken wings, neck, and/or carcass, cut into pieces
4   carrots, roughly chopped
2   onions, roughly chopped
    Half a bunch celery, roughly chopped
2   cloves garlic, minced
3   sprigs thyme
1   bay leaf
    Salt and pepper
¼   cup white wine vinegar

1   tablespoon soy sauce
2   carrots, very thinly sliced
    Second half bunch celery, thinly sliced on the diagonal
    Large handful roughly chopped fresh dill
    Salt and pepper

In a large pot, heat the oil over medium-high heat. Add the pieces of wings, neck, and chicken carcass and cook until golden brown, about 10 minutes. Add the carrots, onions, celery, garlic, thyme, bay leaf, salt, and pepper, and sweat until the vegetables are softened, about 8 minutes. Add the vinegar and stir, scraping the bottom of the pot to loosen the browned bits, until it has evaporated.

Add 12 cups water and simmer, skimming any foam that rises to the surface, for about 35 minutes.

Pour the broth through a fine-mesh strainer into a medium saucepan, add the soy sauce, carrots, thinly sliced celery, and half the dill and bring to a simmer. Add salt, pepper, and remaining dill and ladle into bowls.

CELERY ROOT

I'LL NEVER FORGET the embarrassing lesson I learned about celery root when I was a cook at Restaurant Daniel, from Daniel Boulud himself. One day I felt him breathing down the back of my neck as I peeled celery root in his kitchen. As he watched, I felt quite proud of how I was accomplishing the job quickly and efficiently, cutting away the gnarly celery root to make it look like a perfectly trimmed, symmetric French hexagon. The chef, however, thought otherwise. He pointed out how I was thoughtlessly cutting away the profits of his restaurant by taking off too much of the root with my progressive knife cuts. This guy doesn't miss anything in his kitchen!

That's how I learned to think of trimming celery root as sculpting, removing only the outer skin to reveal the white flesh and a full, rounded globe. I like to use a chef's knife to flatten the top, removing the celery stalks, and then the bottom. I trim off the roots, so it won't roll around on the cutting board. Then, starting from the top, I use my knife to carefully trim away just the thin outer skin. If it's more comfortable, use a vegetable peeler to accomplish this job—not a problem, unless Daniel happens to be in your kitchen.

CELERY ROOT & APPLE PUREE

SERVES 6

THE SECRET TO THIS PUREE is curry powder, turmeric, and brown butter. It might sound strange, but the combination of the warm curry and the nutty butter is fantastic, and turmeric brightens the color. The puree is perfect under a piece of roasted meat or fish, or folded into cooked farro or other grains; it's thin enough to be eaten as a soup.

2   celery roots (about 2 pounds total), peeled and cut into large chunks

1   apple, peeled, cored, and chopped; chop a handful unpeeled, for topping

½   teaspoon mild curry powder
    Large pinch ground turmeric

1   cup milk
    Salt

4   tablespoons (½ stick) butter, cut into small chunks

1   tablespoon olive oil
    Fresh lemon juice

Combine the celery roots, apples, curry powder, turmeric, milk, and 2 cups water in a medium saucepan, add salt, and simmer until the celery root is completely tender, about 20 minutes. Do not worry if the milk curdles; it will be perfectly smooth once it's blended. Set aside.

Meanwhile, make the brown butter. Put the butter in a small saucepan and turn the heat to medium. Swirl the butter around the pan so it melts evenly. When it starts to crackle, that's the sign that the liquid in the butter is evaporating, and the milk solids will start to change color. You're making nutty and lovely brown butter, not burned black butter, so when it stops singing and brown flecks appear throughout, take the pan off the heat. Pour the butter into a small bowl.

Put the celery root mixture into a food processor or blender and add the brown butter. The idea of putting the brown thing into the nice yellow thing might make you nervous, but trust me, it will be delicious. Process into a satiny, smooth puree. Add the oil, a squeeze of lemon juice, and salt, and blend. Serve topped with the chopped apples.

CELERY ROOT & CHESTNUT SOUP

SERVES 8

THE IDEA OF PAIRING celery root with chestnuts came to me from an Austrian chef named Kurt Gutenbrunner. Though his masterful touch included a balancing act of ingredients from prunes to porcini mushrooms, truffles, rich stock, and cream, this recipe focuses on the luxuriousness of celery root, pure and simple, enhanced by the earthy chestnuts.

FOR THE SOUP

- 2 tablespoons grapeseed oil
- 1 small onion, diced
- 1 stalk celery, diced
- 1 clove garlic, minced
- 1 celery root (about 1 pound), peeled and cut into large chunks
- 1½ cups roasted chestnuts (page 199), roughly chopped
  Salt and pepper
- 2 cups half-and-half
  Sprig of thyme
  Pinch grated nutmeg
- 1 tablespoon butter

TO FINISH

- 6 roasted chestnuts (page 199), sliced lengthwise
- ½ tart, crisp apple, peeled and finely diced
  Pumpkin seed oil

Heat the grapeseed oil in a large pot over medium heat. Add the onions, celery, and garlic and stir until softened, about 5 minutes. Add the celery root and chestnuts and cook for a few more minutes. Pour in 5 cups water, add salt and pepper, and simmer, stirring occasionally, until the celery root is tender, about 15 minutes. Add the half-and-half, thyme, and nutmeg and simmer for another 15 minutes. This will infuse the herb and spice into the liquid and reduce the half-and-half a bit.

Discard the thyme and process the mixture in a blender with the butter until silky smooth. Return the soup to the pot and bring to a simmer, thinning with water to the consistency you like. Check the seasonings, then serve the soup in bowls topped with the roasted chestnuts and diced apples. Drizzle with pumpkin seed oil.

Grapeseed Oil

I prefer to use grapeseed oil over other neutral-flavored oils such as canola. I value its purity and its ability to withstand high temperatures.

CHICKPEAS

IS THE CHICKPEA a pea or a bean? The answer is both and neither. I rely on chickpeas so much in my cooking. They're the perfect food: inexpensive, simple to store, easy to soak overnight, full of nutrition, and the cooking process is a snap. I can't understand why we Americans don't use chickpeas more. They're not just that unseasoned thing on the salad bar. Said to be the first domesticated plant, and called *hummus* in Arabic, chickpeas are vital to cuisines from Middle Eastern to Indian to Mediterranean.

Use in Cranberry Beans with Smoky Bacon & Collards (page 34).

CHICKPEA PUREE

MAKES ABOUT 4 CUPS

WHEN I THINK OF PUREED FOODS, I do not consider them baby food (although with three daughters, I've made a lot of that). Purees—like soups, braises, and sauces—are an easy way to achieve complex flavors; purees tap into the alchemy of cooking, the satisfaction of transforming one vegetable into another delicious thing, moving quickly from crunchy to supersmooth. So whether you use chickpea puree as a dip for fresh vegetables, or spoon it over a bowl of rice, or thin it out with some broth for a soup, this recipe is a reminder that purees are a great way to manage your kitchen.

1 cup dried chickpeas, soaked overnight
   in water, drained, and rinsed
½ carrot, finely chopped
½ stalk celery, finely chopped
½ small onion, finely chopped
1 clove garlic
   Salt and pepper
3 tablespoons olive oil
2 tablespoons tahini
2 lemons

Combine the chickpeas, carrots, celery, onions, and garlic in a medium saucepan. Pour in enough water to cover by 2 to 3 inches and simmer until the chickpeas are just tender, about an hour. Throw in a big pinch of salt and let the chickpeas sit for about 30 minutes to absorb the flavor of the liquid and finish cooking. Drain, saving 2 cups of the liquid. At this point, you can serve the chickpeas tossed with a little olive oil, salt, and pepper, or toss them in a salad, a stew, or a soup.

Put the chickpeas in a food processor or blender, saving a handful for topping. Add the oil, tahini, juice of 1 lemon, 1½ cups of the reserved cooking liquid, salt, and pepper. Process until smooth. The puree should be quite thin, with good acidity, so add more cooking liquid and lemon juice if needed. Serve topped with the whole chickpeas.

COLLARD GREENS

THE VERY WORDS *collard greens* evoke huge, fibrous leaves that need hours of boiling, maybe with a ham hock. And they can be delicious that way, with their pot likker. But I love to prepare the younger, more tender plants the way I do chard, kale, and spinach—with a gentle braise. Collard greens capture flavors from the earth and sun, making them more nutrient-dense than their cousins. Their leaves keep their structure, which means they deliver one great bite of greens! Collards thrive in cooler weather, and are available almost year-round.

COLLARD GREENS FRITTATA

SERVES 6

THIS ESPECIALLY LOFTY and majestic layering of greens is held together with sliced potatoes and eggs. As you can see, it is not a thin frittata! I like to make the frittata in my black cast-iron skillet; it's perfect for breakfast, lunch, or dinner. Feel free to use whatever leftover potatoes you may have on hand, or just leave them out.

- 1 bunch collard greens, center ribs removed, leaves blanched, drained, and roughly chopped
  Salt and pepper
- 12 large eggs
- 2 tablespoons chopped fresh flat-leaf parsley
- 1 clove garlic, minced
- 2 tablespoons butter
- 1 pound potatoes, roasted and sliced
- 1 cup grated Parmigiano
  Crushed red pepper flakes

C

Preheat the oven to 325°F. Put the collards in a medium bowl and add salt and pepper. Whisk together the eggs, parsley, garlic, and additional salt and pepper in a large bowl.

Heat the butter in an ovenproof skillet over medium heat, then layer half of the roasted potatoes in the bottom of the pan. Top with half the collards, then pour in half of the egg mixture and sprinkle with half of the cheese and pepper flakes.

Repeat with the remaining potatoes, collards, eggs, and cheese, and some pepper flakes. (The egg mixture will not completely cover the greens.) Transfer the skillet to the oven and bake until slightly soft in the center, puffy, and golden brown, 30 to 40 minutes. (If the frittata is cooked through but hasn't browned, put it under the broiler for a couple of minutes.) Let the frittata cool for a few minutes before serving; it will be easier to cut.

CORN

THE FIRST EAR of corn, eaten like a typewriter, means summer to me—intense, but fleeting. Remember those kitschy corn holders from childhood? They let you eat juicy, buttery corncobs hot—twirl 'em fast, have fun. Fresh corn means a short season of silky corn soups, luscious cheesy corn on the cob, fresh corn pancakes, and corn salad with tomatoes. Corn is perhaps the quintessential American food. It's part of our collective nostalgia, but even today, growers take particular pride in their sweet corn.

Jim Wroble, who grows our Anthony garlic in upstate New York, wears his "Best Corn in the County" pin with pride. It's easy to buy local sweet corn in season and families still prize the precious ritual of putting the pot of water on the stove before they go out to pick (or buy) their corn. Then they gather to shuck it on the back porch. I can't think of another vegetable that draws everyone to the table with such shared joy. Yet no other vegetable has been as distorted, abused, and manipulated as King Corn. But I'm here to remind us that we can still find the real thing: unmodified corn, raised for the table (not cars), sweet (but not supersweet), grown close to home (not flown in), and eaten the day it's picked! The rest of the year, I relish the varieties of corn specially grown to be dried, ground, and cooked for their depth of flavor: cornmeal for corn bread, polenta as a bed for sautéed mushrooms, grits for scooping up with a spoon as fast as you can, and masa, for real tortillas.

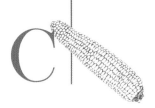

C

Cooking with Water

In all vegetable recipes, adding just enough liquid really matters. Too much water and you lose flavor, but too little water will leave the vegetables undercooked and dry, or worse, scorched. Not a pretty picture. With just the right amount of liquid, you can actually build flavor from the surrounding ingredients. In this book, when I ask you to cover a vegetable with water, I'm very specific about the amount to use. I use the water to communicate flavor, even if it's just salt. When cooking vegetables like turnips and sugar snap peas in just water and salt, the right amount of each makes all the difference. One of the most frequent comments I make in the Gramercy Tavern kitchen is "That dish is not wet enough." And what I mean is there's not enough liquid left in the pan for the ingredients to fully share their flavors. So the last bite is as moist and flavorful as the first. It's hard to communicate these nuances in a recipe.

The best advice I can give you is, when you're finishing a dish, keep in mind that you might need to add a drop or two of liquid to bring out its best qualities. An obvious example is grandma's tomato sauce. She would instinctively add a spoonful or two of pasta cooking water to give the sauce the right consistency and shine. A skillful cook of green beans would want to have just enough liquid in the pan, then add a squeeze of lemon juice, a sliver of garlic, a sprig of thyme, and a drop of olive oil in order to produce a light glaze. Some cooks do it instinctively, others have to be told, but using the right amount of water is directly connected to what makes food delicious.

CORN STOCK
MAKES ABOUT 2 CUPS

HERE'S A WAY TO EXTRACT every luscious drop from an ear of corn. There's still a lot of flavor left in the cobs once the kernels are sliced off. This stock is not a soup in itself; it's a soup base, or a component to other dishes. Cook the stock only for about 20 minutes, because after that, you start to lose the flavor benefits.

3 corncobs, kernels reserved for another use
1 leek (white part), halved lengthwise
1 stalk lemongrass, halved
3 thin slices fresh ginger
1 clove garlic, sliced
  Salt

Cut the corncobs into pieces. Combine the cobs, leeks, lemongrass, ginger, garlic, and 3 cups water in a medium saucepan. Simmer for about 20 minutes, stir in salt, then strain. Corn Stock keeps, covered in the refrigerator, for up to 5 days, or frozen for about 3 months.

CHILLED CORN SOUP WITH COCONUT MILK

SERVES 4

FRESHLY PICKED SWEET CORN hardly requires any help, but there are two elements of this soup that do matter: homemade Corn Stock and the addition of coconut milk. No need for cream or butter; coconut milk and avocado make the soup satiny smooth and give it an unexpected, exotic turn without adding too many ingredients.

4 tablespoons olive oil
1 leek (white and pale green parts), halved lengthwise and sliced
2 cloves garlic, minced
1 (½-inch) piece fresh ginger, minced
2½ cups fresh corn kernels (from about 5 ears)
2 cups Corn Stock (left)
½ cup coconut milk
  Salt
½ avocado, pitted, peeled, and cubed
½ cup sautéed corn
  Olive oil for drizzling

Heat 2 tablespoons of the oil in a medium saucepan over medium heat. Add the leeks, garlic, and ginger, and sweat until softened, about 5 minutes. Add the corn, corn stock, coconut milk, and salt and simmer for about 10 minutes.

Transfer the soup to a blender and process with the remaining 2 tablespoons oil until satiny smooth. Check the seasonings. Refrigerate until cold and then serve topped with the avocado, sautéed corn, and a drizzle of oil.

CORN ON THE COB WITH BASIL

SERVES 4

IT'S TEMPTING to eat corn on the cob totally unadorned, or with just a bit of butter, but this ode to basil is just so good. I love to serve corn seasoned like this boiled or grilled at any summertime party. Add a sprinkle of cayenne if you really want to spice it up.

- 4   tablespoons (½ stick) butter, at room temperature
- 5   fresh basil leaves, finely chopped
      Large pinch fresh cilantro leaves, finely chopped
- 1   tablespoon minced fresh chives
      Pinch paprika
      Fresh lemon juice
      Salt and pepper
- 4   ears corn, shucked and halved crosswise

      Small wedge Pecorino Romano

Bring a large pot of water to a boil. Meanwhile, put the butter, basil, cilantro, chives, and paprika in a small bowl, add lemon juice, salt, and pepper, and stir until thoroughly combined.

Put the corn in the boiling water and boil until just tender, 2 to 3 minutes. Short cooking time is the way to preserve corn's inherent flavor and sweetness. Drain, transfer to a platter, then spread some herb butter on each piece and grate the cheese over the top. Wash down with a chilled beer or tequila and lime.

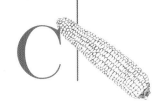

SWEET CORN, TOMATO & CRANBERRY BEAN SALAD

SERVES 4 TO 6

I LOVE THE MIXTURE of fresh corn with colorful and creamy beans. But there's another reason to pair them. Combined, they make a powerful complete protein, better eaten together than separately.

1   cup bean cooking liquid
    (from the cranberry beans)
2   tablespoons sherry vinegar
1   clove garlic, smashed
½   cup olive oil
    Salt

2   tablespoons olive oil
1   small red onion, finely chopped
3   cloves garlic, smashed
    Kernels from 3 ears corn
    Salt
2   cups cooked fresh or dried cranberry beans,
    cooking liquid reserved, at room temperature
8   Sun Gold cherry tomatoes, halved
2   tomatoes, 1 cut into wedges, 1 cubed
    Handful fresh cilantro leaves
    Fresh lemon juice
    Pepper

Combine the bean cooking liquid, vinegar, and garlic in a small saucepan. Bring to a simmer and reduce by three-quarters. Discard the garlic, whisk in the oil, add salt, and set the vinaigrette aside.

Heat the 2 tablespoons oil in a large skillet over medium-high heat. Add half the onions and all the garlic and cook until softened, about 4 minutes. Add the corn and salt and cook until the kernels are tender, about 2 minutes.

Put the corn mixture in a large bowl and add the beans, all the tomatoes, remaining onions, and cilantro. Toss with half the vinaigrette, lemon juice, salt, and pepper. Serve extra vinaigrette on the side.

CORN PANCAKES

MAKES ABOUT 36 (2-INCH) PANCAKES

IN THIS RECIPE, I combine the sweetness of corn kernels with the deeper flavor of stone-ground cornmeal. A hot griddle makes pancakes with irresistible light brown crispy edges. Freshness really matters in cornmeal. Don't buy those packages that have likely sat around on shelves forever. Look for the freshest cold stone-ground meal. I like cornmeal from Wild Hive Farm in New York, McEwen & Sons, in Alabama, and Anson Mills. These pancakes are great dressed down, straight from the griddle, or dressed up with a bit of trout or paddlefish roe and a touch of sour cream. Or, top with seasonal Sun Gold tomatoes, cilantro, and sea salt.

1½	cups fine cornmeal
⅓	cup flour
½	tablespoon baking powder
2	large pinches salt
2	eggs
1	egg white
1	cup milk
1	tablespoon honey
5	tablespoons butter, melted
	Fresh lemon juice
2½	cups corn kernels (from about 5 ears)
2	baby sweet peppers or ¼ bell pepper, minced
½	teaspoon grated jalapeño
	Large pinch fresh cilantro leaves, chopped
	Pepper
	Butter for the skillet
1	pint Sun Gold cherry tomatoes, halved
	Handful fresh cilantro, chopped
	Sea salt

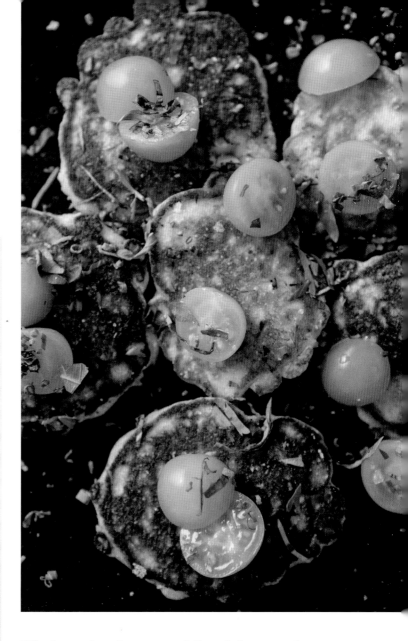

Whisk together the cornmeal, flour, baking powder, and salt in a large bowl. Add the eggs, egg white, milk, honey, butter, and a squeeze of lemon juice and whisk until just combined. Gently stir in the corn kernels, peppers, jalapeño, cilantro, and pepper.

Heat a large skillet over medium heat. Working in batches, melt the butter, then spoon about 2 tablespoonfuls batter for each pancake onto the skillet. Cook until golden, about 3 minutes, then flip and cook about 2 minutes more. Repeat with the remaining batter. Serve topped with the tomatoes, cilantro, and a little sea salt.

CUCUMBERS

WHEN I DREAM of cucumbers, I imagine small, thin-skinned fruits with minuscule seeds— dense and sleek. The kind you needn't peel, the kind that shine raw or cooked. The cucumber I dream of is commonly called Persian, but a bit of research reveals that this Middle Eastern version was perfected in the late 1930s on an Israeli kibbutz. Because these smooth little wonders can be successfully greenhouse-grown, they're blissfully available year-round. They're similar in shape and flavor to the Japanese cucumbers I came to know and love in Tokyo.

CHILLED CUCUMBER SOUP

SERVES 4 TO 6

A COLD CUCUMBER SOUP is a surprising and interesting way to deal with an abundance of cucumbers when they're in season. This soup is light and refreshing and uses both raw and cooked cucumbers as well as their skins, which add great color and flavor. Best of all, there's no waste.

FOR THE SOUP

- 1 tablespoon peanut or grapeseed oil
- 1 small onion, finely chopped
- 1 clove garlic, minced
- 1 teaspoon minced fresh ginger
- 1 cucumber, peeled (peels blanched and kept separate), seeded, and roughly chopped
  Salt and pepper
- 1 cucumber, peeled and seeded, ½ chopped, ½ very thinly sliced
  Large handful fresh flat-leaf parsley, blanched
  Large handful fresh dill, blanched
- 3 tablespoons Greek-style yogurt
- 1 tablespoon honey
- 1 tablespoon olive oil
  Fresh lime juice

FOR THE TOPPING
 Sliced fresh chives
 Chopped fresh dill
 Olive oil for drizzling

Heat the peanut or grapeseed oil in a medium saucepan over medium-low heat. Add the onions, garlic, and ginger and cook until the onions are softened, about 6 minutes. Add two-thirds of the roughly chopped cucumbers and cook for a few minutes more, then add 2 cups water, salt, and pepper and simmer until the cucumbers are tender, about 8 minutes.

Combine the blanched cucumber peels, remaining chopped cucumbers, parsley, dill, yogurt, honey, and olive oil in a blender. Add the cooked cucumber mixture and blend until smooth, then add lime juice, salt, and pepper. Transfer the soup to a covered container and refrigerate. (If you're in a hurry, chill it in an ice bath.) Serve topped with the sliced cucumbers, a sprinkle of chives, dill, and olive oil.

JAPANESE-STYLE SALT-CURED CUCUMBERS

MAKES ABOUT 4 CUPS

WE CALL PREPARATIONS like these pickles, but they're not truly preserved, just salted and seasoned, and meant to be eaten within a week. I learned this humble home technique while living in Japan. First salting, then pressing the cucumbers draws out their vegetal water, which is replaced with a light soy-vinegar seasoning that enhances the cucumbers' natural crunch. I use this technique on daikon, carrots, radishes, turnips, and cabbage. Sometimes I enhance the flavor by adding a 2-inch piece of dried kombu to the marinade.

1½ pounds Persian cucumbers, sliced
3 tablespoons salt
1 tablespoon rice wine vinegar
1 teaspoon soy sauce
1 teaspoon sugar
6 thin slices unpeeled fresh ginger

Toss the cucumbers with the salt in a large bowl and let sit for about 10 minutes. Rinse the cucumbers, pat dry, and return to the bowl. Add the vinegar, soy sauce, sugar, and ginger, and toss.

Transfer the cucumber mixture to a flat container and arrange in an even layer. Cover with plastic wrap, then weight down the cucumbers and let cure at room temperature for about 3 hours or refrigerate for a day. Drain the liquid and discard the ginger. Transfer the pickles to a container; they'll keep, covered and refrigerated, for about a week.

CUCUMBER-YOGURT SAUCE

MAKES ABOUT 1¼ CUPS

THIS EASY, VERSATILE dipping sauce is good with just about any raw vegetable; I like to serve it with delicious thin slices of broccoli stem (page 50), and I like it on garlicky toasted bread with fresh tomatoes; sometimes I spoon it over pan-roasted fish.

In a small bowl, combine ½ cup peeled, seeded, and finely diced cucumbers, ½ cup Greek-style yogurt, ½ teaspoon minced garlic, ½ teaspoon minced shallots, 2 teaspoons finely chopped dill, 1 tablespoon finely chopped fresh flat-leaf parsley, 1 teaspoon finely chopped fresh chives, and 1 teaspoon white balsamic vinegar. Stir together, then add fresh lime juice, salt, and pepper. Top with finely chopped fresh dill.

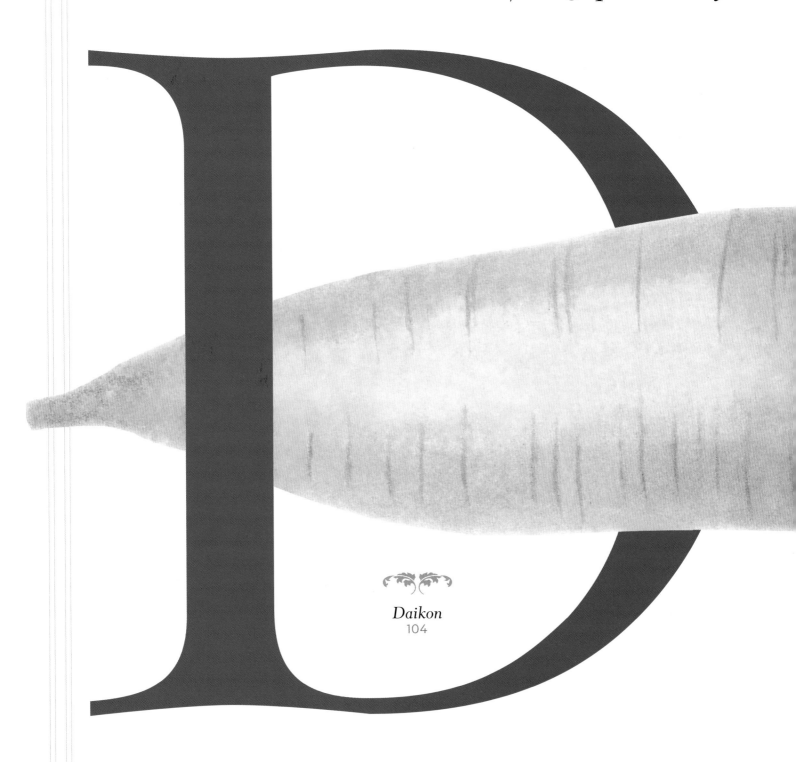

"... winter sustenance comes from Japan's many root

Daikon
104

vegetables ... the icy-white daikon." —YUKARI SAKAMOTO,
Food Sake Tokyo, 2010

DAIKON

BEFORE I WENT to Japan, I had no idea what a daikon was; after living there I can't imagine my kitchen without it. Daikon can seem daunting: It grows fast, large, and very dense, but it's become a staple at our farmers' markets. Less watery than a cucumber, less peppery than most other radishes, there's nothing funky or weird about daikon. And it's super easy to peel. Grated, braised, pickled, or fermented—there are countless ways to discover this fresh, crunchy root.

See Mushroom Hot Pot with Beef & Daikon (page 192).

CLASSIC GRATED DAIKON ON PAN-ROASTED FISH

MAKES ABOUT ⅓ CUP (ENOUGH FOR 4 SERVINGS OF FISH)

GRATED RAW DAIKON is a common condiment in Japan, served with tempura, or over tofu, vegetables, or grilled fish. Here, I spoon it on pan-roasted fish (drizzled with a little lemon-butter sauce and topped with cilantro).

I use a Japanese grater, but the medium holes on a box grater work well, too. Combine ⅓ cup peeled, grated daikon and 1 tablespoon finely grated fresh ginger in a small bowl. Gently squeeze out a little of the liquid, then stir in 1 teaspoon soy sauce.

DAIKON KINPIRA

SERVES 6

THIS VERSION OF THE CLASSIC Japanese vegetable dish that I learned to make when I was a young cook in Tokyo is based on daikon; the traditional dish highlights burdock root, and if you can find it for this recipe, all the better. Now, I make kinpira with any mix of root vegetables, and sometimes with just carrots and daikon. Use what you have; the amount of each vegetable doesn't really matter. Kinpira requires some peeling and cutting, but this delicious salad is well worth it. The flavors are so pure and clean and you feel good just eating it. Refrigerated, it will keep for about 5 days.

2 tablespoons sesame oil

2 stalks salsify, peeled and cut into matchsticks (page 272)

2 stalks burdock root, peeled and cut into matchsticks (optional)

1 clove garlic, minced

2 carrots, cut into matchsticks

½ celery root (about ½ pound), peeled and cut into matchsticks

2 small daikon, peeled and cut into matchsticks

1 cup Dashi (page 109)

3 tablespoons mirin (sweet rice wine)

1 tablespoon sugar

Pinch crushed red pepper flakes

¼ cup soy sauce

2 tablespoons toasted sesame seeds

Fresh lemon juice

3 scallions (green parts), thinly sliced

Heat a tablespoon of the oil in a large skillet over medium-high heat. The vegetables that take the longest to cook go in first: Add the salsify, burdock, and garlic and stir for about a minute. Add the carrots and celery root and stir for another couple of minutes. Add the daikon and stir for about a minute.

Add the dashi, mirin, sugar, and red pepper flakes and simmer, stirring occasionally, until the vegetables are slightly tender and the liquid is almost evaporated, about 5 minutes. Stir in the soy sauce, bring to a simmer, and remove the skillet from the heat. Stir in the remaining tablespoon sesame oil, sesame seeds, and a big squeeze of lemon juice. Let kinpira cool in the skillet or a bowl before serving. Top with the scallions.

Cutting Matchsticks

Cutting vegetables by hand into matchsticks takes a little know-how and practice. Peel the vegetable, cut it into the length you want, and square off the sides. (Save trimmings for stock.) Cut slices about ⅜ inch thick with a knife or a mandoline. Stack the slices into small piles—as high as you're comfortable with—and one by one, with a chef's knife, cut the piles into matchsticks about ⅜ inch wide. That's it!

Making Dashi

The foundational stock of Japanese cooking, dashi provides a basic flavor structure called umami that enhances all other ingredients in the recipe. Umami can be explained chemically, but it is produced naturally in these ingredients and to me it just makes everything taste more delicious. The preparation is so easy compared with the power of the result.

To make about a quart of dashi, put about 5 cups of water in a saucepan with 4 pieces of the dried seaweed called kombu. Bring to a simmer and cook gently for about 20 minutes. Remove the pan from the heat, set aside the kombu, and add 1 cup loosely packed dried bonito flakes *(katsuobushi)*. Let steep off the heat for 15 minutes. Strain before using. Makes 2 cups.

This elemental, subtly flavored Japanese broth is best used the day it's made. If you have any left over, stir in some miso paste and some very thinly sliced button mushrooms and scallions and simmer for 15 minutes for a lovely, simple soup.

"*When I was alone, I lived on eggplant, the stove-top*

Eggplant
112

Escarole
120

cook's greatest ally." —LAURIE COLWIN, *Home Cooking,* 1988

EGGPLANT

THE VERY NAME OF THIS VEGETABLE seems to ricochet into funny places in the minds of people who are unfamiliar with it. That was me as a kid. Eggplant was a strange, foreign object that belonged to another culture and generation. Like dried figs and chewing tobacco, it was what my grandfather loved. For him, as for many first-generation Italian-Americans, eggplant was a family heirloom. He grew them in his garden. Big ones. And he brought them to my grandmother as a treasure from another time. I thought Gramma was the only one who really knew what to do with eggplant. Both my grandparents were born here, in a working-class, mostly Italian community near Syracuse, New York, called Solvay. My grandparents left the neighborhood to take over my great-grandfather's farm outside of Syracuse.

The farmhouse looked out over about a hundred acres of rolling hills that belonged to my grandfather. Like a lot of farmers, when developers offered good money for the land, he sold it. They were dirt-poor. Today, that farm is one huge subdivision. I remember looking out over their yard when I was a little kid, three or four years old, to the landscape beyond, so different from where we lived in Ohio. To me it seemed a foreign kingdom. And what separated my grandparents' kingdom from the neighboring kingdom was a hedgerow of fragrant laurel bushes. Eggplant was like that kingdom, that otherness, that strangeness, the unknown danger it represented.

CAPONATA

SERVES 6

WHAT I FIND INSPIRING about caponata is the idea of a flavorful eggplant-based vegetable condiment that's delicious on its own. It's really like a ratatouille—lightly stewed fresh vegetables—with sweet-and-sour notes. The sweetness is heightened by golden raisins, the tartness by capers, olives, and wine vinegar. Caponata is great at any temperature, on grilled bread, or over pasta or grains.

¼ cup olive oil
1 large eggplant, diced small
  Salt and pepper
1 clove garlic, minced
  Pinch crushed red pepper flakes
3 scallions, thickly sliced, white pieces kept separate from the greens
¼ cup red wine vinegar

6 tomatoes, chopped
  Large handful green or black olives, pitted
  Handful golden raisins
2 tablespoons capers
  Pinch dried basil
  Pinch dried oregano

  Handful fresh basil, roughly chopped

Heat the oil in a large skillet over high heat. Add the eggplant, salt, and pepper, and cook, stirring often, until browned, about 5 minutes. Add the garlic, red pepper flakes, and scallion whites and cook for about 3 minutes more. Add the vinegar, tomatoes, olives, raisins, capers, dried basil, and oregano and cook until the eggplant is tender and the pan is almost dry, about 12 minutes. Stir in the scallion greens, then top with the fresh basil.

GRILLED EGGPLANT WITH MISO GLAZE

SERVES 4

THIS RECIPE TAKES roasted eggplant one step further, roasting the big eggplants, then finishing them with miso paste. This earthy, sweet combination is the tastiest eggplant recipe I know. I use red miso paste here, but white is good too.

- 2 tablespoons olive oil
- 1 large eggplant, halved and scored
  Salt and pepper
- ¼ cup sake
- 1 tablespoon sugar
- 1 tablespoon miso paste

Preheat the grill to medium or heat a grill pan over medium heat. Rub the oil over the eggplant halves and sprinkle with salt and pepper. Grill, turning once or twice, until soft, about 12 minutes.

Meanwhile, bring the sake and sugar to a simmer in a very small pot and cook until the sugar is dissolved. Remove from the heat, add the miso, and stir until smooth. When the eggplant halves are cooked, spread the glaze evenly over the tops. Serve immediately.

ROASTED JAPANESE EGGPLANT

SERVES 4

WHEN I REFER TO JAPANESE EGGPLANTS, those I love are not the long skinny ones. When they're roasted, the skinny ones do not have the luxurious meaty mouthfeel of the small oval ones that I prefer. I like to cook these small eggplants on the stove, halved and scored, in just enough olive oil to brown the outside but not enough to make them soggy. Then I finish them in the oven.

- ¼ cup olive oil, plus more if needed
- 4 small eggplants (about ½ pound each), halved lengthwise and scored
  Salt and pepper
  Brown sugar

Preheat the oven to 400°F. Heat the oil in a large ovenproof skillet over medium-high heat. Add the eggplant cut-side down and cook until lovely and brown, about 4 minutes.

Flip the eggplant, add salt and pepper, and sprinkle lightly with brown sugar to balance any bitterness and caramelize the eggplant. Put the skillet into the oven and roast until the eggplant is tender and the edges are browned and a bit crisp, about 15 minutes. Serve immediately.

GRAMMA ANTHONY'S PICKLED EGGPLANT

SERVES 6

RECIPES TAKE YOU ON A WALK through someone's life. There was always a crock of pickled eggplant on my grandmother's counter and my grandfather would eat it with everything, though his summer favorite was a sandwich, especially on fishing days on Lake Ontario. Like most Italian cooking, it was made with what they had: tons of eggplants and peppers and onions grown in their garden. Pickling meant extending their lifespan. I like pickled eggplant with roasted meats and fish, even with eggs or between two slices of Italian bread, like my grandfather used to do.

1 large eggplant, cut lengthwise into thick slices
¼ cup plus 1 teaspoon kosher salt
2 cups white wine vinegar
2 tablespoons sugar
3 cloves garlic
  Few sprigs oregano
  Pinch fresh thyme leaves
3 tablespoons olive oil
2 bell peppers, halved, seeded, and thinly sliced
1 small onion, halved and thinly sliced

E

Put the eggplant in a baking dish and sprinkle the ¼ cup salt over both sides. Set a slightly smaller dish on top of the eggplant inside the baking dish, weight it down with heavy cans, then let sit at room temperature for about 45 minutes. Weighting down the eggplant is really important to drive the water out so the seasonings can get in. Rinse the salt off the eggplant slices and squeeze out any excess liquid (do not be afraid to squeeze them hard), then firmly press them in paper towels to remove the last bit of liquid. Lay the slices in a baking dish.

Combine the vinegar, sugar, remaining teaspoon salt, garlic, oregano, and thyme in a small saucepan and simmer until the sugar and salt are dissolved.

Meanwhile, heat 2 tablespoons of the oil in a large skillet over medium-high heat. Add the peppers and onions and cook until just tender, about 3 minutes. Spoon them over the eggplant, then drizzle with the remaining tablespoon oil. Pour the vinegar mixture evenly over the vegetables and let cool. Cover and refrigerate for at least a day. The vegetables will keep, refrigerated, for about a week.

BAKED EGGPLANT CASSEROLE

SERVES 6 TO 8

HERE IS MY VERSION of the classic eggplant parmesan. To lighten it up a little, I've omitted the flour, eggs, and bread crumbs. Once baked, it has a completely soft, almost custardlike quality. A grill pan will give you nice marks on the eggplant, but you can brown the slices in a pan too. You can certainly use the homemade My Tomato Sauce (page 300), but a good prepared sauce is fine. I like to add a few roughly chopped tomatoes for texture.

2	large eggplants, thinly sliced
	Salt and pepper
	Olive oil for sautéing
1	tablespoon butter
2	cloves garlic, minced
	Dried oregano
	Crushed red pepper flakes
⅓	cup roughly chopped fresh basil
2	cups My Tomato Sauce (page 300) or other good tomato sauce
6	tomatoes, roughly chopped
¾	pound fresh mozzarella, thinly sliced
1	cup ricotta

Preheat the oven to 375°F. Working in batches, sprinkle both sides of the eggplant slices with salt and pepper. Heat about 2 tablespoons oil in a large skillet or grill pan over medium-high heat and cook the eggplant until it's softened and browned, about 3 minutes per side. Repeat until all the eggplant is cooked.

Butter the bottom of a medium baking dish and add the garlic. Layer in about one-third of the eggplant, slightly overlapping the slices. Top with a small pinch each of the oregano and red pepper flakes, followed by one-third of the basil, tomato sauce, chopped tomatoes, mozzarella, and ricotta. Repeat the layering two more times. Bake until the juices are bubbling and the top is browned, about 45 minutes. Let sit for about 10 minutes before serving.

ESCAROLE

ESCAROLE GROWS readily in cold weather and, for me, is the most accessible of the chicories. Like its cousins, endive, frisée, puntarella, and all the radicchios, these somewhat bitter characters need supporting players to build satisfying combinations with real structure.

Escarole pairs perfectly with strong flavors such as the sweetness of fruit, the acidity of balsamic vinegar, the tang of a farmstead cheese, the caramelization of an onion, the char from a wood-fired grill. The most attractive part of escarole is not the leafy bits but its thick white rib.

ESCAROLE SALAD WITH FENNEL & PEARS

SERVES 4 TO 8

COMPOSED SALADS can be a rich opportunity to layer raw flavors with crunchy textures and a surprising variety of ingredients. The firm heartiness of escarole can be quite filling; if you're creative with the ingredients, a composed salad like this one can become a satisfying meal.

1 tablespoon butter
½ vanilla bean, halved lengthwise
3 ripe pears, half diced, half sliced
3 tablespoons white balsamic vinegar

¼ cup half-and-half
 3 ounces Gorgonzola dolce
    Salt and pepper
12 large handfuls escarole and other
    hearty fall greens, leaves torn
 1 bulb fennel, sliced paper-thin
 1 crisp apple, thinly sliced
    Handful toasted salted sunflower seeds
    Fresh lemon juice

To make the dressing, heat the butter in a small saucepan over medium heat. Scrape the vanilla seeds into the saucepan (save the pod for another recipe), then add the diced pears and cook for about 2 minutes. Add the vinegar and cook until the pears are softened and the vinegar is evaporated, about another 4 minutes. Stir in the half-and-half to get up all the goodness from the saucepan, and pour the mixture into a blender. Add the Gorgonzola and process until smooth. Add salt and pepper, then set the dressing aside to cool.

In a large bowl, combine the escarole and fennel with salt and pepper. Top with the sliced apples and pears, add the sunflower seeds, and toss with enough dressing to lightly coat the salad. Add a squeeze of lemon juice for brightness.

"... find the freshest, brightest, most fragrant fennel ..."

—DAVID TANIS, *Heart of the Artichoke,* 2010

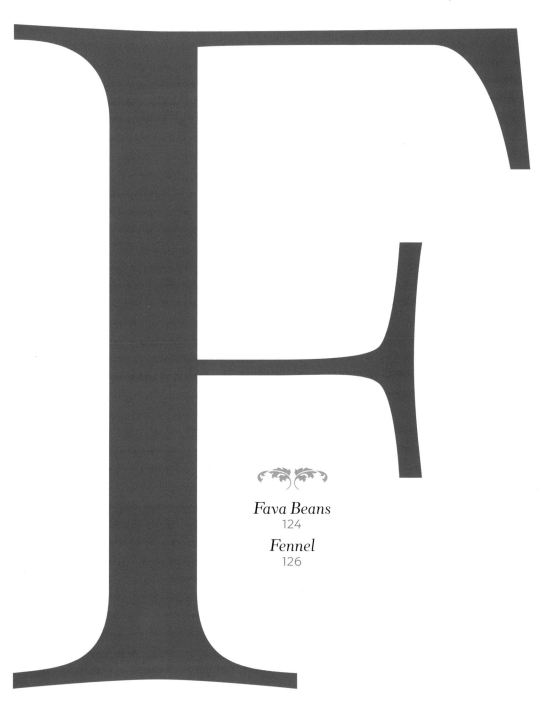

Fava Beans
124

Fennel
126

FAVA BEANS

FAVA BEANS APPEARED on the American culinary scene about twenty years ago, as farmers began to grow them not just as nitrogen-fixing cover crops but also for harvest, and chefs became infatuated with their bright green, right-from-the-garden flavor. I find the architecture of the plant astounding. I love to peel the puffy, fat pods to find those plump beans nestled in the cobwebby interior. Then those beans must be blanched in salted water for just 10 seconds before shocking in ice water. Only then do you get to slip off their pale green jackets and reveal the emeralds within.

FAVAS WITH SEA SALT & OLIVE OIL

MAKES ABOUT 1 CUP

I LOVE TO SNACK ON THESE on a warm summer day with a glass of cold rosé.

In a small bowl, toss together 1 cup blanched, peeled, and rinsed fava beans with a drizzle of olive oil, a sprinkle of sea salt, and some very thinly sliced fresh basil.

FAVA BEAN SALAD

SERVES 4

FAVAS LIKE A QUICK RINSE after peeling to preserve their smooth texture. Here I use the soft and tender leaves as greens in the salad. Makes you want to grow them, mostly because the small beans are more tender and sweeter than those from hulking pods, and you can eat the leaves and flowers too. I like to serve favas with grains or rice, because this way just a few beans go a very long way, yet still they steal the show.

3   cups cooked bulgur wheat,
    at room temperature
1½ cups fava beans, blanched, peeled, and rinsed
2   large handfuls fava bean leaves or
    other salad greens
    Olive oil
    Fresh lemon juice
    Salt and pepper

Combine the bulgur, fava beans, and greens in a large bowl, season with olive oil and lemon juice, add salt and pepper, then gently toss together.

F

FENNEL

WE'RE ATTRACTED TO fennel the way we're drawn to the ocean: They both have something primal and irresistible. Because it grows wild in so many climates, fennel is a true survivor. Greek and Roman myth has Prometheus stealing fire from the gods by hiding it in ... a fennel stalk! In fact, the alluring anise flavor of this ancient plant attracts us.

I'm fascinated by plants with such strong properties. Like mint, nettles, and horseradish, fennel is invasive, and like aggressive plants everywhere, it pulls nutrients from the ground that enhance its flavor. We know the evolution of these plants is linked to ours. The unique strength of its flavor led growers to develop this vegetable with big meaty bulbs and lacy, tender fronds and an almost endless variety of uses, both cooked and raw.

BRAISED FENNEL WITH SAFFRON & ORANGE JUICE

SERVES 6

BRAISING FENNEL SHOWS OFF its tender, fleshy quality. Once cooked, the wedges of the bulb are as soul-satisfying as the soft heart of an artichoke. Sometimes the bulbs can be fibrous on the outside; just peel that layer away. Fennel stalks, fronds, and seeds can be added to the braise for additional flavor. I use all of them in vegetable stock, too.

- 2 tablespoons olive oil
- 1 large onion, halved and thinly sliced
- 3 cloves garlic, minced
- 1 teaspoon fennel seeds
- ½ teaspoon dried oregano
  Pinch crushed red pepper flakes
  Pinch saffron
- 3 tablespoons white balsamic vinegar
- 3 bulbs fennel, cut into 6 wedges

Fennel stalks and fronds
2 cups orange juice
4 shavings orange peel

Heat the oil in a large skillet over medium heat. Add the onions and cook until softened, about 6 minutes. Add the garlic, fennel seeds, oregano, red pepper flakes, and saffron and cook for about a minute. Add the vinegar and cook until evaporated. Add the fennel wedges, fennel stalks and fronds, orange juice, and orange peels, cover, and simmer until the fennel is almost tender, about 20 minutes.

Uncover and continue simmering until the fennel is tender but still holds its shape and the liquid is reduced to almost a glaze, about 10 minutes more. Serve the braised wedges with the braising liquid. Scatter more fronds on top.

FENNEL TABBOULEH

SERVES 4 TO 6

THIS SALAD SHOWS OFF another side of fennel: fresh, crunchy, and full of anise notes. Israeli couscous isn't a grain like bulgur or farro; it's an extruded wheat pasta whose size and texture work well with the fennel dice and other chopped and tossed ingredients.

1 cup Israeli couscous
  Salt
½ bulb fennel (fronds reserved), diced
1 small tomato, diced
½ small red onion, minced
4 large green olives, pitted and sliced
4 large black olives, pitted and sliced
2 tablespoons pomegranate seeds
½ tablespoon capers, chopped
2 tablespoons olive oil
2 tablespoons fresh lime juice
  Pepper

Combine the couscous, 2 cups water, and a pinch of salt in a medium saucepan. Cover and simmer until al dente, about 15 minutes. Remove from the heat and let sit for about 10 minutes, until the liquid is evaporated.

Transfer the couscous to a large bowl and add the diced fennel, tomatoes, onions, green and black olives, pomegranate seeds, capers, olive oil, and lime juice. Add salt and pepper and toss to combine. Scatter fennel fronds over the top.

Garlic
132

Ginger
136

advance flavors, not to club them senseless."
— MARCELLA HAZAN, *Marcella Says ...*, 2004

GARLIC

FOR ME, GARLIC is the starting point of almost every dish. I use it for flavor, sure, but I'm convinced there's an elemental reason garlic helps make food delicious. The very aroma of garlic telegraphs that this is *real* cooking. Based on our primitive reaction to garlic, our evolutionary history, we know this is *safe* food. Raw garlic is generally believed to have antibacterial properties. But I like the way it makes food taste.

Garlic is always present in my kitchen. Always! Each dish I cook calls for a varying amount of garlic; the way you cut and handle it raw defines the dish. For rustic Italian-style cooking, I smash an unpeeled clove with the side of my knife, remove its paperlike skin, and toss it into a pan of sautéed asparagus, or roasting fillet of sea bass, or simmering tomato sauce, then remove it just before serving. For a refined French style, I use a small sharp knife to finely mince garlic and add it in small amounts during the cooking process of silky carrot soups, pungent herbal marinades, and rich potato gratins. For an American-style salsa, I might roughly chop a few cloves and toss them raw with ripe heirloom tomatoes, grilled sweet corn, and smoky peppers. Shockingly, for such a common and easy-to-grow ingredient, the majority of garlic in the world comes from China. You won't be surprised that I prefer to use whole heads of local garlic. I've gone so far as to entrust my family's heirloom garlic (from my great-grandfather's Italian seed) to the stewardship of Jim Wroble, a farmer friend who now supplies the restaurant and my home kitchen, too. *See Garlic Puree (page 282).*

GARLIC CONFIT

MAKES ABOUT 1½ CUPS

MAKING GARLIC CONFIT is my way of turning the sharpness of the raw thing into a sweet, soft condiment that can add rich flavor to even the simplest dish. Fresh garlic arrives at the market all at once, so making confit is a fine way to preserve its fresh goodness. And while you can easily preserve garlic in a dry, dark place, I like to take it one step further—the confit makes it so easy to use in many recipes.

Cooking garlic slowly over a long period of time draws out its sweetness and eliminates its pungency. It also gets you one step closer to cooking a memorable dish. The oil that's left is a fantastic and flavorful cooking oil on its own. I like to fold garlic confit into stewed beans and braised greens; or I coat green beans or bok choy with it in a pan sauté; or I blend it into an avocado mousse.

Combine 1 cup garlic cloves and 1 cup peanut or grapeseed oil in a small saucepan and very gently simmer until the cloves are soft, about 2 hours. Let cool, then transfer the cloves and oil to a covered container. The confit will keep, refrigerated, for about a month.

Mincing Garlic

Choose a chef's knife for this job because mincing garlic requires a big blade that can rock on the cutting board. Only use whole heads of healthy garlic (that is, white, with papery skins, and firm to the touch). Separate the cloves, smash each with the side of the knife, and remove the peel. First, slice the cloves, and then, with one hand on the handle and the other on the top of the blade, mince the slices by rocking the knife back and forth.

Garlic Green & Black

To put it really clearly, green garlic is simply a young garlic plant, pulled in the spring before the bulb is fully formed. Most farmers in North America plant garlic around Columbus Day in the fall, winter it over, then harvest it by mid-July. In early spring, there are fewer sources of revenue, so farmers often pull up 10 to 15 percent of their immature garlic to sell as green garlic. Enthusiastic cooks everywhere benefit from its light, aromatic flavor in spring dishes. I especially love to use green garlic in soups and light vegetable sauces, scrambled eggs, roasted new carrots—I could go on. The rest of the garlic still in the ground has yet another benefit before harvest: garlic scapes. These are the tender shoots of the plant that grow up and out of the stem, curling their way to the sky. Most farmers cut the scapes to preserve the energy of the bulb and thus create yet another spring crop.

Black garlic, on the other hand, uses fully mature garlic bulbs. Whole heads of garlic are very slowly heated and then aged, a process that turns the ivory white cloves coal black. It's an ancient way to generate flavor in Asian cultures, but black garlic has become newly popular today. I add it to fish marinades, mushroom broth, sautéed cabbage, and pickles or other fermented foods, where it lends a satisfying, earthy flavor.

Green garlic is easily found at spring farmers' markets; buy black garlic at Asian specialty stores.

OMELET OF GARLIC SCAPES

SERVES 1

GARLIC SCAPES ARE FAR MORE TENDER and mild than mature garlic. They can be cooked and enjoyed like green beans or thinly sliced and served with pasta, potatoes, or eggs, all of which show off their beautiful aroma. The technique of the omelet is one that I have practiced for years and years, and maybe one day I'll get it exactly right. The size of the pan is important, control of the heat is imperative, and timing is everything. Vigorously stirring the beaten eggs as they slowly cook produces a light and fluffy omelet.

- 2 tablespoons butter
- 1 clove garlic, smashed
- 2 garlic scapes, thinly sliced
  Salt and pepper
- 3 eggs

Heat 1 tablespoon of the butter in a 6-inch skillet over medium heat. Add the garlic clove, scapes, salt, and pepper and cook until the scapes begin to soften, about 2 minutes. Remove the garlic clove and discard, then transfer the scapes to a bowl.

Wipe the skillet clean. Melt the tablespoon butter over medium heat. Beat the eggs well in a small bowl, and add salt and pepper. Add the eggs to the pan and stir vigorously to create small, fine curds. As you work, scrape down the sides of the pan so the eggs cook evenly. Sprinkle one-third of the scapes onto the eggs. When the top is evenly set and not runny, tilt the pan away from you and fold the omelet in half. The lip of the pan will help form the shape of the omelet as it continues to cook gently. Turn out the omelet onto a plate and top with the remaining garlic scapes.

GINGER

WHEN I STARTED COOKING in Japan, I learned what an exciting and foundational ingredient ginger can be, mostly because the Japanese use it young and just-harvested. Then it's far superior to the gnarly, dried fibrous roots we see too frequently. Now this fresh and thin-skinned ginger is available here, and it does make a difference. Mincing ginger together with garlic creates a powerful flavor combination. When cooked in a drop of sesame oil, it can transform almost any raw ingredient into a memorable dish. Add soy sauce and you're headed East; with anchovy and tomato, you're going West. *See Asparagus with Preserved Ginger Relish (page 21).*

GINGER TEA

SERVES 2

WHENEVER ANYONE'S not feeling great in our house, we make them a little ginger tea and watch it work its soothing magic. This is a good way to use fresh ginger scraps.

Put about 8 thin slices of peeled ginger in a teapot. Cover with 3 cups of boiling water, then let steep for about 5 minutes. Serve with honey.

PICKLED GINGER

MAKES ABOUT 1 CUP

USE PICKLED GINGER IN SALADS, serve it with fish, or mince it and add it to sautéed vegetables. A mandoline is perfect for making thin, even slices. Follow the Basic Pickling Recipe (page 66), substituting these ingredients. Refrigerated, it keeps a few weeks.

- 1 cup very thinly sliced fresh young ginger
- 6 tablespoons rice wine vinegar
- 2 tablespoons water
- 2 tablespoons sugar
- ½ tablespoon kosher salt

Peeling Ginger

Young, fresh ginger has paper-thin, tender skin. So as not to waste any of the delicious root, use a teaspoon to scrape away just the outside layer. Or use a peeler.

"*The herbs are left on their stems so that you can make*

*Herbs
(Chives,
Parsley,
Rosemary,
Tarragon &
Thyme)*
140

Horseradish
148

salads, as goats do, while you chew." —TAMAR ADLER,

An Everlasting Meal, 2011

HERBS

VISITING CASA CAPONETTI in Tuscania in central Italy with my daughters, we were asked to forage for salad—gathering wild fennel, mint, and other wild herbs from the fields. It was a late afternoon on a warm spring day and we followed our noses, wandering wherever the smells led. I realized we were doing what people have done forever: finding what is edible in the landscape. Nature has a way of leading you along. It's the business of plants to attract. Curiosity and hunger have encouraged us to discover just which plants in all that wildness are good to eat. Gathering herbs engages our senses. Whether it's a tour of the garden, roaming a farmers' market, or even snipping a pot of thyme on the windowsill, we are repeating a primal act, letting our senses lead us to herbs that will season our food with the aromas of the land.

PARSLEY WITH BROWN BUTTER CROUTONS

MAKES ABOUT 3 CUPS

MAKING CROUTONS is engaging in the essential work of being a cook: making something out of nothing, or almost. It's an idea that appeals to me. The bread can be fresh or a few days old; what really matters is that the loaf is dense. The assertive greenness of parsley is what brings the croutons to life. Try other herbs like lovage, celery leaves, tarragon, or cilantro.

¼ cup olive oil
2 tablespoons butter
5 cloves garlic, smashed
  Pinch crushed red pepper flakes
  Pinch dried oregano
2 heaping cups croutons, diced large
  Salt and pepper
2 cups roughly chopped fresh flat-leaf parsley
½ cup grated Grana Padano

Heat the oil, butter, and garlic in a large skillet over medium heat. When the butter melts, add the red pepper flakes, oregano, croutons, salt, and pepper. Cook, turning the croutons over regularly, until they are golden and have absorbed all the oil and butter, about 5 minutes. Remove from the heat and toss with the parsley and cheese.

Using Croutons

- Toss in a green bean salad, or in a tomato salad like panzanella.
- Add to pasta for crunch.
- Serve with grilled zucchini and fresh goat cheese.
- Pile on top of steamed mussels and tomatoes (page 36).
- Stir into Pepper Stew (page 237).

ALL-HERB SALAD WITH COUSCOUS

SERVES 4

THIS ALMOST INSTANT tabbouleh-like salad enlivens couscous with a mix of almost every herb in the garden. Any combination is delicious, as long as the herbs are super fresh.

	Juice from ½ lemon
¼	preserved lemon (right)
½	tablespoon honey
1½	tablespoons olive oil
	Salt and pepper
2	cups cooked couscous
3	small tomatoes, sliced
⅓	English cucumber, very thinly sliced
1½	cups fresh flat-leaf parsley
1½	cups fresh dill
1	cup fresh tarragon leaves
1	cup small fresh basil leaves
1	cup fresh chives cut into 1-inch pieces

For the dressing, process the lemon juice, preserved lemon pulp and zest, honey, oil, salt, and pepper in a blender until smooth.

Combine the couscous, tomatoes, cucumbers, parsley, dill, tarragon, basil, chives, salt, and pepper in a large bowl, toss with the dressing, and serve.

Preserving Lemons

This is a wonderful way to preserve Meyer lemons in their fleeting season or to build flavor with regular lemons. I use diced preserved lemons in many salads, sauces, and soups, and as a bright accent to roasted vegetables.

Find a large, leak-proof jar. Slice the tops and bottoms off 10 to 12 lemons. Halve the lemons and rub inside and out with plenty of salt. Fit into the container and cover with fresh lemon juice. Refrigerate for about a month, turning the jar upside down every few days to distribute the liquid. I like to use the pulp and the skin, diced, and discard the white pith.

143

CHIMICHURRI ON STEAK

SERVES 4

I LOVE CONDIMENT SAUCES—the kind you chew, not overly refined, or overthought. This is a totally different approach to seasoning: The sauce is *on* the dish, not *in* it.

Chimichurri, while Argentine in origin, works in the same way as a hearty, chunky Mexican salsa. It's dressed down and casual. It's also very easy to make: a rich flavor base (of cooked onions and garlic), a splash of red wine vinegar, and a powerful explosion of freshly chopped herbs. Fresh and dried herbs are the heroes of this piece—they spike the sauce with flavor. Stir them in and enjoy the aromatics immediately, or let it sit until the flavors meld.

This sauce changes over time. Like wine. I serve it with Pan-Roasted Fingerlings (page 241) and this pan-roasted rib-eye steak, but I also slather it on eggplant (page 112), on artichoke hearts (page 16), and on pan-roasted fish (page 104). The recipe makes about 2 cups of sauce, so you'll have extra, but trust me, it won't last long in your refrigerator.

FOR THE CHIMICHURRI
- ½ cup olive oil
- 2 small onions, finely chopped
- 2 cloves garlic, minced
- 1 teaspoon minced fresh thyme
- 1 teaspoon minced fresh rosemary
  Salt and pepper
- 5 Pickled Peppers (page 236), finely diced
- 1 red bell pepper, finely diced
- 1 teaspoon dried oregano
- 1 teaspoon ancho chile powder
  Pinch cayenne
- ¼ cup red wine vinegar
- 1 cup mixed fresh herbs (such as parsley, cilantro, dill, chives), minced

FOR THE STEAK
- 1 (1½-pound) rib-eye steak, 1½ to 2 inches thick
- 1 tablespoon olive oil
  Salt and pepper
- 2 tablespoons butter
- 1 clove garlic, smashed
- 1 sprig thyme
- 1 sprig rosemary

Heat 1 tablespoon of the oil in a small saucepan over medium heat. Add the onions and garlic and sweat until softened, about 6 minutes. Add the thyme, rosemary, salt, and pepper and stir for a minute. Add the pickled peppers, bell peppers, oregano, chile powder, and cayenne and continue to sweat for about 5 minutes.

Add the vinegar and cook until it evaporates, then add the rest of the oil and continue to barely simmer until the onions and peppers are soft, about 7 minutes more. Stir in the herbs, and add salt and pepper. Transfer to a bowl and let cool while you make the steak. The sauce is good warm or at room temperature; store in the refrigerator, where it will keep for about 3 days.

Remove the steak from the refrigerator and let it come to room temperature, about 15 minutes. Heat the oil in a medium skillet over high heat. Generously sprinkle the steak with salt and pepper and add to the skillet. When it starts to brown, reduce the heat to medium and cook until deep brown, about 10 minutes. Flip the steak, cook for 3 minutes, then add the butter, garlic, thyme, and rosemary and regularly baste the steak with pan juices until it's medium-rare, about 6 minutes.

Transfer the steak to a cutting board and let rest for about 10 minutes before cutting against the grain into thick slices. Save the meat juice and add to the sauce. Serve with the sauce. I like to shower the platter with crispy fingerling potatoes, pickled peppers, cherry tomatoes, and more herbs.

CHIVE MATZOH BREI

SERVES 6

I DIDN'T GROW UP EATING matzoh brei; this is an adapted version of my father-in-law Dan Dubin's signature dish, and it took guts to mess with that tradition. But mess I did, first soaking the matzoh, and leaving it in big enough pieces to form an interesting layered effect. We make this at Passover, and it seems only right to include the earliest chives of the year as a real celebration of spring.

2 tablespoons butter
½ small onion, thinly sliced
  Salt and pepper
5 matzohs
1 teaspoon minced fresh rosemary
2 cups whole milk
4 eggs
4 tablespoons minced fresh chives
  Olive oil

Preheat the oven to 350°F. Heat 1 tablespoon of the butter in a medium ovenproof skillet over medium-high heat. Add the onions, salt, and pepper and cook until light brown, 3 minutes.

Meanwhile, break the matzoh into pieces in a large bowl, then add the rosemary and milk and stir to combine. Add the cooked onions and let sit until the matzoh is slightly softened, about 4 minutes. Transfer the solids to a medium bowl, reserving the milk. Add the eggs, ½ cup of the reserved milk, and 2 tablespoons of the chives to the matzoh and stir until well combined.

Heat the remaining tablespoon butter in the same skillet over medium heat. Add the matzoh mixture and let it sit for about 4 minutes. Pop the skillet into the oven and bake until just set, about 8 minutes. At this point, you can unmold the matzoh brei from the pan onto a plate so the bottom is facing up. It looks great that way, but can be tricky to flip. Or just serve it in the skillet. Drizzle with oil and sprinkle generously with the remaining chives.

Blanching Herbs

Blanching herbs adds color and flavor, and softens them so you can make smooth purees to use in many dishes. Pick the tender leaves and stems from whatever herb you're using, then drop into a pot of salted boiling water for a minute. Scoop out the herbs and transfer to a bowl of ice water for 2 or 3 minutes. Drain and squeeze out the excess water.

HORSERADISH

NOW'S THE TIME to go beyond the ubiquitous pickled horseradish that comes in a jar. I want to rescue that hardy, beautiful, long, and sturdy root from its processed state. Fresh horseradish roots are widely available and it's so easy to peel and grate them, thus adding real character to so many dishes. Fresh horseradish is so much more delicate than the processed stuff.

ROOT VEGETABLE STEW IN HORSERADISH BEEF BROTH

SERVES 6

THIS DISH CELEBRATES the welcome sharpness of horseradish in an unconventional way, by bringing a rich beef broth (could be chicken or pork, too) together with mellow vegetables like leeks, potatoes, and rutabaga. The stew is spiked with a horseradish vinaigrette. A Microplane works well to grate the horseradish. Serve with cornichons.

6 fingerling potatoes, halved lengthwise

4 carrots, thickly sliced on the diagonal

4 baby turnips, quartered

2 small leeks (white and pale green parts), thickly sliced on the diagonal

2 parsnips, peeled and thickly sliced

1 rutabaga, peeled and thickly sliced

4 cups beef broth
  Salt and pepper

½ cup olive oil

⅓ cup finely grated fresh horseradish
  Grated zest and juice from ½ lemon

2 tablespoons golden raisins

2 tablespoons red wine vinegar

1½ tablespoons Dijon mustard

1 tablespoon honey

  Small piece fresh horseradish
  Cornichons

Combine the potatoes, carrots, turnips, leeks, parsnips, and rutabaga in a medium saucepan. Add the broth, salt, and pepper and simmer until just tender, about 15 minutes.

Meanwhile, combine the oil, horseradish, lemon zest and juice, raisins, vinegar, mustard, and honey in a blender and process until smooth. Add salt and pepper and thin with 2 tablespoons water. Set the vinaigrette aside.

Serve the braised vegetables in deep bowls. Stir about 3 tablespoons of the vinaigrette into the broth. Fill the bowls with the flavored broth and grate some fresh horseradish on top. Serve with more vinaigrette on the side and the cornichons.

HORSERADISH COMPOUND BUTTER WITH ROASTED SWEET POTATOES

MAKES ABOUT 1 CUP

RAW HORSERADISH IS DECEIVING. It's not nearly as pungent as its pickled state, so be prepared to use more than you think you need. This butter is wonderful on roasted sweet potatoes or carrots, on a mushroom cap, or on pan-roasted fish, a pork chop, or a piece of grilled beef.

- 8   tablespoons (1 stick) butter,
      at room temperature
- ¼   cup finely grated fresh horseradish
- 3   tablespoons chopped fresh flat-leaf parsley
- 3   tablespoons minced fresh chives
- 3   tablespoons panko or dried bread crumbs
      Grated zest and juice from ½ lemon
      Salt and pepper

      Thick slices roasted sweet potato

Put the butter, horseradish, parsley, chives, panko or bread crumbs, lemon zest and juice, salt, and pepper in a small bowl and stir until thoroughly combined.

Use as a topping and spread as is. Or form the butter into a log by transferring it into a small resealable plastic bag and closing it. Then evenly push the butter to the bottom of the bag with the back of a chef's knife. Refrigerate or freeze until firm, then remove the log from the bag and slice. The butter will keep, tightly wrapped, for up to 5 days in the refrigerator and up to 2 months in the freezer.

Preheat the oven to 350°F. Slice the cold butter log, put a thick layer on each roasted sweet potato slice, and transfer to a baking pan or skillet. Put the pan in the oven and heat until the butter softens and browns, up to 15 minutes.

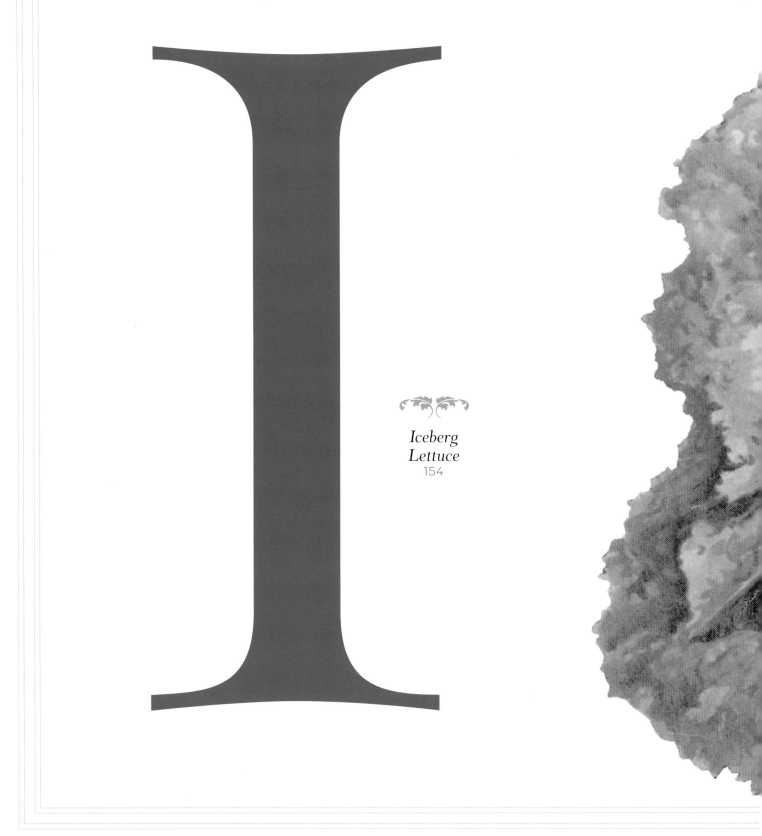

"*Unlike some frail lettuces that wilt and swoon, iceberg*

I

*Iceberg
Lettuce*
154

is stalwart." —MARION CUNNINGHAM, *Lost Recipes*, 2003

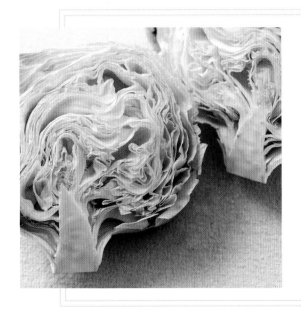

ICEBERG LETTUCE

MOST CHEFS LOOK DOWN their noses at iceberg lettuce, thinking it has no nutritional value, little flavor, and even less style. But what it does have is super crunch. And a kind of all-American nostalgia. The very idea of eating iceberg lettuce makes people smile. Try grilling it for a fresh take on this old favorite.

GRILLED ICEBERG LETTUCE WITH MARINATED TOMATOES

SERVES 4

ICEBERG LETTUCE CAN STAND UP to a hot griddle and an intensely flavorful dressing. This homemade mayonnaise–based dressing has a few steps, but they're easy and the salad that results is surprisingly well worth it. You'll feel accomplished! The tomato-infused oil catapults iceberg lettuce to a whole new level of enjoyment.

½ pint cherry tomatoes

3 cloves garlic, smashed

1 (1½-inch) piece fresh ginger, cut into thirds and smashed

3 strips lemon zest
Juice from ¼ lemon

3 sprigs oregano

2 sprigs basil

⅔ cup plus 1 tablespoon olive oil
Salt and pepper

2 egg yolks

1 heaping teaspoon Dijon mustard

1 tablespoon capers, roughly chopped

5 strips Lemon Zest Confit, shredded (optional, right)

1 head Iceberg lettuce, cut Into 4 wedges

Cut a narrow slit in the bottom of each tomato. Combine the tomatoes, garlic, ginger, lemon zest, lemon juice, oregano, basil, and the ⅔ cup oil in a medium saucepan. Add salt and pepper. Warm the mixture just until it starts to bubble. Off the heat, let the flavors infuse for about 30 minutes. Strain, keeping the tomatoes and oil separate.

Whisk together the yolks and mustard in a medium bowl, and add salt and pepper. Whisk in ½ cup of the flavored oil, then the capers and lemon zest confit, if using.

Heat the remaining tablespoon oil in a grill pan over high heat. Grill the iceberg wedges until lightly charred, about 3 minutes. Transfer to plates, drizzle the dressing, and top with the tomatoes.

Lemon Zest Confit

Lemon confit is simply the skin of lemon (or other citrus fruit) blanched and cooked slowly with sugar and water. The result is a delicious, sweet, and preserved condiment that can add bright notes to many dishes.

Peel the skin of a lemon and remove any white pith. Blanch the skin in boiling water for 1 minute, then place in a small saucepan with 1 cup Simple Syrup (page 66). Bring to a simmer and cook for 25 minutes. Remove from the heat and let the peel cool in the syrup. Submerged in syrup and refrigerated, the confit will keep for a month.

"*Jerusalem artichokes are sweet and almost garlicky and*

J

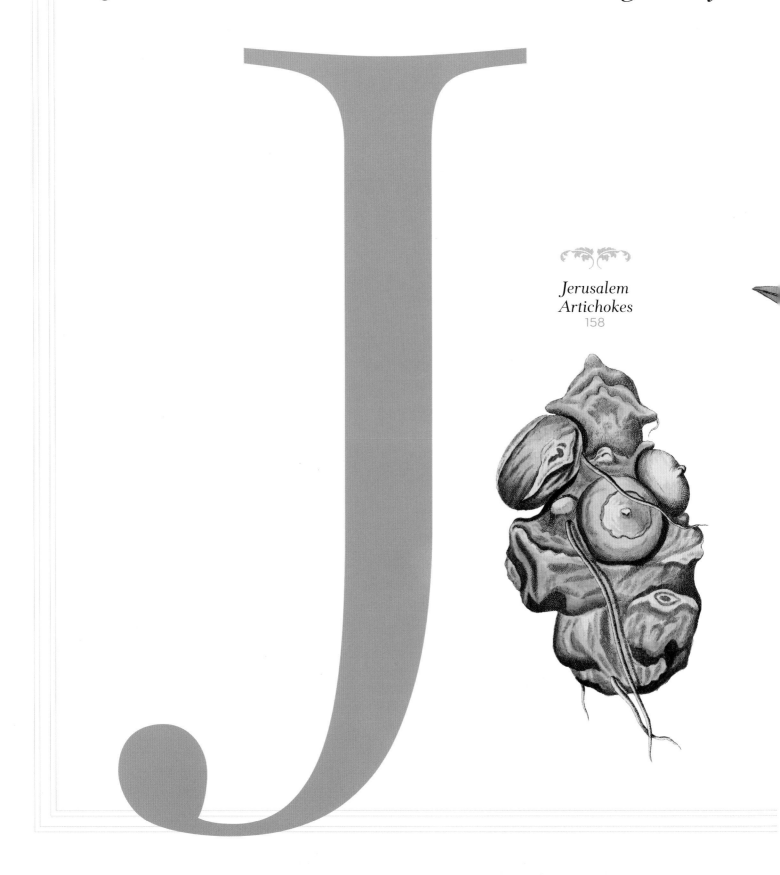

Jerusalem
Artichokes
158

mushroomy and gorgeous." —JAMIE OLIVER, *Jamie's Dinners*, 2004

JERUSALEM ARTICHOKES

DESPITE THE RICH and complex lore surrounding the naming of this indigenous plant, we do know Jerusalem artichokes are neither true artichokes nor do they come from Jerusalem. They are also known as sunchokes, but I have another word for these tubers of a plant in the sunflower family: delicious!

I feel really connected to this tall, leafy plant with bright yellow flowers. Below ground, their intensive system of knobby, oddly shaped tubers can quickly dominate a garden. At first glance, it's not obvious how Jerusalem artichokes can become food. But there are so many ways to use them: Peeled and raw, they're crunchy and cool; roasted, they become amazingly sweet and meaty; pureed, they're silky smooth. Please reconsider the image of the Jerusalem artichoke: Don't connect it with the starchiness of potatoes; it's more like a water chestnut. Can you tell this is one of my favorite things to eat?

SLICED RAW JERUSALEM ARTICHOKE SALAD

SERVES 4

SERVING JERUSALEM ARTICHOKES RAW shows off their light crunchiness. Think of fresh carrots and you get the idea. A handheld mandoline makes the slicing quick, easy, and consistent. Creamy avocado is a perfect contrast. The nuttiness of sunflower seeds is the last touch—a delightful surprise.

1 ripe avocado, pitted and peeled
3 tablespoons yogurt
Fresh lime juice
Salt and pepper
8 Jerusalem artichokes, peeled and cut paper-thin
Olive oil
2 large handfuls baby salad greens

¼ cup toasted sunflower seeds

Mash the avocado in a small bowl with the yogurt and a splash of lime juice until smooth. Add salt and pepper.

Lightly season the Jerusalem artichokes in a medium bowl with oil, lime juice, salt, and pepper.

In another bowl, season the salad greens the same way. Spread the mashed avocado on plates, alternate layers of artichoke and salad greens on top, and sprinkle with the sunflower seeds.

ROASTED JERUSALEM ARTICHOKES & BRUSSELS SPROUT LEAVES

SERVES 4

I LIKE TO COOK Jerusalem artichokes in the same way I'd cook a fish, roasting it whole in the oven, basting it, and then slicing it. For a deep, dark caramelization, start with a skillet on the burner. The direct contact with the high heat and the ability to roll the veggies in the pan results in more even color. And all of that means more flavor.

5 large Jerusalem artichokes
3½ tablespoons olive oil
   Salt and pepper
1 clove garlic, smashed
1 small sprig rosemary

1 tablespoon butter
3 cups Brussels sprout leaves
   (from about 1 pound whole, page 53)
1 shallot, minced
   Fresh lemon juice

Preheat the oven to 375°F. Using a paring knife, cut the knobs off the Jerusalem artichokes. This helps them cook evenly. Cook the smaller cut-off pieces in the same pan with the large pieces and remove them when they're soft.

Heat a tablespoon of the oil in a medium ovenproof skillet over medium-high heat. Add the large Jerusalem artichokes, salt, and pepper, and cook until brown all over, about 6 minutes. Pop the pan into the oven and roast until the artichokes are tender, about 30 minutes. Roll them around every 10 minutes or so, for even roasting and browning.

Remove the skillet from the oven and put it on a burner over medium heat. Add the garlic, rosemary, and butter and, using a spoon, baste the Jerusalem artichokes until they are lightly glazed and light brown all over, tilting the pan so the liquid pools at the bottom edge. Transfer to a cutting board and thickly slice crosswise.

Heat 2 tablespoons of the oil in a large skillet over medium-high heat. Add the Brussels sprout leaves, salt, and pepper, and cook for about a minute, stirring constantly. Add the shallots and cook for another minute, stirring. Add the roasted artichokes and cook until the Brussels sprout leaves are brown in places and crisp-tender, about another minute. Season with lemon juice and stir in the remaining ½ tablespoon oil.

Prepping Jerusalem Artichokes

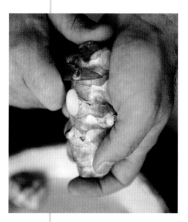

I like to tame these gnarly roots by peeling away uneven knobs and bumps, but you do not really have to peel them at all, unless you want them to be perfectly white, as in the Jerusalem Artichoke Chowder with Monkfish (page 162). Otherwise, I just trim them to make them easy to wash and cook more evenly. I choose tubers more for density than shape, the firmer the better.

JERUSALEM ARTICHOKE CHOWDER WITH MONKFISH

SERVES 4

NEW ENGLAND CHOWDERS are often synonymous with starchy potatoes. Jerusalem artichokes make this soup a silky, sweet, and smooth puree, lending creaminess and a subtle nuttiness. I add dashi, ginger, and mushrooms to round out the flavor and hint at the Japanese influence in my cooking. Dashi adds a foundation of flavor to the chowder, but if you do not have it, the chowder will still be delicious with vegetable stock or water.

- 6 tablespoons olive oil
- 1 large onion, diced
- 3 cloves garlic, 2 minced, 1 smashed
- 1 tablespoon minced fresh ginger
- 12 medium Jerusalem artichokes, peeled and chopped
- 4 cups Dashi (page 109), vegetable stock, or water
   Salt
- 1¼ pounds monkfish or other firm white fish, cut into large pieces
- 1 pound maitake or other locally cultivated mushrooms, cut into large pieces
   Pepper
- 1 tablespoon butter

   Handful fresh flat-leaf parsley, chopped

Heat 2 tablespoons of the oil in a saucepan over medium heat. Add the onions, minced garlic, and 2 teaspoons of the ginger and cook until softened, about 4 minutes. Add the Jerusalem artichokes and dashi and simmer until the artichokes are tender, about 12 minutes.

Transfer the mixture to a blender, add 2 tablespoons of the oil, and season with salt. Process until smooth, then pour through a fine-mesh strainer into a medium saucepan. Straining makes the chowder silkier and more refined. The chowder base should be the consistency of light cream; thin it with a little water if needed. Bring the base to a simmer, add the fish, and poach at just below a simmer until just cooked through—for monkfish, about 3½ minutes.

Meanwhile, heat the remaining 2 tablespoons oil in a large skillet over medium-high heat. Add the mushrooms, salt, and pepper, and brown for about 5 minutes. Add the smashed garlic, remaining teaspoon ginger, and butter and, using a spoon, baste the mushrooms until they are lightly glazed, tilting the pan so the liquid pools at the bottom edge. Serve the chowder in bowls topped with the mushrooms and parsley.

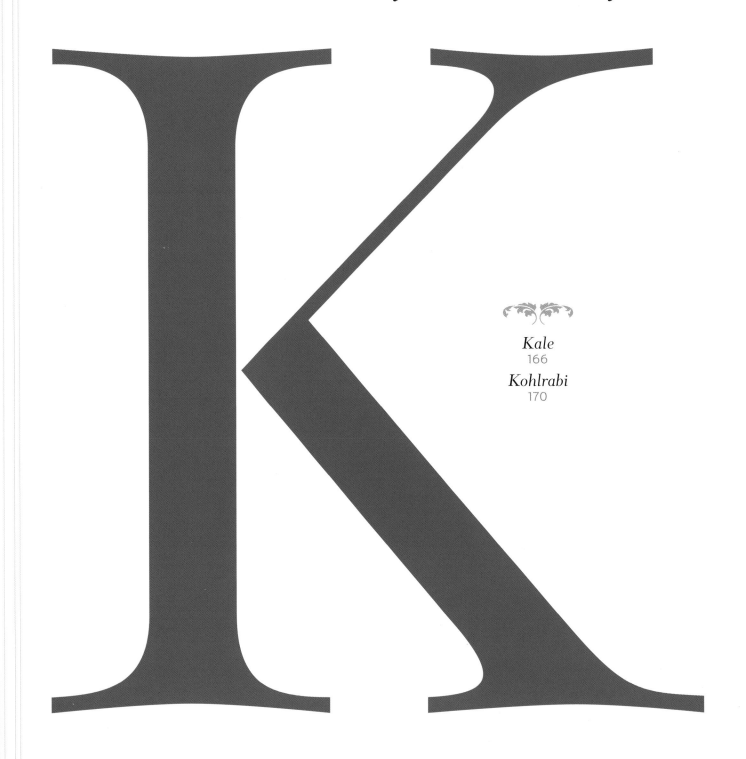

"*...kohlrabi's radishy, water chestnutty crunch.*"

Kale
166

Kohlrabi
170

—HUGH FEARNLEY-WHITTINGSTALL, *River Cottage VEG*, 2013

K

KALE

LONG AFTER THE CURRENT kale frenzy is over, we'll still be loving this healthy, delicious plant that grows in nearly every season. And contrary to our common belief that big leafy plants are difficult, even mysterious, to prepare, kale is a snap. Kale says green; it stays green. It has fueled an entire juicing craze. Unlike spinach, it doesn't wilt as fast or have unpleasant associations from childhood (mostly because we never ate it as children). Trendy or not, kale is a wonderful vegetable to cook. It comes in so many different varieties, each with its distinctive texture, and color. Some of my favorites are Lacinato or Tuscan (aka *cavalo nero*), curly leaved, and Red Russian. They all can be served raw, steamed, sautéed, braised, roasted, and fried—with healthy, terrific results.

KALE SALAD WITH KALE CHIPS & SOY DRESSING

SERVES 4

THE STORY OF THIS kale and kohlrabi salad is like two high-school friends: One grew up to be famous, the other didn't but deserves to be. Together, they make a pretty good team. A good salad is about combining a few crunchy things in a way that lets it feel fresh but still hearty.

This salad is kale times two: The easy-to-make chips are great as a snack, and enhance the overall kaleness of this salad. The kohlrabi is surprisingly refreshing. The dressing is a flavor combination from Southeast Asia—a sweet, sour, and spicy vinaigrette helps the earthiness of kale. I use Tuscan kale here, but any variety works well. Wait until the last moment before dressing the salad so it doesn't become soggy.

1½	bunches kale, center ribs removed
¼	cup olive oil
	Salt and pepper
2	kohlrabi, peeled and cut into matchsticks
¼	cup rice wine vinegar
¼	cup fresh lime juice
2	tablespoons soy sauce
¼	cup sugar
½	teaspoon chile paste
4	lime wedges

For the chips, preheat the oven to 325°F. Wash and pat dry one-third of the kale leaves and toss in a large bowl with the oil, salt, and pepper. Arrange the leaves in a single layer on two baking sheets and bake until just crisp, about 15 minutes. (These are so good, why not make more to eat on their own?)

Meanwhile, cut the remaining kale crosswise into thin slices and put in a large bowl with the kohlrabi. Combine the vinegar, lime juice, soy sauce, sugar, and chile paste in a small bowl and stir the dressing until the sugar is dissolved. Toss the vegetables with just enough dressing to lightly coat them, and add salt and pepper. Serve the salad with the kale chips and lime wedges.

KALE SOUP WITH POTATOES & LEEKS

SERVES 4 TO 6

THINK OF THIS as a vibrant green vichyssoise: It has the requisite leek and potato and is great hot or cold. Kale adds both color and a pleasant earthy flavor.

- 4 tablespoons olive oil
- 1 onion, finely chopped
- 1 leek, diced
- 1 clove garlic, minced
- 3 Yukon Gold potatoes, peeled and cut into large chunks
  Salt and pepper
- ½ bunch kale, center ribs removed and leaves sliced crosswise
  Handful fresh flat-leaf parsley

- 2 baby turnips, peeled and sliced paper-thin

Heat 2 tablespoons of the oil in a medium saucepan over medium heat. Add the onions, leeks, and garlic and cook until softened, about 8 minutes. Add the potatoes, 5 cups water, salt, and pepper, and bring to a boil. Add the kale and simmer until the potatoes are tender, about 15 minutes.

Stir in the parsley and the remaining 2 tablespoons oil, then process in a blender until smooth. Serve hot or cold, topped with the sliced turnips.

KALE COOKED QUICKLY

SERVES 4

I USE THIS TECHNIQUE for cooking most young leafy greens straight from the garden–spinach, collards, Swiss chard, kale. These young greens are tender enough to chop, blanch, and simply sauté. After this quick cooking, the greens can be blended into a puree or turned into a soup.

- 4 tablespoons olive oil
- ½ small onion, finely chopped
- 1 clove garlic, smashed
- 2 bunches kale, center ribs removed, leaves blanched and roughly chopped
  Salt and pepper
  Fresh lemon juice

Heat 2 tablespoons of the oil in a large skillet over medium-high heat. Add the onions and garlic and cook until just starting to brown, about 3 minutes. Add the blanched kale, 1½ cups water, salt, and pepper, and simmer until tender, about 10 minutes. Stir in the remaining 2 tablespoons oil and a big squeeze of lemon juice.

KOHLRABI

YOU'LL LIKE kohlrabi once you get to know it. It has a tender heart, and despite its weirdly protuberant leaves, the young globe (really a succulent stem, not a gnarled root) has no bitterness. Buy kohlrabi no bigger than a baseball, when it's sweet and crunchy raw. It's easy to peel, browns nicely when roasted, and is one of the world's most underrated vegetables.

CRUNCHY SALAD OF KOHLRABI & TOASTED WALNUTS

SERVES 4

I LIKE THE WAY THIS SALAD shows off kohlrabi's brightness of flavor and crunch. Add a handful of chopped parsley if you like. Let it sit for a while to marinate in the walnut vinaigrette before serving.

- ¼ cup fresh lemon juice
- ¼ cup walnut oil
- 2 tablespoons olive oil
  Salt and pepper
- 1 or 2 kohlrabi, peeled and sliced paper-thin
- ½ cup toasted walnuts, roughly chopped

Whisk together the lemon juice, walnut oil, and olive oil in a small bowl, then add lots of salt and pepper. Combine the kohlrabi and walnuts in a medium bowl. Gently toss with enough of the vinaigrette so that the salad is quite moist, separating the kohlrabi slices.

K

Unlocking Kohlrabi

Kohlrabi only looks otherworldly. Its outward appearance is just that: an apparition. It is really a soft stem whose spiky offshoots are merely the ribs of leaves, easily removed with a paring knife. Then kohlrabi is as easy to peel as an apple, revealing its snowy white interior. Sliced, kohlrabi's crunchier than potato chips and just as great to dip.

ROASTED QUARTERED KOHLRABI

SERVES 4

ROASTING KOHLRABI is just as simple as roasting a potato. I like to toss the browned chunks right in the pan with a big pinch of pimentón (smoked paprika), and serve it up immediately.

2   tablespoons olive oil
2   or 3 kohlrabi, peeled and quartered
    Salt and pepper
    Pimentón

Preheat the oven to 350°F. Heat the oil in a large ovenproof skillet over medium-high heat. Add the kohlrabi, salt, and pepper, and cook until the pieces are well browned, about 3 minutes. Kohlrabi browns quickly—even faster than a potato. Put the skillet in the oven and bake until the chunks are just tender, about 12 minutes. Turn into a bowl and sprinkle with pimentón.

"Leeks embody the delicate side of the allium tribe ...

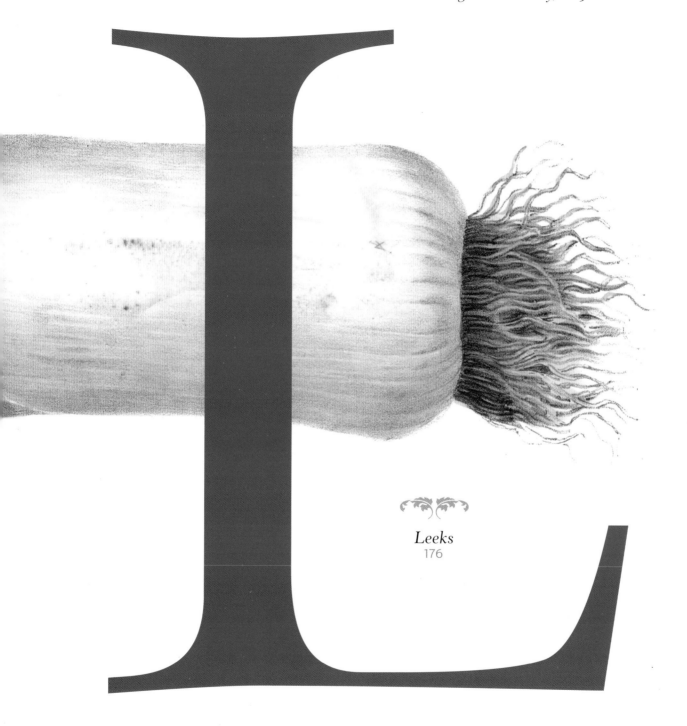

Leeks
176

L

LEEKS

I DIDN'T UNDERSTAND LEEKS when I was growing up; in fact, I never ate them. It took living in France for me to fall for them. The Leek Quiche recipe (page 180) was not only the first thing I learned in cooking school in Paris; it was also part of my final "exam." I had to make it under the close scrutiny of the chefs. So you'd better believe I take leeks seriously.

Leeks are the mildest of the indispensable onion family, less pungent than garlic and shallots, richer and more discreet when cooked. We do not eat them raw, but they soften quickly, and as they warm, their deliciousness is revealed. Minced leeks add flavor as a base in so many recipes. I celebrate whole leeks, too, braised with vinaigrette. They taste mellow tossed with quinoa, or just grilled, sliced in half, and salted. Leeks grow very large in deep, dark soil, and that sturdiness allows them to winter over. Leeks are easy to use. Make sure to wash them thoroughly (soil lodges in their tight layers).

BRAISED LEEKS & YELLOW LENTILS WITH ANCHOVY DRESSING

SERVES 4

LEEKS, WHEN DICED small and simmered with lentils or beans or rice, tend to melt into the mixture, creating a soft and delicious texture. Here a braise is paired with the tanginess of an anchovy dressing to become a seductive dish, a meal in itself. This braise could also be the beginning of a lovely lentil soup, blended with an aromatic leek stock (right).

6	tablespoons olive oil
4	cloves garlic, minced
1	shallot, minced
1½	salted anchovy fillets, rinsed
1	teaspoon grated Parmigiano
	Fresh lemon juice
	Salt and pepper
3	leeks (white parts), minced
½	small onion, minced

- 1 cup yellow lentils, rinsed and picked over
- 1 black radish or 3 large red radishes, cut into thin matchsticks
- 20 tatsoi leaves with stems
- 2 tablespoons white wine vinegar
  Olive oil, for drizzling

Heat a tablespoon of the oil in a small skillet over medium-low heat. Add three-quarters of the garlic and all of the shallots and sweat until soft, about 7 minutes. Transfer the mixture to a blender and add the anchovy fillets, cheese, 1 tablespoon lemon juice, and 2 tablespoons oil. Process until smooth, adding water as needed for a consistency a bit thicker than heavy cream. Add salt and pepper, then set the dressing aside.

Heat 2 tablespoons of the oil in a small saucepan over medium-low heat. Add the leeks, onions, and remaining garlic and cook until softened, about 5 minutes. Add the lentils, salt, and pepper, then pour in 3 cups water and stir. Gently simmer until the lentils are just tender, about 20 minutes. Drain, add a splash of lemon juice, and keep warm.

Heat the remaining tablespoon oil in a large skillet over medium-high heat. Add the radish, toss for a minute, then add the tatsoi, salt, and pepper. Cook, stirring, until just wilted, about 2 minutes. Stir in the vinegar and a drizzle of oil. Serve the tatsoi, radish, and dressing over the lentils.

ROASTED WHOLE LEEKS WITH TANGERINE VINAIGRETTE

SERVES 4 TO 6

WHOLE LEEKS ROASTED OVER COALS, or in the oven, reveal a deep, soulful side of their character—charred on the outside, soft and tender within. I like to use citrus and vinegar to add brightness to their mellow flavor.

- 4 tablespoons olive oil
- 4 leeks, trimmed
  Salt and pepper
- 4 tangerines, peeled and quartered
- ¼ small onion, thinly sliced
- 1 clove garlic, smashed
  Pinch crushed red pepper flakes
  Juice from 1 orange
- 2 tablespoons sherry vinegar
  Small pinch saffron

  Sea salt
- 1 tangerine, segmented
  Small handful fresh cilantro leaves

Preheat the oven to 375°F. Heat 1 tablespoon of the oil in a large ovenproof skillet over medium-high heat. Add the leeks and salt and pepper, then turn the leeks in the oil to coat. Transfer the skillet to the oven and roast, turning once, until brown and tender, about 30 minutes.

Meanwhile, make the vinaigrette. Heat 1 tablespoon of the oil in a small saucepan over medium heat. Add the quartered tangerines, onions, garlic, and red pepper flakes and cook until the onions are softened, about 5 minutes. Add the orange juice, vinegar, and saffron and simmer for about 5 minutes. Strain the

mixture over a bowl, pressing the liquid from the solids. Return the liquid to the saucepan and reduce to about ¼ cup.

Pour the liquid into a small bowl and whisk in the remaining 2 tablespoons oil. Halve the leeks lengthwise, arrange on a platter, and top with the vinaigrette, sea salt, tangerine segments, and cilantro.

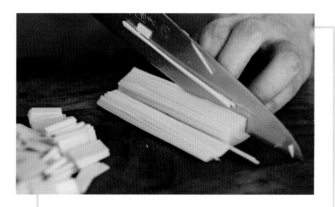

Cutting & Washing Leeks

Trim ⅛ inch off the root ends, then remove the green tops and any tough, damaged outer fronds and save for stock. Cut the leeks in half lengthwise and then into quarters. For matchsticks, continue to slice lengthwise. For dice, cut the quarters crosswise. Each square separates easily.

Leeks can be really sandy, so it's important to clean them well. Fill a bowl with cool water, add the diced leeks, stir them around, then lift them out with your hands or a slotted spoon into another bowl of water and repeat the process. Lift and drain in a colander. This is the way I wash salad greens as well.

LEEK QUICHE

MAKES 1 (10-INCH) QUICHE

I MASTERED THIS QUICHE in cooking school in Paris and I still love to make it today. The tart has three distinctive components: the dough, the filling, and the egg mixture, good things to perfect! The quiche is delicious for breakfast and lunch at home with any number of filling variations: mushrooms, spinach, onions, and so on. The tart comes together pretty quickly if you make the dough in advance. You'll only need the white and pale green leek parts for the quiche, so save the dark greens for stock.

4 tablespoons (½ stick) butter, plus more for the pan
3 large leeks (white and pale green parts), diced
1 large clove garlic, minced
 Salt and pepper
 Small handful fresh flat-leaf parsley, chopped
 Flour (for the pan and rolling the dough)
 Tart Dough (page 182)
½ cup whole milk
½ cup heavy cream
2 eggs
1 egg yolk

 Pinch grated nutmeg
 Salt and pepper
¾ cup grated Parmigiano

Preheat the oven to 350°F. Heat the 4 tablespoons butter in a large skillet over medium heat. Sweat the leeks and garlic with salt and pepper until soft, about 10 minutes. Take off the heat and stir in the parsley, then set the leek mixture aside to cool.

Meanwhile, butter and flour a 10-inch tart pan with a removable bottom, then set it on a baking sheet. Roll out the dough on a floured surface to about ⅛ inch thick. Fit the dough into the tart pan, trim off any excess, and poke the bottom with a fork in several places to let air escape and help the dough keep its shape while cooking.

Line the tart shell with a circle of parchment paper and fill with dried chickpeas, beans, or pie weights. Bake for about 25 minutes, then remove the parchment and beans and bake until the crust is golden and cooked through, another 10 minutes.

When the tart shell is ready, whisk together the milk, cream, eggs, yolk, nutmeg, and 2 pinches each of salt and pepper. Spread the leek mixture evenly in the shell, then gently pour in the milk mixture, leaving the top of the crust exposed. Do not overfill! Top with the cheese and bake until the filling is set and golden brown, about 30 minutes. Let it sit for 10 minutes before serving.

TART DOUGH

MAKES ENOUGH FOR 1 (10-INCH) QUICHE

RIGHT AFTER I LEARNED to make this dough, I was visiting friends outside Lyon who were proud French gastronomes. The matriarch of the family, a grandmother of seven, complained to me about the inconsistent results of her quiche dough. So I cheekily suggested that I would make the dough. The very idea that I, an American boy, could teach a French grandmother to make dough seemed heretical. However, when I successfully made this recipe for her, she became a believer. And so I pass it on to you! You can add ¼ cup sugar to this basic recipe and use it to make a sweet tart or pie. There will be a little left over, just enough to roll out in strips and bake for cookies.

1¾ cups flour
1 teaspoon salt
9 tablespoons butter, cubed and chilled
1 egg yolk
   Up to 4 tablespoons ice water

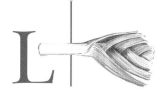

Stir together the flour and salt in a large bowl. Add the butter and, little by little, work it into the flour with your fingertips, flattening it to create a sandy mixture. The idea is not to overwork the dough and the key is to start with cold butter and touch it with only your fingertips.

Add the yolk and 2 tablespoons of the ice water, then lightly stir and fold it in with your fingers.

Do not worry if the mixture seems too dry and like it won't come together. Just add more water, drop by drop, until it does.

When the mixture just barely becomes a dough, transfer to a bowl and cover with plastic wrap. Refrigerate for about an hour. To store the dough longer than a few hours, wrap it well in plastic and refrigerate for up to a couple of days or freeze for up to 6 months.

"*The greater a mushroom's delicacy, the simpler...*

Mushrooms
186

should be its preparation." —RICHARD OLNEY, *Simple French Food*, 1975

MUSHROOMS

FORAGING FOR WILD MUSHROOMS is one of the most exciting adventures in the world of food. However, when I talk about mushrooms in this book, I am generally referring to cultivated mushrooms and not the wild varieties. Let's be honest: The availability of wild mushrooms is very limited, and picking them safely requires special knowledge. Imported wild mushrooms are wildly expensive, and by the time they arrive here, they have but a shadow of the flavor they possessed where they were grown.

Cultivated mushrooms are now abundant. Their quality is excellent, and the flavor you can coax from them is incredible. So I wholeheartedly favor the consistency and availability of the many cultivated varieties such as oyster, hen-of-the-woods, shiitake, cremini, and even white button mushrooms.

SAUTÉED MUSHROOMS ON FLATBREAD WITH BRAISED GREENS

SERVES 2

TWO SIMPLE GESTURES deliver so much. Take a crispy flatbread (or cracker or even grilled bread) and top it with something soft and garlicky, like sautéed mushrooms, then add greens like kale, spinach, or chard. It's the best kind of open-face sandwich–the bread captures the vegetables' succulent juices. I like to use cultivated hen-of-the-woods or maitake mushrooms for their texture.

3   tablespoons olive oil
2   tablespoons butter
2   cloves garlic, smashed
¼   pound mushrooms, thickly sliced
     Salt and pepper
2   pieces flatbread
½   recipe Kale Cooked Quickly (page 169)

Heat 2 tablespoons of the oil and 1 tablespoon of the butter in a large skillet over medium-high heat.

Add 1 clove garlic, the mushrooms, salt, and pepper, and cook until the mushrooms are lightly browned, about 6 minutes. Transfer to a bowl.

Add the remaining oil and butter to the skillet over medium heat. Add the remaining clove garlic and, when the butter starts to brown, slip in the flatbread, a piece at a time, and brown on both sides, about 2 minutes. Spread the sautéed kale over the flatbread, and top with the mushrooms. Serve it up.

MUSHROOM CREPES

MAKES ABOUT 8 (4-INCH) SQUARE CREPES

WHEN I'M MAKING CREPES, I like to make the batter at least an hour ahead and even as far in advance as overnight. This crepe doubles its softness with a flavorful chopped mushroom filling. Keep a few of the sautéed mushrooms whole so there's a mix of textures. You can make the crepes in advance, then fill them just as you're ready to serve them.

FOR THE CREPES

- 2 eggs
- ¾ cup whole milk
- 3 tablespoons butter, melted
  Salt
- 1 cup flour

FOR THE FILLING

- ¼ cup olive oil, plus more for the crepe pan
- 1 pound shiitake or other mushrooms, stemmed and quartered
- 4 tablespoons (½ stick) butter
- 1 onion, thinly sliced
- 2 cloves garlic, chopped
  Salt and pepper
- 2 cups Mushroom Broth (page 191), chicken broth, or water
- 1 tablespoon balsamic vinegar
- 2 cups shredded iceberg lettuce

188

Whisk together the eggs, milk, butter, and a pinch of salt in a medium bowl, then gradually whisk in the flour until smooth. Cover the crepe batter and refrigerate for at least an hour or even overnight.

Heat the ¼ cup oil in a large skillet over medium-high heat. Add the mushrooms and cook until light brown, about 6 minutes. Add the butter, onions, garlic, salt, and pepper, and cook for a few minutes more. Add the broth and simmer until the liquid is almost evaporated, about 15 minutes. Set aside a handful of the mushrooms.

Transfer the rest of the mixture to a food processor, add the vinegar, and pulse until the mushrooms are roughly chopped. Keep the mushroom mixture warm while you make the crepes.

Remove the batter from the refrigerator. It should be the consistency of heavy cream; thin with milk, if needed. Heat an 8-inch crepe pan or skillet over medium-low heat. Brush the hot skillet with oil, then pour in about ¼ cup batter and quickly swirl to coat the bottom evenly. Cook until the crepe is just set and golden on the bottom, about a minute.

Put a couple of tablespoonfuls of the mushroom mixture into a rough square on the center of the crepe (add a few of the reserved sautéed mushrooms now, too), then top with a bit of the lettuce; add salt and pepper. Fold the four sides of the crepe over the filling to make a square package. Flip the crepe over and cook for about 10 seconds more. Transfer the crepe to a plate and make as many crepes as you like.

MUSHROOM BROTH
MAKES ABOUT 8 CUPS

THIS IS THE SIMPLEST BROTH: All it takes is lots of sliced white mushrooms, ample liquid, and an hour. As another flavor boost, I sauté chicken wings as a base for the broth.
This broth is lovely on its own or used as a component of the Mushroom Hot Pot with Beef & Daikon (page 192).

1 tablespoon olive oil
1 pound chicken wings
1 small onion, very thinly sliced
2 cloves garlic, very thinly sliced
2 pounds white button mushrooms, sliced
  Salt and pepper
1 (3-by-3-inch) piece kombu
  Oyster or other whole mushrooms, for topping

Heat the oil in a large pot over medium-high heat. Add the chicken wings and brown on both sides, about 8 minutes. Transfer the wings to a plate, pour off any excess fat, and lower the heat to medium. Add the onions and garlic and sweat for 2 minutes. Add the mushrooms, chicken wings, 9 cups water, salt, and pepper.

Submerge the kombu in the liquid, bring it to a simmer, and cook, uncovered, for about an hour. Strain the broth over a bowl, pressing on the solids. Lightly sauté the oyster or other mushrooms and add to each bowl of hot broth.

MUSHROOM HOT POT WITH BEEF & DAIKON

SERVES 6

WHEN I LIVED IN JAPAN and was cooking in a restaurant in Tokyo, one of my favorite things was to share a hot-pot meal with the family of the head of the women's culture club in the suburb where I lived. We'd gather around the table with a pot of broth, which starts with the classic dashi, set over a portable burner surrounded by platters overflowing with raw vegetables, tofu, meat or fish, and sometimes noodles. The food was cooked right there with everyone helping themselves, and we'd sit there eating, laughing, and drinking until every last morsel was gone. If you do not own such a burner, you can still enjoy my stovetop version of this festive communal dish, bringing the big pot right to the table.

- 4 tablespoons sesame oil
- 1 pound white mushrooms, thinly sliced
- 1 pound shiitake mushrooms, half thinly sliced, half quartered
- ¼ cup Madeira or semisweet sherry
- 1 cup Dashi (page 109)
- ⅓ cup soy sauce
- 2 tablespoons mirin (sweet rice wine)
- 2 tablespoons sugar
- 8 baby turnips, peeled and halved
- 8 scallions
- 1 daikon (8 to 10 inches long), peeled and thickly sliced
- 1 leek, thickly sliced
- 4 large handfuls baby spinach
- 4 baby bok choy, leaves separated
- 1 pound eye-round or top-round beef, very thinly sliced

Heat 2 tablespoons of the oil in a large skillet over high heat. Add the white mushrooms and sauté until well browned and any liquid is evaporated, about 5 minutes. Transfer the mushrooms to a medium saucepan. Then, in the skillet, brown the sliced shiitakes in another tablespoon oil. (It's important not to cook all the mushrooms in one batch. If the skillet is too crowded, they won't brown nicely.) Add the shiitakes to the saucepan, pour in 6 cups water and the Madeira or sherry, and simmer for about 30 minutes.

Strain the mushroom broth into a large pot. Add the dashi, soy sauce, mirin, and sugar and bring to a soft boil. Add the turnips, scallions, daikon, leeks, and quartered shiitakes and simmer until just tender, about 12 minutes. Add the spinach and bok choy and cook until just wilted, about a minute. Add the beef slices at the last moment and gently simmer for about a minute. Stir in the remaining spoonful of oil and serve right away.

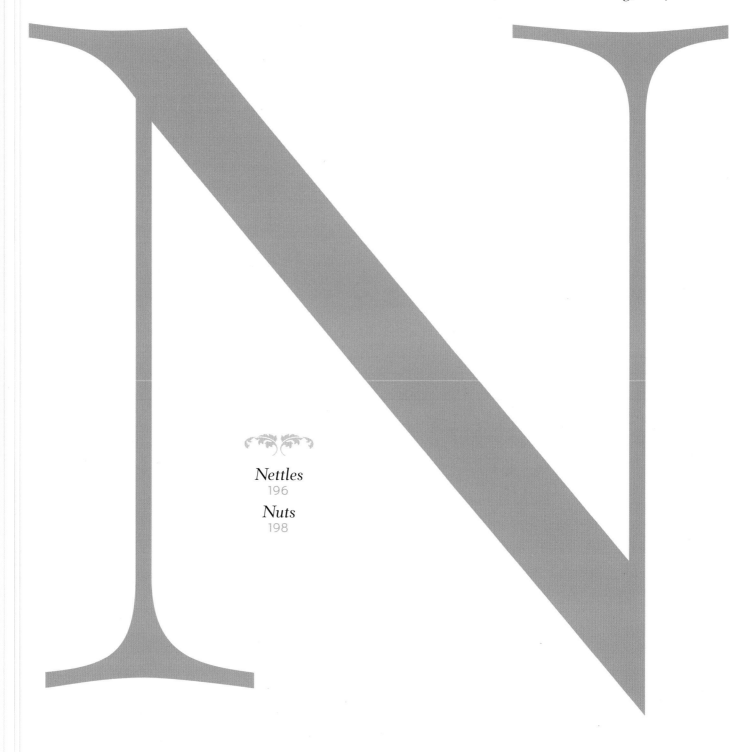

"*Nuttiness: ... slightly sweet, slightly fatty, slightly roasted or toasted ...*" —HAROLD McGEE, *On Food and Cooking*, 2004

Nettles
196

Nuts
198

NETTLES

NETTLES ARE MOST TENDER and delicious in the late spring and early summer. They grow wild everywhere and are one tough plant. Their natural defense system, comprised of microfibers, is a serious skin irritant; unwashed, they must be handled with gloves. But here's the upside: Nettles are the most intense source of chlorophyll and mineral content in the family of leafy greens. So we prize nettles for their deep, dark color and healthy, rich flavor. I like them best for their direct connection to eating wild food.

NETTLE PUREE

MAKES ABOUT 1 CUP

THE INTENSE GREEN of this puree is perfect for blending into an inspired soup. Cook onions, garlic, and leeks softly to build a flavorful soup base, simmer them in vegetable stock, transfer to a blender, and blend the puree into the vegetables and stock to finish with a bright green soup. Or use the puree in Nettle Custard (right).

- 2 cups packed nettle leaves, blanched and roughly chopped
- ½ cup cold vegetable broth or water
- 2 tablespoons olive oil

Combine the nettle leaves, broth, and oil in a blender and process until smooth, adding a little more broth if needed.

NETTLE CUSTARD

SERVES 4

THIS CUSTARD IS MY TAKE on a Japanese dish called *chawanmushi*, a great vehicle for other flavors that sit on this soft, pillowy foundation. I top the custard with peas and pickled mushrooms, but so many other toppings will work.

4   eggs
1   cup silken tofu
¾   cup Nettle Puree (left)
1   teaspoon soy sauce
     Salt

Preheat the oven to 350°F. Combine the eggs, tofu, nettle puree, soy sauce, and 3 large pinches of salt in a blender and process until smooth. Let the mixture sit for about 5 minutes to release any air bubbles.

Pour the custard into four small bowls (with a capacity of about 1¼ cups each), then set them in a larger pan. Add enough boiling water to come about halfway up the sides of the bowls. Put the pan in the oven and bake until the custard is just set, 25 to 35 minutes. Let cool for a couple of minutes before serving.

Handling Nettles

Use gloves to remove the nettle leaves from the stems, rinse the leaves with cold water, blanch, and shock in cold water. Once they're blanched, the leaves are perfectly safe and delicious to eat.

NUTS

USING NUTS IN COOKING is a natural gesture that's akin to today's excitement about wild foraged foods. After all, before nut trees were cultivated, they were precisely that: wild food. Given their botanical purpose, which is, of course, to reproduce—each nut magically contains enough energy to make an entire tree.

Nuts add an extra layer of texture and flavor; warming or toasting them in a dry pan enhances both of these properties. California almonds and walnuts, New York chestnuts, Sicilian pistachios, Oregon hazelnuts, Midwestern hickory nuts, Southern pecans, black walnuts from the Northeast—there's a whole nutty world out there to discover. Instead of reaching for bacon and ham to add richness to a dish, use nuts. They add a sense of place to your cooking as well. Buy whole nuts in small quantities and use them fast, as they tend to lose their character quickly.

TOASTED & SPICED ALMONDS

MAKES 1 CUP

SOMETHING MAGICAL HAPPENS when you heat and season raw almonds. They crisp up and become more flavorful after they're cooked, so make them at least an hour before serving.

1   tablespoon olive oil
1   cup whole raw almonds
1   heaping teaspoon mild curry powder
    Salt

1   teaspoon honey
    Fresh lemon juice

Combine the oil, almonds, curry powder, and a pinch of salt in a large skillet. Cook over medium-high heat, tossing often, until the almonds just start to brown. Add the honey and let it caramelize, about 2 minutes. Add a splash of lemon juice and toss, then transfer to a plate to cool. The nuts will keep, tightly covered, for a few weeks.

PEEL & EAT CHESTNUTS

SERVES 4

A CHRISTMAS CAROL comes to life. Chestnuts roasting on an open fire is an easy image to conjure (well, after you've made the X-cut in the shell) and a totally addictive seasonal treat. Chestnuts in the shell are available only in the fall.

1 pound whole chestnuts in the shell
1 teaspoon olive oil
  Salt

Preheat the oven to 375°F. Using a sharp paring knife, carefully make an X on the flat side of each chestnut, cutting through the leathery shell. This is important so the chestnuts won't burst in the oven. Put the chestnuts on a baking sheet, and toss with the oil and a sprinkle of salt. Roast until the shell around the cut begins to open and the flesh inside looks golden, about 30 minutes. While the chestnuts are still hot, peel off the shell, add a little salt, and devour.

WALNUT MASHED POTATOES

SERVES 6

I LIKE TO IMAGINE a place where potatoes grow in the garden and there's a walnut tree in the backyard, making this combination of buttery mashed potatoes with toasted nuts seem inevitable. Adding a touch of walnut oil makes it beyond delicious. It could become a Thanksgiving classic.

2½	pounds Yukon Gold or other potatoes, peeled and quartered
1	clove garlic
1	bay leaf
	Salt
1½	cups milk
4	tablespoons (½ stick) butter
	Pepper
½	cup toasted walnuts, roughly chopped
¼	cup walnut oil

Put the potatoes in a medium saucepan and cover with water by about 2 inches. Add the garlic, bay leaf, and salt and simmer until the potatoes are just tender, about 15 minutes.

Meanwhile, bring the milk and butter just to a boil, then keep warm. Drain the potatoes, discard the garlic and bay leaf, and toss the potatoes in the hot pan for about a minute to dry. While the potatoes are still warm, pass them through a ricer or food mill back into the saucepan.

Over medium heat, stir in the milk mixture, add salt and pepper, and keep warm. Stir the toasted walnuts and walnut oil into the mashed potatoes, reserving a couple tablespoons of the walnuts and a drizzle of oil for topping.

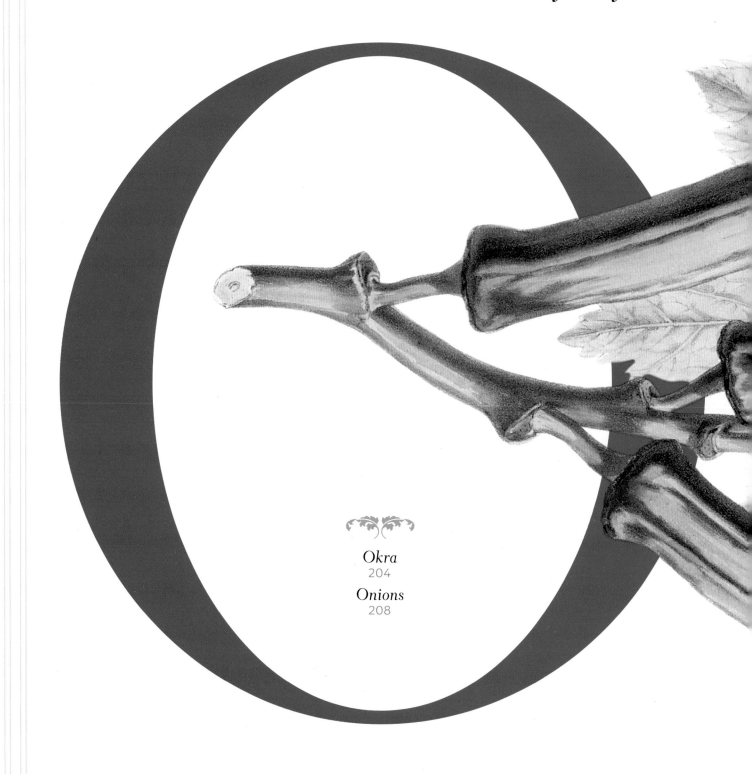

Okra
204

Onions
208

O

OKRA

FOR ME, okra has always been a bountiful late-summer treat. But okra is disdained for the very thing that makes it wonderful to cook with and eat: These little seedpods are a textural delight, becoming more gelatinous as they cook, which adds a lovely quality to light stews and gumbos. But I like to cook okra, too, in ways that make the most of their crisp, fresh green quality.

PICKLED OKRA

MAKES ABOUT 1 PINT

SINCE OKRA GROWS so abundantly in the hottest time of the year, to preserve the crop it's almost imperative to pickle it. Pickled okra is great for a fast lunch with a couple of slices of ham, on a big bowl of rice, or to serve with cocktails. I love to pickle the smallest pods I can find.

Follow the Basic Pickling Recipe (page 66), substituting these ingredients. Refrigerated, the pickles will keep for at least 6 weeks.

    2 cups small okra
    ¾ cup rice wine vinegar
    ¼ cup water
    ¼ cup sugar
    1 tablespoon kosher salt
    2 bay leaves
    1 teaspoon mustard seeds

CORNMEAL-FRIED OKRA

SERVES 4

WHETHER YOU WANT TO reproduce a classic Southern specialty or just simply get fresh okra from the garden to the plate as fast as you possibly can, here is a delicious way to do both at the same time!

Grapeseed oil for frying
1 cup cornmeal
Salt
1 pound okra, halved lengthwise

Heat about 1 inch of oil to about 375°F in a medium skillet. Meanwhile, in a small bowl, stir together the cornmeal and 1 cup water, then add salt. Working in batches, dip the okra in the batter, letting any excess drip off. Drop the battered pieces in the skillet, a few at a time, and cook until they turn golden, about 3 minutes. Remove from the oil with a slotted spoon and drain on paper towels. Sprinkle with salt, then eat 'em up.

OKRA STEW WITH TOMATOES

SERVES 6

IN THIS SIMPLE STEW, the tomatoes and the tomato sauce are cooked separately, or even previously. The okra is simmered, but not longer than 10 or 15 minutes, so it retains its shape and bite. The simmered okra slightly thickens the sauce, giving it just enough body.

2 tablespoons olive oil
1 onion, finely chopped
3 cloves garlic, minced
   Pinch crushed red pepper flakes
3 cups okra, cut crosswise
   Kernels from 2 ears corn
   Salt and pepper
6 halves Oven-Dried Plum Tomatoes (page 299) or plum tomatoes

1 cup My Tomato Sauce (page 300) or other good tomato sauce
   Small handful chopped fresh basil and flat-leaf parsley

Heat the oil in a medium saucepan over medium heat. Add the onions, garlic, and red pepper flakes and sweat until softened, about 6 minutes. Add the okra, corn, salt, and pepper and cook for a few minutes more.

Add the plum tomatoes and 1 cup water and simmer, stirring occasionally, until the okra are almost tender, about 10 minutes. Add the tomato sauce and simmer for a few minutes more, then stir in the herbs.

ONIONS

ONIONS' NATURAL sugars caramelize when heated, and this is the source of their magic. I use different kinds of onions depending on the time of year. In the early spring, I look for the first green shoots that resemble scallions and can be eaten raw. Later, the small young bulbs with their green stems appear, and these can be lightly glazed and eaten whole with their tops attached. The bulbs of summer onions grow big and sweet as their green tops wilt; these are great for grilling. By fall and winter, I use onions that are cured, removing their papery skin.

ONION PUREE

MAKES ABOUT 1 CUP

I DO NOT THINK OF THIS PUREE as a substitute for butter, but I often use it at the point in a classic recipe where butter is called for to add creaminess and mellow flavor.

- 3 tablespoons olive oil
- 2 onions, halved and very thinly sliced
- 1 tablespoon sherry vinegar
  Salt and pepper

Heat the oil in a medium saucepan over medium heat. Add the onions and sweat, stirring often, until they are completely soft but not browned, 15 to 20 minutes. Add the vinegar and cook for about 5 minutes more. Transfer the mixture to a blender and process until satiny smooth, then add salt and pepper. The puree will keep, covered in the refrigerator, for up to 3 days.

Slicing Onions

Cooking onions is all about their sweetness, but slicing them is automatically associated with their assertive, tear-provoking qualities. I am convinced that the way you cut an onion can change the flavor of a dish. Cutting onions demands real attention and a sharp tool—I always use a supersharp knife. This seemingly small detail can really improve the quality of your cooking. I never put onions in a food processor, because I do not like the flavor of crushed or bruised onions.

If you really want to see this difference, make two quick salsas with fresh tomatoes, onions, and a little jalapeño. For one, mince the onion with a sharp knife, and for the other, blend all the ingredients together in a food processor. In a taste test, you will be surprised by how the hand-chopped version shows off the clean freshness of each ingredient, while the processed salsa fills the room (and the salsa) with the onions' not so fresh, pungent aroma.

Or compare chives that have been sliced with a very sharp knife to a batch of chives roughly chopped with a knife so dull that it bruises the chives, causing their water to release. The sliced chives are vivid and green, a pleasure to sprinkle over a dish. But the dull-chopped version is mushy, oxidized in 5 minutes, with an off-putting aroma.

ONION & BACON TART

MAKES 1 (8-BY-12-INCH) TART

FOR THIS QUICK TART I often use store-bought flatbread. My current favorite is the flaky Moroccan bread called m'smen from a bakery called Hot Bread Kitchen in Spanish Harlem, whose mission is to train bakers and celebrate ethnic traditions. For the crispiest texture and great flavor, it's important to toast the bread before you add the onions.

2 tablespoons olive oil
3 thick slices bacon, diced small
6 onions, halved lengthwise and very thinly sliced
  Salt
1 flatbread, about 8 by 12 inches
1 clove garlic, halved
1 tablespoon sherry vinegar
  Pepper
1 tablespoon fresh thyme leaves

Preheat the oven to 400°F. Heat 1 tablespoon of the oil in a large skillet over medium heat. Add the bacon and lightly brown, about 6 minutes. Add the onions and a large pinch of salt and sweat until completely soft and golden, about 20 minutes.

Meanwhile, put the flatbread on a baking sheet, drizzle with the remaining tablespoon oil, and rub with the garlic. Toast lightly for about 10 minutes, then remove, but leave the oven on.

Add the vinegar and pepper to the onion mixture and stir for about a minute, then spoon onto the flatbread, leaving a little border around the edges. Sprinkle the thyme over the top and bake for about 10 minutes.

Caramelizing Onions

An excellent way to boost flavor in a recipe is to caramelize onions. Slice the onions thinly, sweat them in a bit of oil, and in 15 minutes' time they'll brown and become sweet. Then add a pinch of sugar and a drop of vinegar. Continue to cook until the vinegar is absorbed.

Finish by stirring in a bit of butter. You'll end up with an intensely flavorful component not just for soups and stews, but also for the Onion & Bacon Tart (left), Shrimp & Cipollini Stew (page 216), and Spinach Egg Crepes (page 284).

A REAL ONION SOUP
SERVES 10

I HAVE A FOND MEMORY of making onion soup in a village near Lyon. At a French wedding it's traditional to serve onion soup late, very late, after all the festivities, to help folks make it through the long night. When I stumbled upon a group of women making the soup, I watched for a while and then I politely added my two centimes. Why, I asked, had they not added a pinch of flour to the caramelized onions? Of course, this comment from an American didn't go over well, and after some heated discussion, I ended up *wearing* the flour! In the end, I put a little flour in the onions, and everyone loved the soup. But I didn't realize how much until I returned a few years later for another wedding. This time they asked me to make the soup.

One of the keys to great onion soup (aside from that flour) is a flavorful broth. I use beef in this recipe, but sometimes I use Mushroom Broth (page 191) for a lighter, more aromatic version.

2	tablespoons olive oil
¾	pound beef chuck, cubed
5	tablespoons butter
3	pounds onions, halved and thinly sliced
6	cloves garlic, minced
1	tablespoon sugar
5	tablespoons white wine vinegar
5	tablespoons Cognac or brandy
1½	cups Champagne or white wine
2	tablespoons flour
5	cups beef broth
1	sprig rosemary
1	sprig thyme
	Salt and pepper

10	thin slices baguette, cut on the diagonal
1	clove garlic, halved
1½	cups grated Parmigiano or Gruyère

Heat the oil in a large pot over high heat. Add the beef, turning the heat down after a couple minutes, and brown on all sides, about 10 minutes. Raise the heat to high, add 4 tablespoons of the butter and half the onions, and stir. When the onions begin to wilt and the pan begins to sizzle again, it's time to add the rest of the onions. Much of the cooking of the soup can go unattended, but right now you have to be involved and stay close.

Add the garlic and cook over high heat, stirring often and scraping the edges of the pot. After 5 minutes more, stir in the sugar to help the onions caramelize. Continue to cook until the onions are soft and caramelized, about 10 minutes more. Add 4 tablespoons of the vinegar and cook, stirring often, until evaporated. Add 4 tablespoons of the Cognac and cook, stirring often, until evaporated. Add the Champagne and cook until nearly dry. Stir in the remaining tablespoon of butter and then the flour. Add the broth, rosemary, thyme, salt, and pepper and simmer for about 30 minutes.

Meanwhile, make the croutons. Preheat the oven to 375°F. Put the baguette slices on a baking sheet and bake until golden, about 10 minutes. Rub one side with the cut garlic, then top with the cheese and broil until it's melted and brown. Remove the beef from the soup, then stir in the remaining 1 tablespoon each vinegar and Cognac and check seasonings. Ladle the soup into bowls, top with a crouton.

PICKLED ONIONS & LENTIL SALAD
MAKES ABOUT 1 PINT PICKLED ONIONS

PICKLING IS A WAY to enhance a simple ingredient like a sweet garden onion and give it a little extra acidity and crunch. I like pickled onions in a sandwich (Gramma Anthony's Pickled Eggplant, page 116), or in a bowl of peas and rice (page 227). Lentils are a special favorite of mine, and I like to cook them simply with diced onions, garlic, and carrots covered with an inch of water for 20 minutes or until they're soft. In the salad in the photo, I combine Pickled Onions with frisée, radicchio, and parsley, but use whatever greens you have on hand. A bit of the lentil cooking liquid keeps the salad moist.

For the Pickled Onions, follow the Basic Pickling Recipe (page 66), substituting these ingredients.

  2 cups sliced cipollini or other small onions, rings separated
  ¾ cup rice wine vinegar
  ¼ cup water
  ¼ cup sugar
  1 tablespoon kosher salt
  1 teaspoon ground turmeric

SHRIMP & CIPOLLINI STEW WITH ONION PUREE

SERVES 4

IN LIGHT STEWS like this one, Onion Puree becomes a really valuable addition. I fold it in at the end to pull all the disparate ingredients together and give the dish depth.

- 1 cup packed fresh basil
- 1 cup fresh flat-leaf parsley
- 1 large clove garlic
- 3 tablespoons grated Parmigiano
- 2 tablespoons Onion Puree (page 208)
- ½ cup plus 2 tablespoons olive oil
  Salt and pepper
- 4 cipollini onions, quartered
- 2 zucchini, cored and cut into ⅓-inch dice
- 1 cup cooked shell beans
- 4 cups Shrimp Stock (right)
- ¾ pound large shrimp, peeled, deveined, and cut into thirds (peelings saved for stock)
- 3 plum tomatoes, roughly chopped

Blanch the basil and parsley in a pot of salted boiling water for 15 seconds, then shock in a bowl of ice water. Combine the basil, parsley, garlic, cheese, onion puree, and ½ cup of the oil in a blender and puree until smooth. Add salt and pepper, then set the pesto aside.

Heat the remaining 2 tablespoons oil in a medium saucepan over medium-high heat. Add the onions and cook until softened, about 3 minutes. Add the zucchini, beans, and stock and simmer until the zucchini are tender, about 5 minutes.

Add the shrimp and tomatoes and simmer until just cooked through, about 3 minutes. Stir in 3 tablespoons of the pesto, check the seasonings, then serve in bowls.

SHRIMP STOCK

MAKES ABOUT 4 CUPS

SHRIMP STOCK IS SO FAST and easy, but I do recommend making it the same day you plan to use it for the freshest flavor.

- Shells from about ¾ pound shrimp
- 4 scallions, chopped
- 2 carrots, thinly sliced
- 1 stalk celery, sliced
- ½ small onion, chopped
  Pinch coriander seeds
- 1 sprig rosemary
- 1 sprig thyme
  Salt and pepper

Combine the shrimp shells, scallions, carrots, celery, onions, coriander seeds, rosemary, and thyme in a medium saucepan. Cover with 4½ cups water and simmer for about 30 minutes. Strain into a bowl, discarding the solids, and add salt and pepper. Use immediately.

"*In my kitchen, no pepper is used until it has first been peeled.*" —JAMES BEARD, *The New James Beard*, 1981

Parsnips
220

Peas
226

Peppers
234

Potatoes
240

PARSNIPS

PARSNIPS THROUGHOUT HISTORY have been underappreciated. In Europe they fell out of favor, seen as the awful roots of subsistence farming, or worse, as animal feed. Happily, they've gone through a revival, and farmers' markets are piled high with the sweetest of parsnips, just waiting to be roasted, or pureed, or made into fritters. The best place to store parsnips is in the ground, where their natural defense against the cold somehow makes this sweet vegetable even sweeter. You can find parsnips all winter long, and they're as easy to peel as a carrot. I celebrate vegetables like the parsnip that have made a major comeback. Enthusiastic eaters everywhere have had fun rediscovering their awesome flavor.

PARSNIP CHIPS

SERVES 4

Think back to a time when people said: "Kale chips? Really? Are they any good?" Nowadays people recognize how easy to prepare and tasty they are. Well, these sweet Parsnip Chips are every bit as addictive and will be eaten as fast as you can make them. The chips are deep-fried, but if they're drained well and patted dry on a paper towel, they come out amazingly light and crispy.

Grapeseed or peanut oil for frying
3 parsnips, peeled and sliced paper-thin
Salt

Heat about 2 inches of oil to about 375°F in a medium saucepan. Fry the parsnips, a few slices at a time, until they turn golden around the edges, 1 to 2 minutes. They will crisp up as they drain on paper towels. Sprinkle with salt.

PARSNIP & KALE GRATIN

SERVES 6

I USE A CLASSIC RICH combination of cream, butter, and garlic to draw out the seductive qualities of soft parsnips and kale. Together, they make a decadent, delicious dish.

2	tablespoons butter
2	cloves garlic, minced
¼	cup minced shallots
2	cups heavy cream
	Pinch grated nutmeg
	Salt and pepper
1¼	pounds parsnips, peeled and very thinly sliced
1	cup grated Parmigiano
½	pound young, tender kale (center ribs removed), blanched for 10 minutes and patted dry

Preheat the oven to 350°F. Butter a medium baking dish with a tablespoon of the butter, then scatter half of the garlic on the bottom and set aside.

Heat the remaining tablespoon butter in a small saucepan over medium-low heat. Add the shallots and remaining garlic and stir until softened, about 3 minutes. Add the cream and nutmeg, and a generous amount of salt and pepper, and bring to a simmer.

Arrange half the parsnips in the gratin dish, working in a circle and overlapping the edges. Be sure to cover the bottom well because it will cook down to form one thick layer. Sprinkle with half the cheese, then spoon on half the cream. Layer the remaining parsnips, cheese, and cream mixture, then add the kale on the top layer, nestling it in between the slices of parsnip.

Put the dish on a baking sheet (to catch any drips) and bake until the parsnips are tender and the gratin is bubbling and beautifully browned on top, about an hour.

ROASTED PARSNIPS WITH HAZELNUT PESTO

SERVES 4

PARSNIPS, LIKE CARROTS, get sweeter as they roast. In this recipe, I raise the heat to char the outside (grilling does that, too), heightening the experience of eating the soft, creamy parsnips inside. I feel strongly that parsnips (and other root vegetables, for that matter) should be roasted in a heavy skillet, not on a thin baking sheet.

Skillets are designed to transfer heat properly; their flat surface browns vegetables evenly on contact. They won't bend or warp under the heat, and they won't throw off odors as baking sheets might. This is good cooking! It's why grandma's frying pans were so heavy and why enameled cast-iron, stainless-steel-clad, or copper cookware is worth investing in. It's what makes food taste good.

The Hazelnut Pesto is a great partner for these rustic parsnips, but I also like it drizzled over Escarole Salad with Fennel & Pears (page 120), on Sliced Raw Jerusalem Artichoke Salad (page 158), and with Roasted Whole Leeks (page 179). To maximize the pesto's fresh flavor, make it in small quantities in a mortar and pestle.

6   tablespoons olive oil
4   parsnips, peeled

Salt and pepper
¼ cup roughly chopped fresh flat-leaf parsley
¼ cup roughly chopped fresh cilantro
1 large clove garlic, minced
¼ cup toasted and skinned hazelnuts, halved

Preheat the oven to 400°F. Heat 2 tablespoons of the oil in a large ovenproof skillet over medium-high heat. Add the parsnips, salt, and pepper and cook, turning them a few times, until they start to brown,

about 3 minutes. Pop the skillet into the oven and roast until the parsnips are tender, about 40 minutes.

Meanwhile, in a mortar, combine the parsley, cilantro, garlic, and salt. Smash into a coarse paste while drizzling in the remaining 4 tablespoons oil, then stir in the nuts. Cut the roasted parsnips in half lengthwise and spoon on the pesto.

PEAS

I'D LIKE TO MAKE AN ARGUMENT for cooking with garden fresh peas. I know that's not always easy-peasy. Frozen peas are frequently sweeter and available year-round, but I'm not excited about supporting the industrialized systems that facilitate their harvest. If you're lucky enough to find tiny, fresh-picked peas from the garden—anybody's garden or at a local farmers' market—cherish them. Those peas are beautiful, a rare luxury, and require next to no cooking or seasoning. As peas mature in the field, however, and as hours pass from their moment of harvest, they lose their sweetness. But the complexity of their flavor increases. They become different, not less interesting. Let's embrace the true nature of later peas, and cook them with different techniques and seasonings.

For example, eat them with rice and pickled vegetables to show off their vegetal crunch. We need to celebrate the natural life cycle of the pea—it is short and fleeting, just like ours. Amazingly, some pea breeders are focusing on flavor rather than just pest resistance and production. Sugar snaps—a wonderful variety—did not even exist before 1968, when Dr. Calvin Lamborn recognized a mutation in his field studies of Idaho snow peas and created a brand-new delicious variety. His sugar snaps are now grown around the world. In fact, Dr. Lamborn's son, Rod, hand-delivered his father's pea shoots, left, for us to photograph.

BOWL OF PEAS, RICE & PICKLED ONIONS

SERVES 4

THIS SIMPLE DISH IS INSPIRED BY the way people commonly eat inexpensively and every day in India and Japan. Making a bowl of healthy rice is easy (I happen to love my programmable rice cooker), and it can be topped with flavorful vegetables of all kinds, raw, cooked, or preserved. The luxury of this dish is to enjoy fresh peas by the spoonful.

1½ cups peas, blanched
Olive oil

1 to 2 teaspoons pickling liquid from Pickled Onions (page 215)
Salt

4 cups cooked basmati rice

12 slices Pickled Onions (page 215)
1 tablespoon thinly sliced scallion greens

In a small bowl, season the peas with oil, the pickling liquid, and salt. Spoon the rice into 4 bowls, then top with the peas, pickled onions, and scallions.

P

Peeling Sugar Snaps

No matter what folks tell you, you really do have to peel the strings off sugar snap pods before using them in a recipe. For me, there is something so satisfying in the unzipping: literally pinching off both ends and pulling off the strings from both sides of the pods.

SUGAR SNAP SALAD WITH QUINOA
SERVES 4

I LOVE GRAINS MIXED WITH fresh, crunchy vegetables—it's my favorite thing to eat. And there are infinite combinations that work. But this mix of soft quinoa and crispy, just-blanched sugar snaps is my very favorite.

3 cups cooked quinoa, cooled
   Olive oil
   Fresh lime juice
   Salt and pepper
1 tablespoon pickling liquid from Pickled Baby Carrots (page 66)
1 tablespoon sherry vinegar
½ teaspoon Dijon mustard
2 cups sugar snap peas, blanched and thinly sliced crosswise
1 kohlrabi, peeled and very thinly sliced
6 Pickled Baby Carrots (page 66), halved lengthwise

In a medium bowl, season the quinoa with oil, lime juice, salt, and pepper, then spoon into bowls. In a small bowl, whisk together ¼ cup oil, the pickling liquid, vinegar, mustard, lime juice, salt, and pepper. Toss the sugar snap peas, kohlrabi, and pickled baby carrots with enough of the dressing to lightly coat, then spoon over the quinoa.

WARM WILTED PEA SHOOTS

SERVES 4

THERE'S MORE THAN JUST the pods to eat from a pea plant. In fact, some farmers are growing peas especially for their shoots and leaves, so look for them in late spring to add to the wide variety of greens like spinach, Swiss chard, and kale to eat raw or wilted.

- 2 tablespoons olive oil
- 1 tablespoon sesame oil
- 1 large clove garlic, smashed

- 4 large handfuls pea shoots
   Handful snow pea pods, blanched
   Salt and pepper

Heat the olive and sesame oils in a large skillet over medium-high heat. Add the garlic, pea shoots, snow pea pods, salt, and pepper and cook, stirring often, until the pea shoots are just wilted, about a minute.

FRESH PEAS WITH BRAISED MORELS
SERVES 4

WHEN YOU THINK about braised morels, you imagine them cooked in cream, which is one of my favorite ways to eat them. But in this version the Mushroom Broth–braised morels are so much more aromatic and light against the clean pop and sweetness of the peas and onions. This is the best way to enjoy the rare delicacy of morels.

3 cups Mushroom Broth (page 191) or water
½ pound morel mushrooms
   Salt and pepper
4 small onions with stem attached, halved
2 cups peas, briefly blanched

Bring the broth to a simmer in a small saucepan. Add the morels and a pinch of salt and pepper and gently simmer for about 10 minutes. Add the onions and cook for about 10 minutes more. Combine the morels, onions, and broth with the peas in a medium bowl.

WARM SALAD OF SNOW PEAS, CHERRIES & BABY CHARD

SERVES 4

HERE'S A WAY to tenderize sturdier greens like Swiss chard and still serve them in a fresh and warm salad of contrasting textures.

- ¼   cup Simple Syrup (page 66)
- 1   teaspoon plus 1 tablespoon cider vinegar
- ¼   cup dried cherries
     Small pinch coarsely ground black pepper
- ½   tablespoon Dijon mustard
     Salt
- 4   tablespoons olive oil
- ¼   cup raw almonds
- 4   large handfuls baby Swiss chard leaves
     Fresh lemon juice
- 2   cups snow peas, blanched
     Handful fresh basil, chopped

Combine the simple syrup, 1 teaspoon of the vinegar, cherries, and pepper in a very small pot, bring to a simmer, then set aside off the heat so the cherries plump up. Drain, reserving the liquid.

In a large bowl, combine the cherries, 1 tablespoon of the reserved liquid, the remaining tablespoon vinegar, mustard, and salt. Whisk in 3 tablespoons of the oil, then set the vinaigrette aside.

Heat the remaining tablespoon oil in a medium skillet over medium-high heat. Add the almonds and salt and cook for a minute, then a handful of the Swiss chard and a squeeze of lemon juice and cook until the chard is barely wilted.

Scatter the wilted chard mixture on a platter, add the remaining chard, snow peas, and basil to the vinaigrette and toss. Pile on the platter and serve!

PEPPERS

IT'S SURPRISING that in most of the United States we have such a limited vocabulary for and understanding of the dazzling variety of peppers grown here. Like tomatoes, there's an intriguing range of flavors and shapes, but these distinctions remain highly regionalized. Granted, the heat packed in some peppers is often surprisingly (and even thrillingly) dangerous to cook with. But, judiciously cooking with peppers—and the tantalizing heat that they impart—has become a defining characteristic of American food.

Like many American chefs, my cooking is influenced by many different culinary traditions: French food is all about harmony; Japanese food is all about nature's subtlety; but for me, American cooking is liberated by peppers. The acidity of citrus and vinegar, the flavor of cooking over wood, combined with the long, slow, persistent heat of peppers—these define American cooking for me. I like to use the American words for foods. Instead of worrying about *chillis,* or *chiles,* I call them *hot peppers* and *sweet peppers.*

Making Hot Pepper Oil

I love the flavor of so many different hot peppers, but taming the heat can be really challenging. Just a couple of seeds, or even a rogue piece of pepper, can ruin a dish (and your eyes, hands, and mouth!).

Infusing oils with the aromatics of peppers allows us to use heat in more controllable amounts. I like to add a couple of drops to stews, soups, and vegetable mixes, to impart just the heat I want in each recipe. Infused oils are a smart way to stretch an ingredient's season and preserve flavor.

In a very small bowl, combine 2 seeded and halved hot peppers, such as habaneros, 1 seeded and thinly sliced hot pepper like serrano, 1 thinly sliced clove garlic, 1 thin slice fresh ginger, 1 teaspoon mustard seeds, a pinch of fennel seeds, 1 bay leaf, a few slivers of lemon peel, and ½ cup warm olive oil. Let the mixture infuse in a warm place for about 2 hours, then cover and refrigerate. The oil will keep for a few weeks. Makes about ½ cup.

Drying Seasoning Peppers

Drying peppers is another natural way of preserving flavor. In the garden, peppers ripen all at the same time, and it can be difficult to use that harvest all at once. My dad has experimented with many simple techniques for drying his hot pepper crop in the sun.

Here's his method: He slices the peppers in half, removes most (but not all) of the seeds, and lays them on a repurposed screen door, set on cement blocks, in the sunlight. He leaves them there for 5 days, taking them in at night to avoid moisture from the dew. He's been known to use a dehydrator to make sure they're really dry (and says since it's faster and less work, he may do it all in a dehydrator next year). He then grinds the dried peppers in a blender and stores them in jars. Cooking with these dried peppers—and sprinkling on their warmth as a finishing touch—has become essential to me.

PICKLED PEPPERS

MAKES ABOUT 1 PINT

SIMILAR TO INFUSING peppers in oil, pickling peppers stretches the season, preserves the flavor, and with the addition of vinegar, sugar, salt, and spice, pickling them heightens the peppers' aromatic quality. This way they can brighten up any dish, bringing delicious acidity without being overpowering. I like the mild quality of ají dulce, jalapeño, and Trinidad seasoning peppers. They all have great flavor without searingly intense heat. Refrigerated, they'll keep for a few weeks.

Follow the Basic Pickling Recipe (page 66), substituting these ingredients.

- 2 cups ají dulce or other small mild, aromatic peppers, stemmed
- ¾ cup rice wine vinegar
- ¼ cup water
- ¼ cup sugar
- 1 tablespoon kosher salt

PEPPER STEW

SERVES 4 TO 6

THE ORIGIN OF THIS STEW may be in the piperades of the Basque country of south-western France and northeastern Spain, but my version is lighter, brighter, and easier to cook. It's all about building a sweet foundational flavor of onions and peppers. Sure, ginger and lemongrass are not traditional, but I like what they do to peppers. It's up to you to decide if you'd like to include hot peppers or Hot Pepper Oil (page 235) to increase the intensity of heat.

¼ cup olive oil

1½ pounds sweet, mild peppers, halved, seeded, and sliced

1 (4-inch) piece lemongrass, bruised

1 clove garlic, smashed

1 teaspoon minced fresh ginger

Salt and pepper

Handful black olives, pitted

1 tablespoon capers, drained

2 tablespoons red wine vinegar

Pinch crushed red pepper flakes

Pinch dried oregano

1 onion, halved and thinly sliced

Fresh lemon juice

Handful fresh flat-leaf parsley, roughly chopped

Handful fresh basil, roughly chopped

Heat the oil in a medium saucepan over medium-high heat. Add the peppers, lemongrass, garlic, ginger, salt, and pepper, and give it a stir. Turn the heat down to medium-low and let the mixture stew, stirring occasionally, until the peppers are just soft, 15 to 20 minutes.

Add the olives, capers, vinegar, red pepper flakes, and oregano and stir for about a minute, letting the vinegar evaporate. Add the onions and a nice splash of lemon juice and cook, stirring occasionally, until the onions are softened but still have a crunch, 5 to 10 minutes. (It might seem strange to save the onions until the end, but it lets them have more texture rather than melting into the stew.) Stir in the parsley and basil and serve hot or at room temperature.

P

STUFFED PEPPERS WITH CHORIZO & WILD RICE

SERVES 4

HOW CAN ANYONE NOT LOVE to make stuffed peppers? Cut a pepper in half and it becomes nature's bowl! I like to use all kinds of colors and sizes of peppers and fill them with rice, grain, sausage, fish, or eggs. It's your decision whether you cook them for 25 minutes, as I do here, so the peppers retain their identity, or cook them longer, so the peppers almost melt, roasted, into the stuffing. Both are impossibly delicious.

- ¼ cup olive oil, plus more for drizzling
- 2 pounds chorizo sausage, removed from the casing
- 4 cups cooked wild rice
  Large handful finely chopped fresh chives
  Salt and pepper
- 4 large bell peppers, or a mix of sizes, halved lengthwise, seeded, and ribs trimmed
- 4 tablespoons (½ stick) butter, cut into 8 pieces

Preheat the oven to 375°F. Heat the oil in a very large skillet over medium heat. Add the chorizo and cook, stirring occasionally and breaking up any large clumps, until it's cooked through, about 8 minutes. Drain any rendered fat. Transfer to a large bowl, add the rice, chives, salt, and pepper to the bowl, and stir to combine.

Lay the pepper halves cut-side up in a baking dish. Drizzle with oil, then add salt and pepper and a piece of butter to each. Spoon the chorizo filling into each half. Bake until the peppers are soft and the filling is steaming hot, about 25 minutes.

POTATOES

HISTORICALLY, potatoes have taught us how precarious it is to rely too heavily on one crop, proving once again the urgency of diversity and how susceptible monocultures are to disease. These conditions that led to the Irish Potato Famine are scarily similar: We favor too few food crops. That's a lesson sitting right in front of us. And it's not for lack of potato diversity. In fact, there's an amazing variety of colors, sizes, shapes, and textures of potatoes, as well as inspiring ways to handle them. The recipes here do involve a little technique—humble potatoes thrive with exciting preparation—but technique doesn't drive the story, flavor does.

While I was in cooking school in Paris, I externed at a restaurant called Le Toit de Passy, a great Michelin-starred place. I worked as a *commis* on the fish station with a salty old cook who, it seemed to me, had been there forever (he was 26). I was quite a proud cook: I knew I needed to please the hungry crew, so for family meal I made mashed potatoes. Again! Jean Pierre shot me a look that went right through me: "That's all you know how to do?" In a flash, he grabbed a fistful of flour, a little butter, and set a pan of oil on a burner. In no time, he had folded my potato puree into a soft dough called *pâte à choux,* then nudged me to plop the mixture into the hot oil. Without the slightest idea of what would happen, I just did it. What did happen was golden puffs of deliciousness, crunchy on the outside, soft and buttery on the inside. Best potato I had ever tasted. Made the whole kitchen smile. He looked at me with a half grin that made me understand that I still had a lot of work to do. For me, this defines a cook's job: making something out of nothing. In other words, a magician! *See Walnut Mashed Potatoes (page 200).*

PAN-ROASTED FINGERLINGS

SERVES 4

THIS IS MY GO-TO METHOD for cooking fingerling potatoes really crispy on the outside, really tender within. With small potatoes, you can brown them raw, or as I do here, simmer them first until tender, and then brown them. Use a generous amount of oil in the pan and be patient: Let the potatoes cook cut-side down in the pan for longer than you think, so they'll brown beautifully. At the very end, turn off the heat and sprinkle chopped herbs and/or minced onions or red pepper flakes over the potatoes in the hot pan before serving.

1½   pounds fingerling potatoes
        Salt
¼   cup olive oil
        Handful fresh flat-leaf parsley or tarragon,
        chopped
        Crushed red pepper flakes

Put the potatoes in a medium saucepan, cover with water by an inch, and add a large pinch of salt. Simmer until the potatoes are just tender, about 15 minutes. Test them by piercing with a sharp knife; if it slips in without resistance, the potatoes are ready. Drain the potatoes, pat dry, halve lengthwise, and sprinkle with salt. You can do this step well ahead, even the day before, then brown them just before you're ready to serve.

Heat the oil in a large skillet over medium-high heat. Add the potatoes flat-side down and cook without moving until they are deep brown and crispy, about 4 minutes. The beautiful crispiness develops when you don't move the potatoes, so resist the impulse. Flip the potatoes over and repeat on the other side. Serve flat-side up sprinkled with the herbs and red pepper flakes.

P

POTATO PANCAKE

SERVES 4 TO 6

I ENCOUNTERED THIS CLASSIC of French cooking called *pommes Darphin* in the kitchen at March restaurant in Manhattan, where it was perfected; the cooks there made it every day. This pancake does require a bit of practice to get it right. But man, is it worth it! The more you practice, the better you'll get. Try doing it without the onion filling at first to get a sense of how the potatoes brown on the outside and cook on the inside. The thinner the pancake, the easier it is to handle, so as you practice, start small.

6 tablespoons olive oil
1 large onion, quartered and thinly sliced
2 tablespoons red wine vinegar
  Salt
2½ pounds potatoes, such as Yukon Gold or russet, peeled and cut into matchsticks
  Pepper
  Handful fresh flat-leaf parsley, chopped

Preheat the oven to 400°F. Heat 2 tablespoons of the oil in a large skillet over medium heat. Add the onions and caramelize (page 211). Take your time. This is where the special flavor is born! Add the vinegar and cook until it's evaporated. Add salt, then set the caramelized onions aside.

Combine the potatoes and a tablespoon of the oil in a large bowl, and add salt and pepper. Heat the remaining 3 tablespoons oil in a large ovenproof skillet over medium-high heat. Pour the potatoes into a strainer, then spread half evenly into the bottom of the skillet.

Pile the caramelized onions on the center of the potatoes and sprinkle with the parsley. Spread the remaining potatoes on top, covering the onion mixture completely. Cook until the potatoes on the bottom are well browned and crispy, about 5 minutes. Pop the skillet into the oven and roast until the bottom becomes a sturdy crust, about 8 minutes.

Remove the skillet from the oven, run a spatula under the pancake all around, then flatten the top a bit into an even layer. Continue to bake until the pancake holds together, about 10 minutes more. Remove the skillet from the oven and, with a spatula and a little shake of the pan, confirm that the pancake is detached and not sticking. Here comes the fun part. Cover the skillet with a large inverted plate, then flip the pancake onto the plate.

Slide the pancake back into the skillet, browned side up, then smooth the sides of the pancake with the spatula to form a compact, round shape. Heat the skillet over medium-high heat, return to the oven, and bake until the potatoes are tender and browned on the bottom, about another 10 minutes. This crispy pancake is irresistible, so serve it right away.

P

POTATO & CHEESE CROQUETTES

MAKES 16

I PREFER TO MAKE THESE croquettes with dense potatoes like Yukon Gold, Russian Bananas, or German Butterballs. These super-delicious cheesy bites are best eaten just as they're made, so I make them at home as a pre-dinner snack. This version shows off the tangy, semisoft Reading cheese from Vermont; Gruyère is fine, too. Experiment! Try stirring herbs, sautéed corn, other vegetables like caramelized onions, or even smoked fish into the potato mixture.

1½	pounds potatoes, peeled and quartered
	Salt
¾	cup flour
3	eggs, whisked
1	cup panko or dried bread crumbs
	Grapeseed or peanut oil for frying
1	cup grated Gruyère
2	egg yolks
	Pinch grated nutmeg
	Pepper

Put the potatoes in a medium saucepan and cover with water by about 2 inches. Add salt and simmer until the potatoes are just tender, about 15 minutes. Meanwhile, put ½ cup of the flour, whisked eggs, and panko or bread crumbs into 3 separate shallow bowls.

Drain the potatoes, toss in the pan for about a minute to dry them out, then pass them through a ricer or food mill into a large bowl. Heat 2 inches of oil to 350°F in a medium saucepan, then add the remaining ¼ cup flour, cheese, yolks, nutmeg, and pepper to the potatoes and stir well to combine.

Scoop 2 rounded tablespoons of the potato mixture into your hand, shape into an oval, and set on a plate. Repeat with the remaining potato mixture, then bread each one, first by dusting with flour, shaking off any excess, then dipping into the beaten eggs, and then coating with panko.

When the oil is hot, fry the croquettes in batches, turning occasionally. They're done as soon as they turn golden brown on the outside, about 2 minutes. Sprinkle with salt and serve immediately.

P

GRANMAW HARTLE'S POTATO DUMPLINGS

SERVES 4

I WAS VERY EXCITED TO UPDATE this standard of the supper table that my mother grew up eating in her German parents' kitchen, a recipe that came from their family in Indiana and Ohio. Turns out that this recipe, known as "pot pie," was a cornerstone of Pennsylvania Dutch cooking. As in the kitchens of all working-class families, the dumplings were simplified over the years to match families' limited time and budgets. My grandfather worked on a railroad; my grandmother ran a school cafeteria.

For me, the most interesting part of this recipe is not the culinary complexity—in my childhood I considered these dumplings literally cooked starch—but I love the idea of using the emotions of home cooking as a starting point for soulful dishes. So, when

I began to experiment with the dumplings, I didn't look to my technical background to remake this recipe; instead, I started with the love that my mother has for this recipe, then I lightened the dumplings with vegetables and simmering broth. Now these dumplings are more than comfort food; they remind us that there's nothing more contemporary than being inspired by the soulfulness of the past.

¾   pound unpeeled Yukon Gold potatoes
     Olive oil
     Salt and pepper
5   cups chicken broth
2   carrots, diced
1   stalk salsify, peeled and diced
1   leek (white and pale green parts),
     halved and thickly sliced

1 boneless, skinless chicken breast, cut into large dice
½ cup flour, plus more for rolling
½ teaspoon baking powder
2 tablespoons grated Gruyère
1 egg, whisked
    Small handful roughly chopped fresh dill

Preheat the oven to 375°F. Lightly coat the potatoes with oil, sprinkle with salt and pepper, then wrap them in aluminum foil. Bake until tender, about 45 minutes.

Meanwhile, bring the broth to a boil in a medium saucepan. Add the carrots, salsify, salt, and pepper and simmer until just tender, about 10 minutes. Add the leeks, simmer for a couple minutes, then add the chicken and poach until just cooked through, about 5 minutes. Turn off the heat, remove the chicken from the broth, and set aside.

Peel the baked potatoes, then pass them through a ricer or food mill into a large bowl. Add the flour, baking powder, cheese, egg, salt, and pepper and stir to combine. If the mixture is too dry to form a dough, add a couple drops of water. Turn the dough onto a floured work surface and knead for a minute or two, then roll out and fold it onto itself a couple of times to give it a little body. Roll out the dough to a rectangle about ¼ inch thick and cut into rough squares.

Return the broth to a brisk simmer, add the dumplings, and cook until they float, about 3 minutes. Add the poached chicken back to the pan and add the dill, salt, and pepper. Serve in shallow bowls.

P

MY POTATO SALAD

SERVES 6

MY POTATO SALAD encompasses a wildly
varying number of other ingredients. Sure,
potato salad can be made using only potatoes.
But it's so much more satisfying to add other
vegetables, such as the sweet potato and
rutabaga I use here. Enliven your potato salad
with any firm-textured vegetable: on the
lighter side, avocado and artichoke; or on the
more substantial, carrots, fennel, and celery root.
Homemade mayonnaise brings these humble
ingredients together, and it makes all the
difference in this salad. Scatter plenty of fresh
herbs over the top before serving.

      Salt
  1   rutabaga, peeled
  4   Yukon Gold potatoes, unpeeled
  1   sweet potato, peeled
  2   tablespoons olive oil
  2   onions, finely chopped
  6   scallions (white and pale green parts), sliced
  2   cloves garlic, minced
  ½   teaspoon ground cumin
  1   small red onion, minced
  2   tablespoons grated fresh horseradish
      Small handful fresh flat-leaf parsley,
      finely chopped
1½   tablespoons minced fresh chives
  1   recipe Mayonnaise (page 58)
  1   tablespoon white wine vinegar
      Pepper

Bring a large pot of water to a boil over
medium-high heat and add 2 pinches salt. Add
the rutabaga and simmer for 15 minutes. Add
the Yukon Golds and sweet potatoes and simmer
until tender, about 30 minutes more.

Meanwhile, heat the oil in a medium saucepan over
medium heat. Add the onions and scallions and
sweat until softened, about 10 minutes. Add the
garlic, cumin, and a pinch of salt and sweat for
another couple minutes. Transfer the onion
mixture to a large bowl, add the red onions, horseradish, parsley, and chives, and stir until combined.

Drain the rutabaga and potatoes and remove the
skin from the potatoes. Then dice the potatoes and
rutabaga. Add them to the onion mixture, along
with about two-thirds of the mayonnaise, the
vinegar, and pepper. Gently stir to combine, adding a
little more mayonnaise and/or vinegar, if needed.

Quince
252

"*Quince, in my book, is an honorary vegetable.*"
—MICHAEL ANTHONY, *V is for Vegetables*, 2015

QUINCE

I KNOW FALL has truly arrived when I walk through the front door of Gramercy Tavern and am greeted by the heady aroma of crates and crates of flowery quinces. While the fruit smells lovely and looks like a pear, quince is much too bitter to eat raw. This is great news for a cook, because you must use your tricks to render it edible. Quince retains its signature aroma and texture, even after long slow cooking, which makes it a wonderful companion to autumn salads and desserts, and for the mostarda that follows. Do not be put off by the fruit's exterior fuzz; it's easily rinsed off. A quince should feel very firm when you buy it.

QUINCE MOSTARDA

MAKES ABOUT 2 CUPS

I CREATED THIS RECIPE based on the traditional sweet and spicy Italian condiment called mostarda. This version shows off the actual fruit and keeps the sweetness in the background, making it a perfect partner to charcuterie and for cheese. I love to serve Mostarda with cheese from my favorite producer in the Northeast: Jasper Hill Farm in Greensboro, Vermont. From top right, Bayley Hazen Blue, Moses Sleeper, Winnimere, and Cabot Clothbound Cheddar.

1   bottle dry white wine
½   cup sugar
1   quince, peeled and cubed
1   pear, peeled and cubed
1   apple, peeled and cubed
1   tablespoon dry mustard powder
2   teaspoons mustard seeds
½   teaspoon white wine vinegar
⅓   cup toasted walnut halves, roughly chopped

Combine the wine and sugar in a medium saucepan and simmer until the sugar is dissolved. Add the quince and simmer for 10 minutes, then add the pears and apples and simmer, stirring occasionally, for another 15 minutes, or until the fruit is tender but still holds its shape.

With a slotted spoon, remove the fruit from the pan. Boil the liquid until reduced to about 1 cup, then add the mustard powder, stirring to dissolve any clumps. Add the mustard seeds and vinegar, stir in the cooked fruit and walnuts, then let cool to room temperature. Transfer to a covered container. The mostarda will keep, refrigerated, for about 2 weeks. Bring to room temperature before serving.

"Rutabaga, Rutabaga, Rutabaga, Rutabaga,

Radishes
256

Ramps
262

Rhubarb
265

Rutabaga
268

Rutabay-y-y-y..." —FRANK ZAPPA, *Call Any Vegetable*, 1967

RADISHES

*"The man pulling radishes
pointed my way
with a radish."*

THAT 18TH-CENTURY HAIKU is by one of my favorite Japanese poets, Issa. Everyone who loves to eat appreciates the beauty and bounty of radishes, but it's not always clear how to make the most of them. I think of remarkable restaurant settings where radishes are the star: part of a bouquet of vegetables right on the table at La Colombe d'Or in sun-drenched Provence; their beauty celebrated by Alice Waters at Chez Panisse as a simple welcome; their purity by Fergus Henderson at St. John in London—red radishes on a small white plate with a block of the best butter and flaky sea salt. I love to call radishes by their names, like superheroes: the long red and white-tipped French Breakfast, the pure white Icicle radish, the red-hearted watermelon radish (page 322), the purple plums, the red globes, the black radish, the green Korean moo radish, and the massive heft of the daikon (page 104).

Eating radishes whole is its own pleasure, but it may be a discovery that the roots, leaves, sprouts, and seedpods are all edible, too. Three ways to use them raw: Shaved, especially the long ones, then put in ice water to curl beautifully (right); grated, as a topping for fish or other vegetables; and sliced, cutting them into superfine matchsticks with red tips. Yet radishes are wonderful braised, roasted, fermented, salted, and even fried. Pairing radishes with such sweet things as honey, fruit (like peaches), and juices (like apple cider) mellows their sharpness.

SALTED RADISH SALAD WITH BLACK BASS

SERVES 4

HERE'S WHERE the simplest things matter most: a pinch of salt, a crunchy radish, and the barely touched slices of pristine fish.

- 4 large radishes, sliced paper-thin
- 2 tablespoons salt
- 1 (¾-pound) skinless sushi-quality black sea bass fillet, sliced crosswise
  Olive oil
  Sea salt
  Zest from 1 lime

- ¼ cup trout roe
- 3 large radishes, peeled and grated

In a small bowl, combine the sliced radishes and 2 tablespoons salt and let sit for about 10 minutes. Rinse the radishes, pat them dry, then lay them, slightly overlapping, on 4 plates. Top with the fish, drizzle with oil, and sprinkle with a little sea salt and the lime zest. Spoon the trout roe, then the grated radish, around the fish.

Slicing Radishes

One of my indispensable tools in the kitchen is a mandoline, either a light, handheld plastic one or a metal slicer that stands on the countertop. Use whichever you have or feel most comfortable with. Mandolines help make the magic happen with so many vegetables.

BRAISED RADISHES WITH HONEY & BLACK PEPPER

SERVES 4

BRAISING IS A GREAT WAY to soften radish roots and remove their spicy rawness. Without losing the character of the radish, this braise enhances it with the sweetness of honey, the aromatic quality of the black pepper, and the browned edges of the radish itself. This is an entirely different way to love radishes. If you can find (or grow) multicolored Easter Egg radishes, they'll look great in this braise.

- 2 tablespoons olive oil
- 1 pound radishes, halved
- 1 clove garlic, smashed
- 2 tablespoons honey
- 1 teaspoon coarsely cracked black pepper
- 2 tablespoons cider vinegar
  Salt

Heat the oil in a medium saucepan over medium-high heat. Add half the radishes and all the garlic and cook until lightly browned, about 5 minutes. Add the honey and pepper and let the honey caramelize, about a minute. Add the vinegar, the remaining radishes, and salt and cook until all the radishes are just warmed but not cooked soft.

RAMPS

RAMPS ARE WILD LEEKS and a celebrated first sign of spring. When the forest floor is still cold and brown, hardy ramps poke out their spade-shaped leaves (skunk cabbage comes along at that time, too, and is actually edible, but you'd have to be starving to death to consider it). Ramps grow plentifully and indigenously on the East Coast and as far west as the Great Lakes. In Appalachia, entire festivals are devoted to gathering and eating them; ramps have been a localized part of our culture and economy for generations.

The truth is, however, that ramps have become so popular in restaurants in the past several decades that their brief, wild existence is compromised. As a chef, I feel a bit responsible. I do not think anyone celebrates ramps more than we do at Gramercy Tavern. But as the trend of using wild food has amplified, and ramps are over-harvested, we have to consider how to manage this natural resource more responsibly. Ramps should be considered a rare delicacy; a connection to the fragile, natural world around us.

PICKLED RAMPS

MAKES ABOUT 1 PINT

WHETHER YOU COME out of the woods with
your basket of ramps or buy them at the
farmers' market, like every plant, from the
second they're harvested, ramps lose flavor.
So eat the fragile leaves quickly. First separate
the leaves, wash them, and set aside for dishes
like Ramps & Spaghetti (page 264). Then trim
off the roots and outer skin, rinse, and pickle,
following the Basic Pickling Recipe (page 66),
substituting these ingredients. These pickles
can be enjoyed long after the ramps have
succumbed to warmer weather.

2 cups ramps with about ¼ inch of
  green attached

¾ cup rice wine vinegar

¼ cup water

¼ cup sugar

1 tablespoon kosher salt

½ teaspoon coriander seeds

½ teaspoon fennel seeds

½ teaspoon mustard seeds

½ teaspoon black peppercorns

RAMPS & SPAGHETTI

SERVES 4

RAMPS CAN EASILY BE TURNED INTO pesto and compound butter to season risotto and pastas. In this dish, I celebrate the entire ramp, using the texture of their smooth leaves, their aromatic chopped stems, and their bulbs to turn the simplest plate of spaghetti into an explosive springtime meal.

¾ pound spaghetti
   Salt
4 tablespoons olive oil
24 ramps, roughly chopped, whites and greens separated
   Pinch crushed red pepper flakes
2 cups spinach leaves, stemmed and washed
   Small pinch dried basil
   Small pinch dried oregano
   Pepper
⅓ cup grated Parmigiano

Cook the pasta in a large pot of salted boiling water until just tender, then drain (reserving ¼ to ½ cup of the cooking water). Stir in a tablespoon of the oil.

While the pasta is cooking, heat the remaining 3 tablespoons oil in a large skillet over medium heat. Add the ramp whites and red pepper flakes and cook for about 2 minutes. Add the ramp greens, spinach, basil, oregano, salt, and pepper and cook for about a minute more. Add the spaghetti, about ¼ cup of the pasta cooking water, and the cheese and toss to combine.

RHUBARB

MY MOM'S favorite pie in the world is strawberry rhubarb, and for pastry chefs after a long winter, rhubarb marks the reentry to the garden. With rhubarb, the answer to the oft-asked question "Can you eat that?" is emphatically "yes" when it comes to the celery-like stalks, and even more emphatically "NO!" if you're referring to their enormous leaves, which are toxic. The redness of the stems is not a sign of ripeness; each variety has its own signature color ranging from green to pink to crimson. Rhubarb, for me, represents a plant from an earlier time, when we were less certain to find abundance in our markets and it was necessary to find ingenious ways to use this strange, extremely hardy plant. Rhubarb's flavor reminds us of our past even as it opens our taste buds to new possibilities.

SWEET & SOUR RHUBARB SAUCE

MAKES ABOUT 1½ CUPS

RHUBARB IS MOST FREQUENTLY used as a dessert, mostly because it needs sweetness to soften its tart flavor. But I imagine this homey barbecue-like sauce to be like a famous French recipe called *saumon à l'oseille*, salmon with sorrel, created by Jean and Pierre Troisgros in the early 1960s. That creation opened the door to using tart sorrel in a savory dish. In fact, rhubarb is related to sorrel, and I made this tart sauce to work as a luscious contrast to the crispy skin and meaty quality of a great farm-raised bird.

⅓ cup brown sugar
⅓ cup sherry vinegar
2 stalks rhubarb (about 6 ounces), chopped
2 cloves garlic, chopped
½ small onion, chopped
   Pinch coarsely ground black pepper
   Pinch crushed red pepper flakes
   Salt
1 cup tomato pulp (fresh or canned)
   Small pinch dried basil
   Small pinch dried oregano

1 teaspoon Dijon mustard
1 teaspoon sesame oil
1 teaspoon soy sauce

Put the brown sugar in a saucepan over medium heat and cook until it's caramelized, a few minutes. Add the vinegar (watch out for sputtering) and let it bubble for another minute. Add the rhubarb, garlic, onions, pepper, red pepper flakes, and salt and simmer until the vinegar is almost evaporated, about 5 minutes. Add the tomato, basil, and oregano and simmer until the rhubarb has softened and the sauce has thickened slightly, about 10 minutes. Remove from the heat and stir in the mustard, sesame oil, and soy sauce. The sauce will keep, covered in the refrigerator, for about 5 days.

RUTABAGA

HOW TO MAKE rutabaga taste good? We do not often dream about this vegetable, saying, "Ummmm, I can't wait to sink my teeth into that yellow turnip that's been in the ground all winter!" This hardy vegetable, able to survive the most punishingly cold weather, first became popular, not surprisingly, in Northern Europe. Hence its vernacular nickname, Swede. For me, the secret to bringing out the hidden value of this rough-looking vegetable is to add the richness of butter and the sweetness of fruit. Both will make a virtue of the bitter, turnip-y quality of cooked rutabaga. The Rutabaga Gratin (right) relies on dates to fill the fruit requirement, but think about using dried figs, cherries, or cranberries to play the same role. Or make a puree of the cooked rutabaga with baked apples, quince, or pears, just a touch of brown butter, and a speck of vanilla bean. Choose the smallest rutabaga in the market, as they're never waxed and often the best tasting.

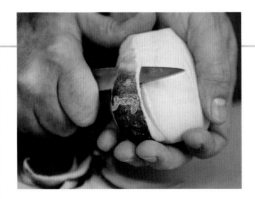

Prepping Rutabaga

So if you promise not to buy the big, hulking waxed roots of rutabaga, I'll promise you can make short work of getting to the heart of this vegetable. Forget the vegetable peeler; use a sharp paring knife to remove the tough outer skin in strips. Then the root is easily sliced.

RUTABAGA GRATIN

SERVES 6

THIS IS ONE VEGETABLE that needs all the help it can get. I cut the rutabaga thin for a reason: It can be a tough customer and needs to cook until it's completely soft. Since a shot of brandy along with a fair amount of cream and butter paired with garlic and shallots tastes so good with potatoes, turnips, and cauliflower, I use this same combination to tame rutabaga. But the key to this recipe is to enhance rutabaga's mellow earthiness with the sweetness of dates. Dates make rutabaga lovable.

2   tablespoons butter
2   cloves garlic, minced
¼   cup minced shallots
¼   cup brandy
¼   cup white wine
2   cups heavy cream
4   Medjool dates, pitted and roughly chopped
    Salt and pepper
1¼ pounds rutabaga, peeled and very thinly sliced
1   cup grated Parmigiano

Preheat the oven to 350°F with a rack in the center of the oven. Butter a medium baking dish with a tablespoon of the butter, scatter half the garlic on the bottom, and set aside.

Heat the remaining tablespoon of butter in a small saucepan over medium-low heat. Add the shallots and remaining garlic and stir until softened, about 3 minutes. Pour in the brandy and cook until the liquid has almost evaporated. Repeat with the wine. Take your time. This is where the special flavor is born! Add the cream and dates, season assertively with salt and pepper, and bring to a simmer.

Arrange half the rutabaga in the gratin dish, working in a circle and overlapping the edges. Be sure to cover the bottom well because it will cook down to form one thick layer. Sprinkle with half the cheese, then spoon on half the cream-date mixture. Layer on the remaining rutabaga, cheese, and cream-date mixture. Put the dish on a baking sheet (to catch any drips) and bake until the rutabaga is tender, about an hour. Increase the heat to 375°F and continue to bake until the gratin is bubbling and beautifully browned on top.

"*Few vegetables look more handsome growing in a*

kitchen garden than chard."—ALICE WATERS, *Chez Panisse Vegetables*, 1996

Salsify
272

Scallions
274

Shallots
278

Spinach
280

Swiss Chard
286

SALSIFY

A VERY LONG dark-skinned root that grows deep in the soil and has the ability to pull out amazing mineral content, salsify is not easy to harvest, but it is surprisingly abundant in wintertime. The leafy tops are chicory-like and edible, but it is much more satisfying to peel off its dark skin to reveal a perfectly white interior. Once peeled, the root oxidizes quickly, so keep it in lemon water to prevent it from turning brown. Similar in color to a parsnip, salsify's flavor is not as sweet. When cooked with a drop of lemon juice, salsify softens beautifully, like a carrot. In vegetable braises, it enhances the flavor of its supporting characters in a way that is hard to describe. Salsify somehow makes each component of a dish taste better. I've never found it to taste like oysters, as reputed, but I'm convinced eating salsify brings with it some kind of ancient wisdom.

GLAZED SALSIFY & CARROTS

SERVES 4

SALSIFY IS A VEGETABLE whose flavor improves immensely with a light touch of garlic and butter. This recipe is a classic way to glaze root vegetables. *See Glazed Hakurei Turnips with Turnip & Mustard Greens (page 309).*

3 salsify, peeled and sliced on the diagonal
2 carrots, sliced on the diagonal
1 clove garlic, smashed
2 tablespoons butter
1 tablespoon sugar
   Salt
   Fresh lemon juice
   Ancho chile powder

Combine the salsify, carrots, garlic, butter, sugar, salt, a squeeze of lemon juice, and 2 cups of water in a medium saucepan. Simmer until the vegetables are tender, the liquid has evaporated, and the vegetables are lightly glazed, about 20 minutes. Swirl the vegetables in the saucepan so the glaze evenly coats them. Sprinkle with ancho chile powder just before serving.

SCALLIONS

IS A SCALLION just an immature onion? Well, *no!* Scallions are in the onion family and are even, in some parts of the country, called green onions. But to clarify, scallions are a different variety of allium that will not form a bulb. Seed catalogues call them "bunching onions," prized for their slim, straight white (sometimes red) stalks and abundant, tender green tops. For me, scallions (especially from a garden and not from a supermarket) are great raw in salads, or chopped and lightly cooked in a stir-fry, and are really delicious grilled whole. Scallion greens sliced into thin rounds are a nice finishing touch on so many dishes, and they curl amazingly when cut into very thin matchsticks and soaked in ice water for a couple of hours.

SCALLION PANCAKES

MAKES 4 (6-INCH) PANCAKES

WORKING ON THIS BOOK has been such a joy, partly due to the creative collaboration of our acting sous chef, Sue Li. Talking about scallions, Sue showed us the authentic way her Taiwanese mother taught her to make delicious scallion pancakes. This is the recipe she shared with us.

2 cups flour, plus more for kneading and rolling
⅔ cup boiling water
4 teaspoons peanut oil, plus more for frying

   Salt
1 cup sliced scallions
   Hot sauce, chile oil, and/or soy sauce

Put the 2 cups flour in a large bowl and gradually stir in the boiling water until a rough dough forms. Dust a work surface with flour, turn the dough out of the bowl, and knead until it is somewhat smooth and starts to feel firm, about 5 minutes. Flatten it into a disk, wrap in plastic, and let it cool, about 2 hours.

Divide the cooled dough into 4 pieces. Lightly flour a work surface and roll out a piece of dough into about an 8-inch circle. Brush the top with a teaspoon of the oil, then sprinkle with salt and one-quarter of the scallions. Form the circle of dough into a long roll, then twist into a coiled shape like a snail shell. Cover with plastic wrap, set aside, and repeat the process with the remaining 3 pieces of dough.

Use a rolling pin to roll the coils into 6-inch rounds. Heat 2 teaspoons oil in a medium skillet over medium heat. Add one of the pancakes, cook until golden on one side, about 4 minutes, then start flipping it every 30 seconds or so until it is crispy on both sides and cooked through, about 10 minutes longer. Swirl the pancake in the pan. The contact with the side of the skillet will help it puff up. Repeat with the remaining pancakes, using more oil as needed. Cut into quarters and serve with the hot sauce, chile oil, and/or soy sauce.

STEAMED CLAMS WITH SCALLION & TARRAGON SAUCE

SERVES 4

THIS IS A STRAIGHTFORWARD and classic way to prepare shellfish, but I chose it specifically to illustrate the whole scallion. The flavor of scallions is so light, its subtlety lets the brininess of the clams shine through the broth, mellowing the acidity from the wine. I use scallion greens as an herb, in the same way as tarragon.

2   tablespoons olive oil
2   bunches scallions, chopped, greens from 1 bunch thinly sliced and reserved
1   cup dry white wine
    Leaves from 1 sprig tarragon, 5 leaves reserved
    Pinch fennel seeds
3   pounds littleneck clams
2   tablespoons butter

Heat the oil in a large pot over high heat. Add the chopped scallions and cook for about 2 minutes, then add the wine, tarragon, fennel seeds, and clams. Cover the pot and steam, shaking the pot occasionally to help the clams pop open. After about 6 minutes, the clams will start to open; transfer to a large bowl. Discard any clams that do not open.

When the clams are steamed, remove the meat from the shells. Strain the liquid from the clams and any remaining in the pot into a small saucepan, bring to a simmer, and reduce slightly. Turn off the heat and add the butter and the reserved thinly sliced scallion greens and tarragon leaves. Put the clams in small bowls and pour the sauce over them.

SHALLOTS

SHALLOTS REMIND ME of my firm and nurturing culinary instructor in Paris (think Tom Hanks in *Saving Private Ryan*). He told us of his apprenticeship in a classic French kitchen called La Grande Cascade, where once a year in the late spring, they would buy a specific variety of shallot called *échalote grise,* also known as *griselle,* that's famous for its flavor. They'd treat those shallots as prized possessions, peeling mountains of them and preserving every last one in white wine vinegar to last through an entire year of vinaigrettes, beurre blancs, and béarnaises.

Shallots really do impart deeper flavor and longer-lasting aromatics in cooking, without the harshness of onions. I took so much away from that teacher's experience. His way with shallots inspired me to celebrate modest ingredients; to learn the varietal names of the foods I cook; and to try to keep an open mind and an eager palate, always searching for distinctive flavors.

SWEET & SOUR SHALLOTS

MAKES ABOUT 2 CUPS

THIS AMAZING CONDIMENT can enliven grilled, fried, steamed, and raw foods. It enhances and amplifies the shallots' inherent qualities. Since the shallots are cooked with vinegar, the condiment keeps for a long time and is a great homemade preparation to brighten all sorts of dishes, such as fried oysters.

1¼ pounds shallots, finely chopped
1 cup port
1 cup red wine vinegar
   Salt and pepper

Combine the shallots, port, vinegar, salt, and pepper in a medium saucepan. Simmer, stirring occasionally, until the liquid is evaporated, about 45 minutes. Let cool, then transfer to a covered container. The shallots will keep, refrigerated, for about 2 weeks.

SPINACH

WHEN I LIVED IN FRANCE, it was charming to me how vegetables—in this case spinach—have influenced the language. I love that vegetables were important enough for kings and queens to make a fuss over them and still feed the imagination of regular folks to create so many colorful slang expressions: *Mettre du beurre dans les épinards* means to "sweeten the pot," in the sense of working another job, or overtime. I love that *à la Florentine* signifies that a dish focuses on spinach. Of all the greens that we commonly eat at home—like chard, kale, collards—spinach is the most accessible. Tender enough to eat raw, dense enough to enjoy wilted, packed with color to make bright purees, flavorful enough to stand up in a stir-fry, completely alive for fresh soups. It may be one of the world's healthiest foods.

I love spinach because it's so easy to understand and prepare, and it just tastes wonderful. Spinach is really a seasonal green, best enjoyed in the cooler, damp weather of spring and fall. I do not trust or enjoy prepackaged, prewashed bags or clamshells of spinach, now available under fluorescent lights 24/7 in big box stores everywhere. What I do not like about the aforementioned packaged greens, without even getting into how they're produced, is that the leaves have lost every sign of vibrancy. A fresh bowl of beautiful spinach should actually make a kind of squeaking noise when you rub the leaves together. So buy your spinach fresh and alive, cook it right away, and eat it before it loses its glory.

Washing Greens

Spinach, like any leafy green, can be sandy, so it's a good idea to make sure to rinse it thoroughly. Running water over the leaves in a strainer won't clean them well enough. A better method is to fill a large bowl with water, add the leaves, swish them around with your hands several times, then pull them out and transfer to another large bowl of water. Repeating this one more time is usually enough to ensure bright green leaves with no grit. Now you're ready to cook.

SPINACH & GARLIC PUREE WITH SCALLOPS

SERVES 2 TO 4

MOST OFTEN I LIKE TO COOK spinach without water. I sweat or steam it in a large skillet or sauté a small amount of leaves in just a little bit of oil, concentrating the flavor. But blanching spinach in water is sometimes practical. It takes a rather large amount of raw spinach (8 cups, here) to make a dense puree. Adding the smooth Garlic Puree enhances the flavor of the spinach, but is not mandatory. Spinach puree can give a bright, rich color to soups and sauces. It's a perfect accompaniment to scallops. Lightly scoring the scallops' tops is easy and adds a beautiful decorative effect.

- 8 cups packed spinach (stems removed), blanched, and shocked (below right)
- 1 heaping tablespoon Garlic Puree (right)
- 3 tablespoons olive oil
   Salt and pepper
- 12 sea scallops
- 2 tablespoons butter
- 1 clove garlic, smashed
- 2 sprigs thyme

   Coarse sea salt
   Handful baby watercress or spinach

Put the spinach in a blender, breaking it up into chunks. Add the garlic puree (if you like), 2 tablespoons of the oil, ¼ cup water, salt, and pepper, and puree until smooth. Add a bit more water to help with the blending, if needed. The consistency should be silky smooth. Set the spinach puree aside.

Heat the remaining tablespoon oil in a large skillet over high heat. Sprinkle the scallops with salt and pepper, add them to the pan (scored side down),

then reduce the heat to medium-high. Brown evenly, about 2 minutes, then add the butter, garlic, and thyme. Flip the scallops over, baste for about a minute, then remove from the heat.

Spoon the puree into bowls, add the scallops, and scatter the greens on top.

GARLIC PUREE

MAKES ABOUT ½ CUP

THIS BLANCHING PROCESS is repetitive but easy and is guaranteed to remove garlic's bitterness and amplify its sweetness. Garlic Puree can add body and shine to so many dishes.

- ½ cup cloves garlic (about 20)
- 1 cup whole milk
   Salt

Put the garlic in a small saucepan and add enough cold water to cover. Bring to a boil, then drain the garlic. Return the garlic to the pan, cover with cold water, and repeat the process five more times. (Sounds tedious, but it's not!)

After the last draining, return the garlic to the pan, add the milk and a pinch of salt. Bring to a simmer and cook until the garlic is soft, about 15 minutes.

Transfer the garlic to a blender and process with just enough of the milk to create a satiny light puree. Cool and refrigerate up to 5 days.

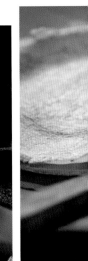

SPINACH EGG CREPES

MAKES ABOUT 8 (6-INCH) ROLLS

EATING SPINACH SOMETIMES leaves a funny feeling in people's mouths, caused by the oxalic acid in the leaves. Nigel Slater, a British food writer I admire, calls it "furry teeth." Lemon juice can soften that effect and mellow its flavor. These crepes are a wonderful way to highlight many garden greens—kale, collards, chard—and are filled here with potatoes, too. I often add other ingredients to the filling, such as grains, peppers, fish, or meat.

6 eggs
1 tablespoon butter, melted
3 tablespoons flour
4 tablespoons olive oil, plus more for the skillet
½ small onion, thinly sliced
1 clove garlic, minced
1 teaspoon mild curry powder
2 medium potatoes, boiled, peeled, and lightly crushed with a fork
Fresh lemon juice
Salt and pepper
14 cups spinach, sautéed (see Kale Cooked Quickly, page 169)

Combine the eggs, butter, and flour in a medium bowl and whisk until smooth. Pour through a fine-mesh strainer to remove any lumps.

Heat an 8-inch crepe pan or nonstick skillet over medium-low heat. Brush the hot skillet with oil, then pour in about ¼ cup batter and quickly swirl to coat the bottom evenly. Cook until the egg crepe is set and starting to brown, about a minute. Carefully

flip the crepe and cook on the other side, about 30 seconds. Transfer to a plate and repeat the process with more oil and the remaining batter, stacking the crepes as you go. Set aside.

Heat 1 tablespoon of the oil in a small saucepan over medium heat. Add the onions and garlic and sweat until softened, about 5 minutes. Add the curry powder and cook for a minute more. Add the crushed potatoes, remaining 3 tablespoons oil, lemon juice, salt, and pepper. Transfer to a bowl.

Lay one crepe on a plate. Spoon some of the potato mixture in the center almost from edge to edge, top with some sautéed spinach, then roll up. Repeat with the remaining crepes, potatoes, and spinach.

SWISS CHARD

SWISS CHARD IS A BIT OF A MYSTERY for home cooks. It was developed by plantsmen who valued the pleasure of eating the leaves and stems of beetroots. Eventually, a separate species emerged: plants with leaves, no globe root, and named for the homeland of its botanist-inventor. While chard leaves are voluptuous, the edible stems are succulent, too, sautéed or used like celery in soups. Red stems are beautiful peeled and cut into matchsticks, or pickled to use all year long.

Here's my fanciful notion of the Swiss part of the drama: visiting the gardens at the Château de Villandry in France, and seeing lines of red chard with their billowing tops marching down the allées, I thought of Swiss Guards at the Vatican, their helmets flamboyant with red feathers. I thought: Swiss chard! When my weekly CSA box arrives at home, and I show my daughters the vegetables, nothing excites them more than chard. They get to eat a rainbow.

CHARD SHAKSHOUKA

SERVES 6

I'VE ALWAYS LOVED savory egg dishes, such as red wine–poached eggs, so when a cook in our Gramercy Tavern kitchen made the classic Israeli shakshouka for a daily family meal, I thought: what a wonderful idea! In this version, I add the substantial nature of Swiss chard to amplify the flavor of tomatoes and peppers. What grows together goes together!

4 tablespoons olive oil
½ small onion, diced
2 cloves garlic, 1 minced, 1 smashed
1 teaspoon crushed red pepper flakes
1 teaspoon smoked paprika
1 bell pepper, cut into matchsticks
1 sprig thyme
1 sprig rosemary
8 canned plum tomatoes, plus juices

Pinch sugar
Salt and pepper
1 tablespoon butter
2 bunches Swiss chard, center ribs removed
6 eggs
¼ cup fresh flat-leaf parsley leaves
2 tablespoons fresh tarragon leaves
Leaves from 3 sprigs thyme
Pinch dried oregano

Preheat the oven to 375°F. Heat 1 tablespoon of the oil in a medium saucepan over medium heat. Sweat the onions, minced garlic, red pepper flakes, and paprika for about 3 minutes. Add the peppers, thyme, and rosemary and continue to cook for

5 minutes more. Add the tomatoes, sugar, salt, and pepper, and simmer until the peppers are soft and the sauce has thickened, about 30 minutes (try to leave the tomatoes intact).

Meanwhile, cook the chard. Heat the remaining 3 tablespoons oil and the butter in a large cast-iron skillet over medium-high heat. Add the smashed garlic, Swiss chard, salt, and pepper and sauté until completely wilted, about 4 minutes. Spoon the tomato mixture over the cooked chard. Make little indentations and break the eggs into them. Sprinkle with half of the herbs.

Bake until the yolks are just set, about 8 minutes. Sprinkle the remaining herbs on top and serve.

SAUTÉED CHARD ARANCINI

MAKES ABOUT 24

THESE FRIED ITALIAN RICE BALLS are named after the "little oranges" they resemble, arancini. This is an amazing way to use up leftover rice, so plan to make a bit more rice than you'll need for dinner. Or just make the risotto from scratch. Sometimes I serve these rice balls with tomato sauce.

- 4 tablespoons olive oil
- ½ small onion, finely chopped
- 1 cup risotto rice
- ¼ cup dry white wine
- 4 cups chicken broth or water, heated to a simmer
- 3 tablespoons butter, at room temperature
- 2 cups grated Parmigiano
  Salt and pepper
- 1 clove garlic, smashed
- 1 bunch Swiss chard, center ribs removed
- ¼ cup flour
- 2 eggs, lightly beaten
- 1 cup bread crumbs
- 1 large egg yolk
- 2 teaspoons fresh lemon juice
- 1 teaspoon grated lemon zest
  Pinch dried oregano
  Grapeseed or vegetable oil for frying

Make the risotto. Heat 2 tablespoons of the olive oil in a small saucepan over medium heat. Add the onions and sweat until softened, about 5 minutes. Add the rice and toast, stirring, about 3 minutes. Add the wine and simmer until it's almost evaporated.

Add the broth or water in increments of ½ cup, waiting to add the next until the liquid has been almost completely absorbed. Cook, stirring constantly, until the rice is al dente, about 15 minutes. Stir in the butter, 1 cup of the cheese, salt, and pepper. Spread the risotto on a plate and let cool.

Meanwhile, cook the chard. Heat the remaining 2 tablespoons olive oil in a large skillet over medium-high heat. Add the garlic, Swiss chard, salt, and pepper and cook until completely wilted, about 4 minutes. Cool, then finely chop.

To make the arancini, put the flour, eggs, and bread crumbs in 3 separate small bowls. Combine the risotto, cooked chard, egg yolk, lemon juice, lemon zest, oregano, salt, and pepper and the remaining cup cheese in a medium bowl. Roll about 2 tablespoons of the risotto mixture in your hands to form a ball. Set the rice ball on a plate and repeat with the remaining mixture.

Heat about 2 inches grapeseed or vegetable oil in a medium saucepan to 350°F. Working in batches, cover each rice ball in the flour, then the eggs, then the bread crumbs. Fry until golden brown, crispy, and heated through, about 2 minutes. Repeat with the remaining rice balls and serve the arancini while still warm with tomato sauce, if you like.

"*The word tomato now embraces the best and worst of*

Tatsoi
292

Tomatillo
294

Tomatoes
296

Turnips
306

the vegetable kingdom." —JANE GRIGSON, *Jane Grigson's Vegetable Book*, 1978

TATSOI

TATSOI IS A MILD AND JUICY Asian green similar to the familiar bok choy (page 46); pak choy; and yu choy, along with hundreds of other varieties. Tatsoi's glamorous whole head is a glory in the garden. Tatsoi's small leaves, like mizuna, mustard greens, and turnip tops (page 309), are tender enough to eat raw in a salad and take only the briefest cooking to soften; tatsoi stems pack a satisfying crunch. Its flowers are delicious, too. A favorite way to practice hands-off cooking is to heat sesame oil in a heavy saucepan with a smashed clove of garlic and a piece of ginger, and throw in several handfuls of washed and still-damp tatsoi or bok choy. Cover the pot, walk away, and come back for the succulent greens when the rice is steamed. Now you have dinner!

SAUTÉED TATSOI WITH MATCHSTICK RADISHES

SERVES 2

SOMETIMES IT'S NOT IMMEDIATELY obvious how to use the wide variety of greens found in farmers' markets. But this simple sauté couldn't be easier. It's fast, too. Tatsoi stems keep their lovely shape and crunch even as their leaves soften in the pan. I love to cut all types of radishes into matchsticks to show off the skin color on their tips and soften their bite.

2 tablespoons garlic oil, from Garlic Confit (page 133)

2 large handfuls tatsoi leaves

1 large black radish, cut into matchsticks

1 teaspoon soy sauce

Fresh lemon juice

Salt and pepper

Chile paste (optional)

Heat the garlic oil in a large skillet over medium heat. Add the tatsoi and radishes and cook until wilted, about 3 minutes. Remove from the heat and stir in the soy sauce, a squeeze of lemon juice, salt, and pepper. Serve with a bit of chile paste on the side, if you like.

TOMATILLO

A TOMATILLO IS NOT A GREEN, unripe tomato, but it is certainly a close Mexican cousin, with an inedible papery husk that makes it look like a Chinese lantern. I like to use tomatillos in salsas, stews, and salads because they can be eaten raw, blanched, and best of all, roasted. I think of tomatillos as little treasures, beautifully round, beautifully wrapped, blushed with purple. I can imagine some potentate carrying a basket of tomatillos as a cherished present to another head of state.

ROASTED TOMATILLO & PEPPER SALSA

MAKES ABOUT 2 CUPS

WHAT TO DO WITH TOMATILLOS? This smooth tomatillo-based salsa is an answer to that very question. Serve it with crispy tortillas or, even better, quickly blanched vegetables, like Romano beans.

- 10 tomatillos, husked and rinsed
- ½ cup olive oil
- 4 Hungarian sweet peppers, or 1 large bell pepper, halved and seeded
- 1 small clove garlic, minced
- 1 teaspoon minced shallots
- 1 teaspoon minced fresh ginger
     Large pinch dried oregano

- 1 teaspoon sherry vinegar
     Salt and pepper
- 1 pound Romano beans, blanched until tender, for dipping

Preheat the oven to 350°F. Put the tomatillos in a baking dish and toss with a tablespoon of the oil. Roast until soft, about 30 minutes, then let cool slightly. Transfer the tomatillos to a blender and add the peppers, garlic, shallots, ginger, oregano, sherry vinegar, and remaining oil. Process until smooth (if you prefer a chunkier salsa, pulse the blender until you like the consistency), then add salt and pepper. Stir in a little more vinegar for a brighter, sharper flavor.

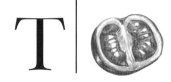

TOMATOES

THE OBVIOUS AND IRONIC POINT of including tomatoes in this book is that the tomato is technically not a vegetable. But technicalities aside, in practice we treat tomatoes as one of our most important vegetables. I gravitate toward open-pollinated tomatoes (those not overly manipulated by industry). Varieties that predate 1940 are called heirlooms because they contain the most concentrated flavors, and appear in summer months in an astounding array of sizes, shapes, and colors. Their names speak volumes: Cherokee Purple, Black Prince, German Striped, Green Zebra, Great White; the list goes on for a country mile. Some more contemporary varieties, though not heirlooms, are equally delicious and have proven to be sturdy and steady crops for tomato growers: the cherry Sun Golds, Mortgage Lifters, Red Devils. The commercial tomato industry is plagued with abuse of all kinds, of the land, of the workers, and of the product.

One way to keep from drowning in the ugly politics of tomato growing is to demand access to high-quality tomatoes; to eat (and cook with) tomatoes that are in season, fully ripened, and grown close to home. A good tomato should not be considered an elitist food! Access to delicious, nutritious, and affordable vegetables should be part of our American birthright.

TOMATO WATER COCKTAIL
SERVES 2

TOMATO WATER IS a surprisingly flavorful and subtle way to enjoy ripe tomatoes. For cooking, I make tomato water by mixing the strained juice with onions and peppers and letting it drip overnight. This simpler version collects the essence of tomatoes. Tomato water is wonderful to cook with as a flavor base for soups and sauces and simmering diced vegetables. But you may just want to drink it! There's a very exciting revival of locally produced vermouths (a fortified wine) infused with seasonal botanicals, like herbs and spices. A family favorite is produced by my brother-in-law and sister-in-law at Channing Daughters Winery on eastern Long Island.

- 1 large very ripe tomato, halved
- 3 tablespoons dry vermouth
- 3 tablespoons bourbon
- 1 tablespoon Simple Syrup (page 66)
- 1 sliver peeled fresh ginger
- 3 ice cubes
- 2 Sun Gold cherry tomatoes, for serving

Squeeze the juice and soft flesh from the tomato into a fine-mesh strainer set over a bowl. Press on the pulpy liquid with the back of a spoon to release as much juice as possible. Combine 3 tablespoons of the resulting tomato water in a cocktail shaker with the vermouth, bourbon, simple syrup, ginger, and ice cubes. Shake well, then pour into 2 small glasses. Cut a slit in each Sun Gold tomato and slip onto each glass.

TOMATO SASHIMI

SERVES 4

MY INSPIRATION was a brilliant creation of chef Wayne Nish's that he served at his late restaurant March in Manhattan, where I cooked in the '90s. Here, I treat the fleshy, silky quality of thinly sliced ripe tomatoes the way he used paper-thin slices of fatty hamachi.

Choose the ripest garden tomatoes you can find; different colors enhance the magic. The tomatoes add a nuanced umami quality in combination with the salty, smoky white soy sauce (or shiro dashi), and the olive oil brings a luscious mouthfeel. Sometimes simple ingredients produce complex results.

2 large tomatoes, thinly sliced
2 tablespoons olive oil
2 tablespoons white soy sauce or shiro dashi
1 tablespoon white sesame seeds
   Sea salt

Overlap the tomato slices on a platter. Drizzle with the oil and drops of white soy sauce or shiro dashi, then sprinkle with the sesame seeds and sea salt.

OVEN-DRIED PLUM TOMATOES

MAKES 16 HALVES

PLUM TOMATOES HAVE A THICK fleshiness that suggests cooking rather than eating raw. Their flavor is intensified by a light seasoning and then a slow concentration in the oven. For me, they are like tomato raisins, and I use them to add body and flavor to pasta dishes and vegetable stir-fries. These tomatoes will keep for several weeks, covered with olive oil and wrapped tightly; or they can be frozen.

8 plum tomatoes, skinned, halved lengthwise, and seeded
   Olive oil
   Salt and pepper
   Dried or fresh rosemary leaves
   Sugar
1 small head garlic, cut crosswise into thirds

Preheat the oven to 350°F. Put the tomatoes in a baking dish, cut-side down. Drizzle with oil, then sprinkle with salt, pepper, rosemary, and a little sugar. Add the garlic and bake for an hour, then baste with the juices. Return the tomatoes to the oven and bake until totally soft and slightly collapsed, about 30 minutes more.

MY TOMATO SAUCE

MAKES ABOUT 5 CUPS

THIS IS NOT GRANDMA'S Sunday "gravy"— tomatoes cooked all day into a thick, red sauce. Rather, this sauce captures the bright acidity of fresh tomatoes in season; cooking time is brief. It's orange because I blended olive oil with lighter-colored tomatoes and vinegar. For a deeper red, you'd need a ton of tomato paste. There's deliberately none in this sauce, because my goal is freshness.

- 2 tablespoons olive oil
- ½ red onion, thinly sliced
- 2 large cloves garlic, minced
  Large pinch crushed red pepper flakes
  Pinch dried oregano
- 1 tablespoon red wine vinegar

- 4 large beefsteak tomatoes
  (about 3½ pounds), roughly chopped
  Pinch sugar
  Salt and pepper
  Handful fresh basil leaves

Heat the oil in a medium saucepan over medium heat. Add the onions and garlic and sweat for a couple of minutes. Add the red pepper flakes and oregano and cook for another minute, then add the vinegar and cook until it's almost evaporated.

Raise the heat to high, then add about one-third of the tomatoes and cook until they start to break down, about 3 minutes. Repeat twice more with the remaining tomatoes. Reduce the heat, add the sugar, salt, and pepper, and simmer, stirring occasionally, until the tomatoes are softened and the sauce has thickened, about 15 minutes. Add the basil and cook for a couple of minutes more.

Transfer the mixture to a blender and process until smooth. For an even smoother texture (seductive, but hardly necessary), pass the blended sauce through a fine-mesh strainer.

From Barely Touched to Completely Transformed

Tomatoes give us an excellent way to amplify the point I made in Cooking with Water (page 92). My thought process in creating a new vegetable dish follows a spectrum of possibilities. I ask myself: How much liquid, if any, must I add to these vegetables to make them fully express their flavor?

My first step is to ask if it can stand on its own. Just a drop of olive oil or a splash of vinegar can be enough to make a simple preparation like Tomato Sashimi (page 299, and on the cover) come alive. It needs just a delicate nudge.

In other cases, I'll choose to cook a vegetable in a small amount of liquid, allowing ingredients to share their flavors. Take for example, Tomato & Roasted Peach Salad (right). By pan-roasting the peaches and nectarines, even for a minute or two, I generate a light sauce that softens and changes the tomatoes ever so slightly and gives each bite a shiny glaze.

In the progression of increasing liquid, I use vinegar, wine, soy sauce, stock, even water, to simmer ingredients quickly in a weightless sauce that brings together disparate elements. In Tomato & Shrimp Pasta (page 304), the magic lies in how the pan sauce plays a supporting role to complement the other ingredients.

Further along the liquid spectrum are the wettest dishes, full-on stews and braises, like Ratatouille (page 347). Some vegetables benefit from a total immersion in a flavorful liquid. There are almost infinite variables: subtle nuances, but possibly, more reward. Time and heat are essential. When things get super-wet—in a broth like Mushroom Hot Pot with Beef & Daikon (page 192)—the resulting liquid becomes the focal point of the dish. In the final example, My Tomato Sauce (page 300), the goal is to completely transform the texture, shape, and color of the ingredients.

TOMATO & ROASTED PEACH SALAD

SERVES 4

THIS SALAD SCREAMS "Summer!" Its goal is to amplify the intensity of raw tomatoes of many colors. Pan-roasting the peaches brings out their sweetness, watermelon adds a welcome fruity quality, and just a splash of vinegar enhances the tomatoes' natural acidity.

- 2 cups cubed watermelon
- 2 tomatoes, cut into wedges
- 2 tablespoons olive oil
- 1½ tablespoons white balsamic vinegar
  Salt and pepper
- 2 peaches, cut into wedges
- 1 small nectarine, cut into wedges
  Pinch sugar
  Fresh lemon juice

Put the watermelon and tomatoes in a large bowl and toss with 1 tablespoon of the oil, 1 tablespoon of the vinegar, salt, and pepper.

Heat the remaining tablespoon oil in a large skillet over high heat. Add the peaches and nectarines and cook until they are heated through and starting to soften, about 3 minutes. Add the sugar, a pinch of salt, and the remaining ½ tablespoon vinegar. Toss for about a minute more, then add a splash of lemon juice. Add the roasted peaches and nectarines to the watermelon and tomatoes and gently toss to combine.

TOMATO & SHRIMP PASTA

SERVES 2

THE TECHNIQUE I USE to cook this pasta is completely different from boiling it in water. I add the dried pasta to a dry pan and gradually add liquid—a small amount of oil and water. This produces a light, flavorful sauce that's naturally shiny and slightly thickened by the pasta's starch. The pasta takes on an irresistible flavor from the combination of the tomato, shrimp, and peppers. I prefer to use only wild American shrimp; the pasta I use here is called *foglie d'ulivo*, olive leaves, but any small, dense pasta shapes, such as orecchiette or cavatelli, will work.

3 tablespoons olive oil

3 thin slices fresh ginger

3 cloves garlic, 2 thinly sliced, 1 smashed

1 shallot, thinly sliced
  Pinch crushed red pepper flakes

1 heaping cup small pasta
  Salt and pepper

1 slice fresh ginger, smashed

3 baby sweet peppers or ⅓ bell pepper, sliced crosswise

½ pound wild American shrimp, shelled and deveined

1 cup My Tomato Sauce (page 300) or other good tomato sauce

  Small handful fresh flat-leaf parsley, chopped

Heat 2 tablespoons of the oil in a medium skillet over medium heat. Add the sliced ginger, sliced garlic, shallots, and red pepper flakes and sweat until the shallots are softened, about 4 minutes. Add the pasta, 2 cups water, salt, and pepper and simmer, stirring occasionally, until the pasta is almost al dente, about 15 minutes.

Meanwhile, heat the remaining tablespoon oil in a medium saucepan over medium heat. Add the smashed garlic, smashed ginger, and peppers and sweat until the peppers are softened, about 4 minutes.

Add the pepper mixture to the pasta along with ½ cup water. Return to a simmer, then add the shrimp and tomato sauce and simmer, stirring occasionally, until the shrimp are just cooked through, about 3 minutes more. Scatter the parsley on top.

TURNIPS

SAY ALL YOU WILL ABOUT HOW SWEET and delicious turnips can be, some people have difficulty getting beyond their negative impressions. I never ate them as a child. In France, I was happy to discover the dense, purple-shouldered globes you'd find in *boeuf bourguignon,* so delicious braised for hours in that beefy red wine sauce. But it was not until I lived in Japan that I really fell in love with eating turnips: the small, round white hakurei, the long, slim, purple-topped hinona, the red-tinted akakabura— all thin skinned, sweet, and crunchy, with their smooth and crispy greens always beautifully intact. Specific varieties, harvested younger, and handled with particular care: *That's* what it takes to make turnips lovable. I couldn't be more excited to see these very turnips show up, grown and handled so perfectly, in our own greenmarket. Some of those turnips actually come from seeds I've brought from Kyoto to our farmers. This discovery of new varieties is an important part of the development of delicious vegetables.

TURNIP & SQUASH STEW WITH CHICKEN

SERVES 4

SIMMERING ROOT VEGETABLES with dashi, soy sauce, mirin, sake, and sugar is a classic way to cook them in Japan. It's also a great way to generate flavor from vegetables that are sometimes hard to love, like squash and turnips, which become the "meaty" part of this dish. You only need a little bit of chicken to finish it. Pair the stew with rice, lentils, beans, or grains.

3 tablespoons sesame oil
1 small onion, chopped
1 large clove garlic, smashed

1 (2-inch) piece fresh ginger, peeled and smashed
1 small winter squash, peeled and cut into wedges
6 medium turnips, peeled and cut into wedges
3 cups Dashi (page 109)
¾ cup soy sauce
¾ cup mirin (sweet rice wine)
¾ cup sake
Large pinch sugar
1 boneless, skinless chicken breast, cut into small pieces

Heat the oil in a medium saucepan over medium heat. Add the onions, garlic, and ginger and sweat for

I often consider *kyo-yasai* as a role model—traditional vegetables that are grown specifically near Kyoto (*kyo,* from Kyoto, *yasai* meaning "vegetables"). In all, forty-one kinds of vegetables have been recognized on the *kyo-yasai* list, each with its unique shape, vivid color, and distinct taste, and rich in nutritional value. Kintoki carrots (orange and purple), kamo eggplants, shishigatani kabocha squash, and the turnips, akakabura and shogoin-kabu. All were developed over centuries, initially for the Imperial court, through an ongoing dialogue between gardeners and cooks. And if you walk through the Nishiki Market in Kyoto today, you will find these same vibrant, amazing-tasting vegetables. I'm working toward developing such intense relationships with the growers I know and admire.

about 3 minutes. Add the squash, turnips, dashi, soy sauce, mirin, sake, and sugar and simmer, stirring occasionally, until the vegetables are tender, about 15 minutes.

Add the chicken and reduce the heat to a low simmer. Cover the saucepan and stir occasionally to help the stew cook slowly and evenly. The dish will be ready in about 5 minutes, or when the chicken is moist and cooked through and all the vegetables are tender. Remove the garlic and ginger before serving.

GLAZED HAKUREI TURNIPS WITH TURNIP & MUSTARD GREENS

SERVES 4

BEGIN WITH TURNIPS that are all the same size. Cut them into pieces if needed to ensure even cooking. The sugar and butter and the drop of vinegar really help make these turnips irresistible. Browning the turnips adds to their great flavor, and wilting the greens at the very end amplifies that gesture.

1 tablespoon olive oil

2 bunches hakurei or baby Tokyo turnips, peeled and halved, greens reserved

1 tablespoon butter

1½ tablespoons sugar

Salt and pepper

1 tablespoon soy sauce

1 tablespoon rice wine vinegar

2 tablespoons fresh lime juice

2 tablespoons fresh lemon juice

1 small bunch mustard greens, thick stems removed

Heat the oil in a large skillet over medium-high heat. Add the turnips and toss to coat in the oil. Stir in the butter and sprinkle the sugar over the turnips. Add ½ cup water, salt, and pepper and simmer briskly until the liquid is thickened and shiny, about 5 minutes.

Stir in the soy sauce, vinegar, 1 tablespoon of the lime juice, 1 tablespoon of the lemon juice, mustard greens, and the turnip greens. Cook until the greens are wilted, about 4 minutes. Stir in the remaining lime juice and lemon juice.

JAPANESE FERMENTED TURNIPS

MAKES 12 TO 15

NUKAZUKE—THE ANCIENT ART of fermenting vegetables in rice bran, deeply rooted in Japanese culture—is quickly becoming popular here, too. Traditionally these pickles were eaten with rice as their own course, but in the United States we use them to add interesting flavor to a whole range of dishes. Fermenting vegetables is considered to be one of the most intriguing aspects of contemporary American cooking, showing how our cuisine has come full circle. Now we're eager to explore these traditional techniques to preserve food and create interesting flavors at the same time.

Fermenting does not demand any special equipment, but it does take time. And attention. It's a real project, taking a couple of weeks to introduce starter vegetables (you'll use about 6 pieces of turnip, carrot, and/or daikon a day for 10 days) to the moist rice bran before it actively ferments. You can use any kind of bowl to mix the rice bran, salt, and vegetables. Fermentation is best in the cool temperature of a basement at around 60°F, but you can do it in a kitchen. There's no need to trim or peel the vegetables first, you can ferment with water as well as beer, and once the fermentation of the rice bran begins with the turnips, you can pickle other vegetables, such as cucumbers and radishes.

4 cups rice bran (available at Japanese food stores)

¼ cup kosher salt

1 (2-inch) piece fresh ginger

1 (12-ounce) beer

Each day for 10 days, 2 or 3 of each starter vegetable: turnips, carrots, and/or daikon

12 to 15 small turnips

Combine the rice bran with the salt and ginger in a large nonreactive bowl. Slowly stir in the beer. The mixture will have the consistency of wet sand. Cut the starter vegetables into pieces, add to the bowl, and toss with your hands until they are evenly distributed and coated with the bran mixture. Cover the surface with cheesecloth, and a plate to weight it down, and store in a cool spot.

Each day for 10 days, remove and discard the pieces of starter vegetables. Stir the rice bran mixture so that it remains active and healthy. Then add 6 more pieces of starter vegetables. Repeat the process every day. (You can skip a day, but only one, otherwise it'll turn sour and you'll have to begin again.) After 10 days, the bran mixture is ready to be used as a pickling medium. It's alive! Bury the turnips in the mixture, cover the bowl with cheesecloth, and set aside in a cool spot.

The texture and flavor of the vegetables will indicate doneness, so check them every day or so. Most vegetables take between 3 and 7 days. Wash the vegetables before peeling, cutting, and serving. The pickling mixture, like a bread starter, needs constant care (stirring and feeding), but it can be used indefinitely.

"... a cool, lush watercress sandwich eaten on a baking

Upland Cress
314

hot summer's afternoon, ranks higher than anything."

—NIGEL SLATER, *Tender*, 2009

UPLAND CRESS

THIS ANCIENT PLANT and its many cress cousins have been known forever to provide exceptional nutritive and restorative qualities. I like the sturdy, round leaves of upland cress for their versatility—used raw or cooked like spinach and kale—but especially for the peppery flavor cress brings to composed salads. Upland cress is grown in soil as well as hydroponically; often you see it with its roots attached. That way, it doesn't fade as quickly as cut lettuce, and you can use it a leaf at a time. Rather than sprinkle fading parsley or limp chives over a dish, why not scatter something more meaningful and powerful? Upland cress delivers brightness and bite.

UPLAND CRESS SALAD WITH CARROT DRESSING

SERVES 6 TO 8

WE COOKS ARE ALWAYS LOOKING for clever ways to season raw vegetables without spoiling their pristine nature. An advantage to using upland cress over other greens is that it stands up loud and proud, making a bouquet in a bowl. You can enjoy eating the tender, flavorful stems as well as the leaves, and what a background for thin slices of colorful vegetables and a hearty, cooked vinaigrette.

2 bunches upland cress
2 radishes, thinly sliced
5 baby carrots, thinly shaved
  Cooked Carrot Dressing (right)

Gently wash the cress leaves in cool water and spin dry in a salad spinner. Mix in a large bowl with the radishes and carrots. Serve with the cooked carrot dressing on the side.

COOKED CARROT DRESSING

MAKES 1 CUP

THIS STYLE OF COOKED DRESSING suggests a whole range of vegetable sauces, from fresh juices to silky purees to chunky salsas, that can be used to season so much more than salads. The dressing turns a bowl of raw vegetables into a complete dish.

- 6 tablespoons olive oil
- 5 baby carrots, chopped
- ½ small sweet onion, thinly sliced
- ¼ teaspoon coriander seeds
- ¼ cup white wine vinegar
- 2 tablespoons fresh lemon juice
  Salt and pepper

Heat 2 tablespoons of the oil in a small saucepan over medium-high heat. Add the carrots, onions, and coriander seeds. Sweat for about 2 minutes, but do not brown at all. Add the vinegar and a cup of water and simmer until the carrots are tender, about 10 minutes. Transfer to a blender, add the lemon juice and the remaining 4 tablespoons oil, and process until smooth. Stir in salt and pepper. Allow the vinaigrette to cool completely before serving.

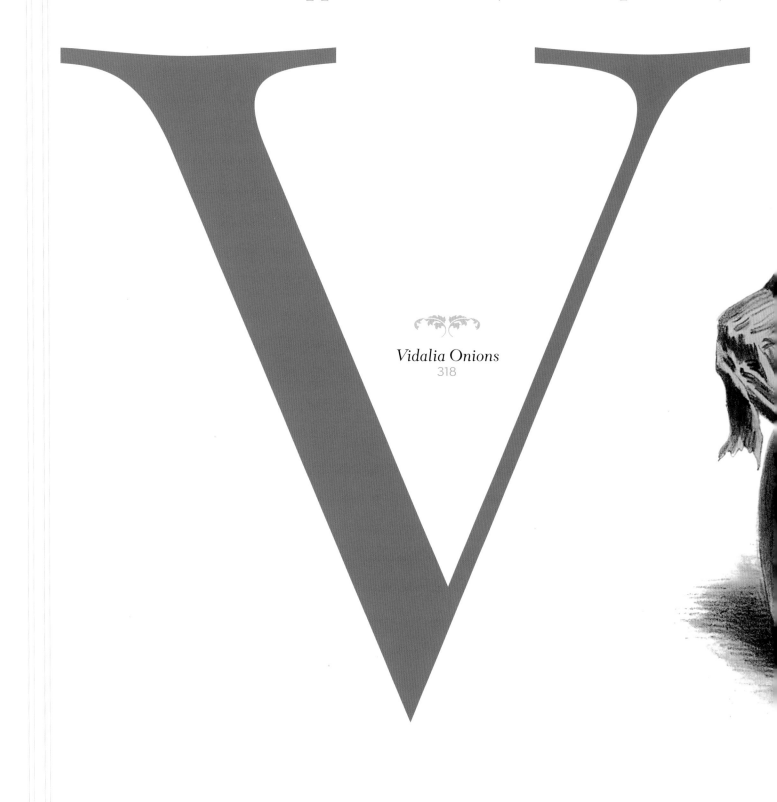

"Onions happen to be one of the most potent of all

Vidalia Onions
318

antimicrobial food plants." —MICHAEL POLLAN, *Cooked*, 2013

VIDALIA ONIONS

THE HISTORY of this vegetable is special not just because it is a distinct hybrid of onion, the yellow granex, but because by growing *that* variety in thirteen specific counties, in *that* particular soil (sulfurous and sandy), and in *that* climate (warm and mild), hand-harvested around the town of Vidalia, in southern Georgia, Vidalia onions have become famous for their sweet flavor. Vidalia isn't the only place in the country that can grow sweet onions, but folks down there paid attention; they worked hard and gave their onion value. I think I like the story of Vidalias most because I believe in celebrating a sense of place.

CHARRED VIDALIA ONIONS WITH PEAS & BEANS

SERVES 4

THE INSPIRATION for this dish came from a recent trip to a teppanyaki restaurant in Kyoto. In this style of cooking, the chef uses a flat griddle to quickly prepare fresh vegetables, right in front of the guests. The light caramelization on these sweet onions is irresistible. As the heat softens them, they become a great partner for the seasonal beans. Those big caramelized onion slices are a wonderful platform for serving chili. Or just sprinkle them with grated cheese, slide them under the broiler, and enjoy. Here, the mellow onion slices are topped with the brightest peas and beans, briefly blanched and shocked.

½ cup plus 2 tablespoons olive oil
1 large Vidalia onion, cut crosswise into 4 slices
Salt and pepper
¼ cup red wine vinegar
1 tablespoon whole-grain mustard
Handful snow peas, blanched and shocked
Handful sugar snap peas, blanched and shocked
Handful string beans, tips trimmed, blanched, and shocked
⅓ cup fava beans, blanched, peeled, and rinsed (optional)
2 tablespoons finely chopped onion
2 heaping tablespoons Caramelized Onions (page 211, optional)

Preheat the oven to 375°F. Heat 2 tablespoons of the oil in a large ovenproof skillet over medium-high heat. Add the onion slices, sprinkle with salt and pepper, and cook until brown on the bottom, about 3 minutes. Pop the skillet in the oven and roast until soft, about 15 minutes.

Meanwhile, make the vinaigrette. In a large bowl, whisk together the ½ cup oil, vinegar, mustard, salt, and pepper. Toss in all the peas and beans, chopped onions, and caramelized onions, if you like.

When the onion slices are browned and soft, transfer to a platter and top with the bean mixture.

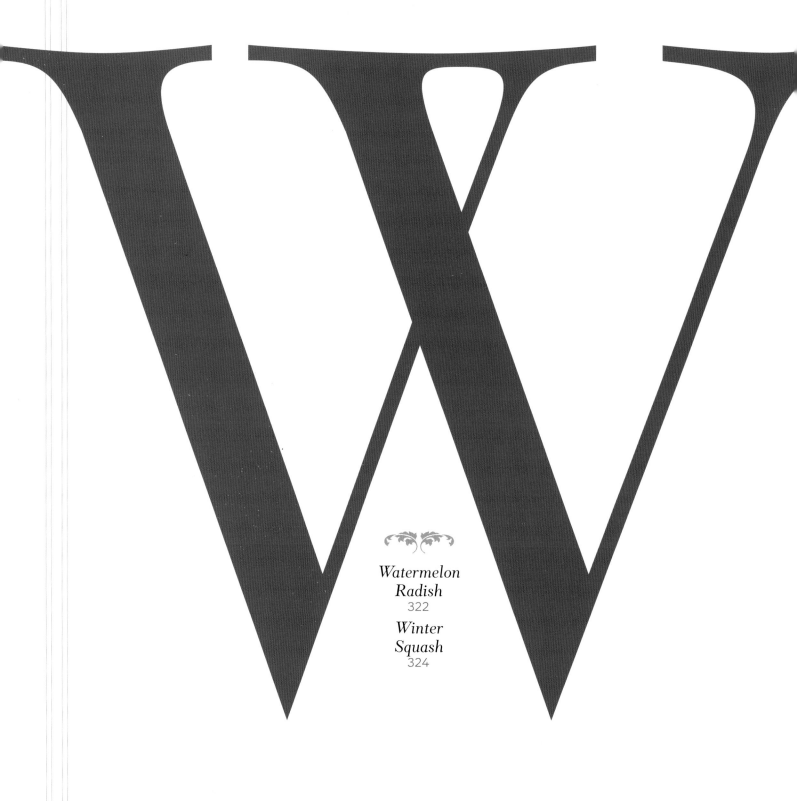

"*Winter squashes ... are real characters with big,*

Watermelon
Radish
322

Winter
Squash
324

and in some cases, unforgettable personalities."
—DEBORAH MADISON, *Local Flavors*, 2002

WATERMELON RADISH

IT'S EASY TO BE SEDUCED by a vegetable's bright color, but that color often fades the second it's seasoned. Or cooked. But the watermelon radish—aka Chinese Red Meat—never disappoints. Only in the past decade has this firm Asian winter variety been grown regularly here. The beating heart of the radish cheers us up when we're starved for color. Splash slices with white balsamic vinegar and fruity olive oil to intensify their raw crunch; grill or braise to enhance their sweetness.

WATERMELON RADISH SALAD WITH GINGER VINAIGRETTE

SERVES 4

RADISHES ARE PLENTIFUL all year long, and of all the colorful, crunchy, peppery radishes, the winter watermelon stands out for its glorious color and size. But it's deceptive: Unsliced in the farmers' market, it looks like a sad greenish-white turnip! The watermelon, unlike its domestic cousins, is for much more than nibbling. Use it abundantly in salads like this one, sliced thin to reveal its bright red heart, dressed with a simple vinaigrette.

¼ cup olive oil

3 tablespoons white wine vinegar

1 (1-inch) piece fresh ginger, peeled and thinly sliced

Pinch crushed red pepper flakes

Fresh lemon juice

Salt and pepper

1 watermelon radish, thinly sliced

3 or 4 radishes, mixed colors, sizes, and shapes, thinly sliced

2 large handfuls mizuna or arugula

1 tablespoon toasted sunflower seeds (optional)

Sea salt

Combine the oil, vinegar, ginger, and red pepper flakes in a medium bowl and let infuse for about 20 minutes. Discard the ginger, then add lemon juice, salt, and pepper. Add the radishes to the vinaigrette, toss, and let them sit for a few minutes to soak up all that good flavor. (Separate the slices so the vinaigrette touches all of them.) Remove the radishes and toss with the greens in a large bowl. Sunflower seeds add a nice crunch, if you like. Sprinkle with sea salt and serve.

WINTER SQUASH

SQUASH IS AMAZING. Isn't it crazy that a plant could make such a complex thing from one slim seed? When I think of squash, I imagine this rough, rugged, almost mutantlike indigenous plant of North America that's both grotesque and fascinating at the same time. Squash have a rough-hewn quality that masks their sweet interior, much like the tough-looking young cooks who come to interview with me at the restaurant—and then I discover how soft-hearted and thoughtful they are. Winter squash is one of the three sisters—squash, corn, and beans—that Native Americans grew together. Many varieties of winter squash have flesh that's generally darker and denser than summer squash, with less fiber and a higher sugar content. Each squash I love has its own distinct story: shape, color, country of origin, name. The Japanese varieties red kuri and kabocha taste exceptionally good, and I love the French *Rouge vif d'Etampes,* aka Cinderella pumpkin; the Long Island Cheese pumpkin; as well as butternut, delicata, and spaghetti squash. I like my squash on the smaller side: They're easier to lug home and cut.

Besides these practical reasons, the flesh of smaller squash is denser, with less water to dilute their intense flavor. You could pull many other vegetables out of the garden and not even come close to the primitive and transporting, colorful, and delicious experience of preparing and eating one winter squash.

WINTER SQUASH STUFFING

SERVES 8

SOMEHOW THANKSGIVING STUFFING can be the best thing on the holiday table. I use winter squash combined with mushrooms to make a delicious dish for our celebration or for any day of the week.

- 3 tablespoons olive oil
- 2 large onions, minced
- 3 cloves garlic, minced
- 1 stalk celery, diced
- 1 cup shiitake mushrooms, quartered
- 1 (3-pound) kabocha squash, roasted (page 326), peeled, and diced
- 1 bunch kale, stemmed and blanched
- 4 cups day-old sourdough bread cut into large chunks
- 1 cup diced fresh mozzarella
  Big pinch dried herbs
  Salt and pepper
- 2 quarts turkey or chicken stock

Preheat the oven to 325°F. Heat the oil in a large, deep skillet over medium heat and cook the onions, garlic, celery, and mushrooms until lightly browned and soft. Add the squash, kale, bread chunks, and cheese and toss. Season with the dried herbs and add salt and pepper. Add the stock until it reaches the top of the bread (remember, the ingredients will soak up the stock as it cooks).

Cover and bake for 40 minutes, or until all the liquid has been absorbed. Remove from the oven and let sit for at least a half hour.

Cutting Winter Squash

Because winter squash are so heavy, make sure your cutting board is stabilized with a damp cloth beneath it. Put the squash on the board and with the blade of a heavy chef's knife on the center of the squash, push the knife down through the squash, cutting it in half. Then, with the flat side of the squash on the board, cut it into quarters. I might decide to peel the squash if I'm going to braise it in water or stock for a soup or puree.

Roasting Squash with Wild Rice

The sweet heartiness of roasted winter squash combines with the particular nuttiness of Minnesota wild rice to deliver a satisfying experience. Dinner can simply mean many plates of delicious food that taste good together. Thinking like this eliminates the rules. Why manipulate these beauties further?

There's a real pleasure in spooning out the browned honeyed bits of roasted squash from its shell. Cut, seed, and season the squash with olive oil, a drizzle of local honey, a dusting of smoked paprika, a couple drops of sherry vinegar, and lots of salt and pepper, and roast it on a baking sheet for about 1½ hours at 375°F. Wild rice is easy to cook if you respect the basic proportion of a cup of rice to 3 cups water; cover and simmer for about 45 minutes. Finish with butter and a squeeze of lemon juice, and chopped parsley.

ROASTED SPAGHETTI SQUASH WITH COUNTRY HAM

SERVES 6

THE UNIQUE ASPECT of spaghetti squash is its texture: It really does look and act like spaghetti. That first wonderful bite is so unique. Here I pair it with country ham cut thin to resemble the squash strands. The ham brings a little salty element that gives the squash another layer of flavor and fun. American country ham is an underrated delicacy; just a little goes a long way. I like to use Allan Benton's country ham from Madisonville, Tennessee.

1 small spaghetti squash (about 2 pounds), halved lengthwise and seeded
1 tablespoon olive oil, plus more for finishing
2 teaspoons maple syrup, plus more for finishing
1 teaspoon dried oregano
   Salt and pepper
1 clove garlic, smashed and halved
   Fresh lemon juice
2 teaspoons sherry vinegar
   Pinch crushed red pepper flakes
¼ pound country ham, cut into matchsticks
   Large handful toasted salted pumpkin seeds
   Handful fresh flat-leaf parsley, chopped

Preheat the oven to 375°F. Rub the cut sides of the squash with the oil and place cut-side up on a baking sheet. Drizzle with the maple syrup, sprinkle with the oregano, then sprinkle with salt and pepper. Put half a clove of garlic in each cavity and roast until you can easily pierce the flesh with the tip of a sharp knife but it still has some texture, about

35 minutes. If you're not sure if it's ready, it's better to undercook it a little rather than overcook it. Pull the squash out of the oven and let cool.

Remove the garlic and reserve. Hold a squash half in one hand over a medium bowl and gently scrape out the flesh with a fork, using short strokes to make spaghetti-like strands; you do not want big clumps, just let gravity pull it out. The browned roasted bits add flavor, so be sure to get everything but the waxy peel. Discard the skin. Repeat with the other half.

Mince the reserved garlic and add it to the bowl. Season the squash generously with oil, lemon juice, salt, and pepper (it'll soak the flavor right up), then stir in the vinegar, red pepper flakes, and a drizzle of maple syrup. You want a nice balance of acidity, sweetness, and heat. Put the squash on a platter and sprinkle with the ham, pumpkin seeds, and parsley; or toss everything together in a bowl.

LACY WINTER SQUASH TEMPURA

SERVES 4

YOU CAN USE pretty much any vegetable for tempura: carrots, broccoli, mushrooms, sweet potatoes, even zucchini blossoms (page 350). I like the combination of squash and onions. The keys to light, crispy tempura are to keep the batter lumpy and very cold and to fry in oil that's about 375°F. If you do not have a thermometer, that's okay. Test the temperature by dropping a bit of batter in the oil; if it sinks and returns to the surface, the oil is ready.

Grapeseed oil for frying
½ cup flour
½ cup cornstarch
1 pound winter squash, peeled, halved, seeded, and sliced into very thin crescents, then halved crosswise
½ small onion, halved and very thinly sliced crosswise
Salt

Add enough oil to a medium saucepan to reach a depth of 2 inches and heat over medium-high heat to about 375°F.

Combine the flour and cornstarch in a medium bowl, then gently whisk in a cup of very cold water until a batter just begins to form. The lightest, crispiest batter is achieved by barely mixing the flour with cold water. Add the squash and onions to the batter and gently stir to combine and coat.

Carefully lay several pieces of squash and onion in the oil, overlapping them a bit so they form a palm-size "fritter." Shape a few in the pan and cook until you see a light crust on the bottoms, about 2 minutes. Flip the fritters over and cook for about 2 minutes more. Remove from the oil with a slotted spoon and drain on paper towels. Sprinkle with salt and serve immediately.

X

Extra-Virgin
Olive Oil
334

EXTRA-VIRGIN OLIVE OIL

COOKS AROUND THE WORLD (myself included) have, for years, believed that you do not cook with extra-virgin olive oil: You cook with a lesser olive oil and finish with the more expensive extra-virgin. But I've been rethinking the issue. Since extra-virgin olive oil simply means *oil pressed naturally from olives with no additives,* I suggest that when you're cooking with olive oil, use only extra-virgin. I can't be sure that anything other than extra-virgin is indeed even olive oil. Bottles marked just "olive oil" could be blends of lower-grade oils, and their country of origin is murky at best. California olive oils seem to be well-regulated. So when I call for olive oil in this book, I always mean extra-virgin olive oil, marked with its place of origin. Find one that you like and can afford (sure, there are the rarified extra-virgins that, like wine, you'd rather drink than cook with, but I'm not talking about those) and use it.

OLIVE OIL–POACHED SQUID

SERVES 2

HERE'S AN INTERESTING WAY to think about cooking with olive oil—not to sauté vegetables in a skillet, but to use lots of oil to gently cook the squid at a low temperature. Lightly scoring the *outside* of the squid bodies in a crosshatch pattern is the secret to those delicate little rolls, such a pleasure to eat. Buy American squid, locally caught and, when possible, fresh not frozen. Delicate fish fillets such as halibut, and the firmer swordfish and albacore, are wonderful cooked this way, too.

- 2 cups olive oil
- 1 zucchini, seeded and cut into matchsticks
- 1 garlic scape, sliced, or 1 clove garlic, halved
- 1 young garlic or onion bulb
  Pinch coriander seeds

1 pound squid bodies, cleaned, scored, and
   cut into rectangles
   Fresh lemon juice
   Sea salt

Warm the oil in a medium saucepan over low heat
until just a few small bubbles appear, about 225°F,
then add the zucchini, garlic scape or garlic clove,
young garlic or onion bulb, and coriander seeds.

Heat for 5 minutes,
then add the squid and
cook just until the squid
curls. Remove the pan from the heat and let sit
for about 5 minutes.

Lift the solids from the pan with a slotted spoon,
then serve the squid and vegetables sprinkled with
lemon juice and sea salt.

OLIVE OIL–BRAISED VEGETABLES

SERVES 4 TO 6

THE INSPIRATION FOR THIS DISH comes from a classic Mediterranean technique called *à la grecque:* simmering vegetables in olive oil and vinegar that become emulsified into a sauce. This is completely different from the poached squid technique (page 334) that uses only low-temperature olive oil.

Traditionally the vegetables were preserved in a vinegar broth with lots of olive oil. A more modern way to cook it is to minimize the vinegar, so that the vinegar and herbs just season, not preserve, the vegetables. Swirling the vegetables together in the pan encourages the liquid to emulsify. The vinaigrette comes together as the vegetables cook.

2 cups olive oil

1 cup dry white wine

1 cup white wine vinegar

6 bulbs spring onion or small onions, halved lengthwise

2 small bulbs fennel, sliced lengthwise

2 artichoke hearts, cut into wedges

2 carrots, sliced

3 strips lemon zest

1 bay leaf

Pinch crushed red pepper flakes

Salt

Pinch coarsely cracked black pepper

Several fresh dill or fennel fronds, chopped

Small handful fresh basil leaves

½ cup fava beans, blanched, peeled, and rinsed (optional)

In a large skillet, combine the oil, wine, vinegar, onions, fennel, artichoke hearts, carrots, lemon zest, bay leaf, red pepper flakes, salt, and pepper. Cover with parchment paper and gently simmer until the vegetables are tender, about 30 minutes. Remove from the heat, then swirl the pan to emulsify the remaining liquid. Add half the dill or fennel and half the basil. Transfer to a large serving dish and let the vegetables cool to room temperature. When cooled, toss in the favas, if you like, and the rest of the herbs.

"*[The yam is] a living artifact of African American*

history."—WILLIAM WOYS WEAVER, *100 Vegetables and Where They Came From*, 2000

Yams
340

YAMS

I'LL BE STRAIGHT WITH YOU: We needed a Y to complete our alphabet! And since in this country the word *yam* is used completely interchangeably with *sweet potato,* I feel like I'm on safe ground. The food historian Jessica Harris points out that in fact, the true yam is an African tuber that is *not* grown in North America. The confusion, she says, came from early African slaves in the South, who when they arrived and saw the root of a morning glory–like vine, the sweet potato, called it by the name they knew at home. And the name stuck. Today both names are used by farmers and eaters alike. But even if it's called a yam in your store, unless it was imported from Africa, what you're eating is a sweet potato. *See Warm Red Cabbage Salad with Sweet Potatoes (page 60).*

BAKED SWEET POTATO FRIES

SERVES 4

I LIKE ALL KINDS of yams and sweet potatoes: white, orange, purple. I like them roasted and fluffy, or moist and dense. I like them crisply fried and I like them softly braised. But I think these easy baked fries are my favorites.

2 large unpeeled sweet potatoes, cut lengthwise into 6 wedges

3 tablespoons olive oil
  Salt and pepper

Preheat the oven to 375°F. Put the potatoes in a deep baking pan large enough to fit them in one layer, then add the oil, salt, and pepper. Over medium-high heat on the stove, cook the potatoes until well browned, about 10 minutes. Transfer the pan to the oven and bake until the potatoes are tender inside and crispy outside, about 20 minutes. Broil them for a few minutes to crisp the skins.

"Could they design an automobile engine that runs

Zucchini
& Other
Summer Squash
344

on zucchini?" —BARBARA KINGSOLVER, *Animal, Vegetable, Miracle*, 2007

ZUCCHINI

FOR SO LONG, ZUCCHINI WASN'T JUST A UBIQUITOUS plant that grew out of control in the summer. It was a symbol of Mediterranean cooking and represented a very different way of eating. Zucchini is a pillar of Provence, is deeply connected to Greece, and is inseparable from Italian cooking. In other words, zucchini thrives in the warm climate where civilization began. When you think about it that way, this delicate squash becomes something to celebrate. There are so few vegetables that are at once so tender and so immediately accessible. Compared to winter squash, say, which involves peeling and roasting and scraping, getting at the heart of this vegetable is easy and immediate.

Its skin is soft as a baby's, especially when just picked. Slice into a super fresh zucchini and see the beads of moisture that result—the squash stores an amazing amount of flavor. Fresh zucchini is a treasure. Whether it's yellow crookneck or pattypan, whether you eat it raw, lightly seasoned, or completely cooked, its soft flavors are inextricably linked to the sun, to summer. This vegetable relies on surrounding flavors to truly express its virtues. Zucchini is a call to arms, a blank canvas. Zucchini encourages us to cook.

WARM ZUCCHINI SALAD

SERVES 4

THIS SALAD MAKES the most of as many shapes and sizes of zucchini as you can find. I like to make it in the summertime when fresh shell beans and all sorts of fresh vegetables like sugar snaps, favas, and/or artichokes come to market. Any of these are excellent companions to the zucchini.

- 2   tablespoons olive oil
- 1   clove garlic, smashed
- 1   pound mixed zucchini, cut into wedges
- Pinch crushed red pepper flakes
- Pinch dried oregano
- Pinch dried basil
- Salt and pepper
- ½   cup fava or any shell beans, blanched, peeled, and rinsed
- 4   ounces goat cheese, crumbled
- Handful fresh basil, roughly chopped

Heat the oil in a large skillet over medium-high heat. Add the garlic, zucchini, red pepper flakes, oregano, basil, salt, and pepper and cook until the squash is tender, about 5 minutes. Add the favas, goat cheese, and basil, then toss and serve.

RATATOUILLE

SERVES 10

MY RATATOUILLE is a colorful vegetable stew that's light, hearty, and flavorful. I like to cook it for less time than the classic French version, to celebrate the brightness of each vegetable. The result is more a light sauce than a heavy stew. But you can cook it longer to generate a softer stew, hearty enough to serve over grains or rice to become a meal.

1¼ cups olive oil

2 pounds eggplant, roughly chopped (about 6 cups)

4 cloves garlic, chopped

2 pinches crushed red pepper flakes
 Salt and pepper

1 onion, chopped
 Large pinch fresh or dried rosemary leaves
 Pinch dried oregano

1½ pounds green zucchini (about 3 medium), roughly chopped

1½ pounds yellow zucchini (about 3 medium), roughly chopped

3 pounds tomatoes (about 4 large), chopped

4 cups My Tomato Sauce (page 300) or other good tomato sauce
 Handful fresh basil leaves, chopped

Heat ½ cup of the oil in a large pot over high heat. Add the eggplant, a pinch of the chopped garlic and a pinch of the red pepper flakes, salt, and pepper and cook, stirring often, until the eggplant is golden and almost cooked through, about 5 minutes. Transfer to a medium bowl and set aside.

Heat the remaining ¾ cup oil in the same pot over medium heat. Add the onions, rosemary, oregano, remaining garlic, remaining pinch of pepper flakes, salt, and pepper and cook, stirring often, until the onions are soft, about 8 minutes.

Add the green and yellow zucchini, salt, and pepper and sweat for about 5 minutes. Add two-thirds of the tomatoes, salt, and pepper and cook until the liquid has thickened a bit but the tomatoes still hold their shape, about 5 minutes. Return the cooked eggplant to the pot and cook for a couple minutes. Add the tomato sauce and bring to a simmer. Stir in the remaining tomatoes and the basil. Serve the ratatouille hot, warm, or cold.

SAUTÉED SUMMER SQUASH WITH FRIED ZUCCHINI BLOSSOMS

SERVES 4

FRIED ZUCCHINI BLOSSOMS are a delicate favorite. On their own, they make a great chip, dipped in Roasted Tomatillo & Pepper Salsa (page 294). I like to get the best of both worlds—crispy and soft—by pairing the fried blossoms with sautéed summer squash.

> Grapeseed oil for frying
> ½ cup flour
> ½ cup cornstarch
> 8 large zucchini blossoms, base trimmed, pistils removed, and cut open
> Salt
> 2 tablespoons olive oil
> 1 pound assorted summer squash, roughly chopped
> 2 cloves garlic, smashed
> 1 (1-inch) piece fresh ginger, peeled and smashed
> Pepper
> 2 heads baby bok choy, stems and leaves separated

Heat about 1 inch of grapeseed oil to 375°F in a medium skillet. Meanwhile, combine the flour and cornstarch in a medium bowl, then gently stir in a cup of very cold water until a batter just begins to form. The lightest, crispiest batter is achieved by barely mixing the flour with cold water.

Working in batches, dip the zucchini blossoms in the batter, letting any excess drip off. Fry until you start to see a light crust form on one side, about 2 minutes. Turn the blossoms over and cook for about 2 minutes more. Remove from the oil with a slotted spoon and drain on paper towels. Sprinkle with salt, then set aside.

Heat the olive oil in a large skillet over medium-high heat. Add the squash, garlic, ginger, salt, and pepper and cook until the squash are just tender, about 4 minutes. Add the bok choy stems and cook for about 2 minutes. Reduce the heat to medium, then add the bok choy leaves and cook until just wilted, about a minute. Transfer to a platter and top with the fried zucchini blossoms.

STUFFED ZUCCHINI BLOSSOMS WITH SUN GOLD TOMATO SAUCE

SERVES 4

ANOTHER FINE WAY TO ENJOY zucchini blossoms is to simply fill them with a delicious stuffing. The blossoms are so thin and delicate that they're a perfect wrapper for all kinds of preparations. They will wilt quickly in the steamer basket, so the stuffing must only require a minute of heat.

1 pound jumbo lump crabmeat
8 fresh basil leaves, chopped
  Olive oil
  Fresh lemon juice
  Salt and pepper
16 large zucchini blossoms, base trimmed, pistils removed, and cut open
1 cup Sun Gold Tomato Sauce (right) or My Tomato Sauce (page 300), warmed
2 fresh basil leaves, chopped

Bring a pot of water fitted with a steamer basket to a boil. Meanwhile, toss the crabmeat and shiso or basil in a small bowl with some oil, lemon juice, salt, and pepper.

Lay 2 zucchini blossoms on a cutting board so that they form a rough circle with the bottoms toward the center and overlapping. Repeat, using 2 blossoms for each dumpling, so you have a total of 8 wrappers. Drizzle with oil and lemon juice, then spoon the crabmeat mixture onto the center of each blossom wrapper.

Carefully fold the tops of the blossoms over the crabmeat to form a package. The ends should stick together; if they need help, moisten them with a bit more oil. Put the blossoms in the steamer, in batches if needed, and steam until the crab is just warmed and the blossoms are just wilted, about a minute.

Spoon the sun gold tomato sauce into individual bowls and top with the stuffed blossoms (right). Top with the basil leaves.

SUN GOLD TOMATO SAUCE

MAKES ABOUT 1 CUP

THE PROCESS OF THIS IS SIMILAR to My Tomato Sauce (page 300) using Sun Gold cherry tomatoes as a base. This makes a small amount; for more sauce, increase the amounts proportionally.

- 2 tablespoons olive oil
- ½ onion, chopped
- 1 clove garlic, minced
- 1 (½-inch) piece fresh ginger, minced

  Pinch crushed red pepper flakes
- 1 pint Sun Gold tomatoes, halved

  Salt and pepper
- 1 tablespoon sherry vinegar
- 2 fresh basil leaves

Heat 1 tablespoon of the oil in a medium saucepan over medium heat. Add the onions, garlic, and ginger and sweat until softened, about 5 minutes. Add the red pepper flakes and stir, then add the tomatoes, salt, and pepper. Stir in the vinegar and cook until it's almost evaporated, then simmer until the tomatoes are softened and the liquid is syrupy, about 12 minutes. Add the basil and cook for a couple minutes more.

Transfer the mixture to a blender. Add the remaining tablespoon oil and process until smooth, then pass through a fine-mesh strainer.

OPEN "RAVIOLI" OF SUMMER SQUASH

SERVES 6

THE TASTE AND TEXTURE of fresh, raw aromatic summer squash makes a perfect bite. Sliced thin on a mandoline, they're summer's gift; they're beautiful and smell a bit like their blossoms. Gently softened by the marinade, squash slices pair easily with so many different ingredients. The filling should be soft (here, oven-dried tomatoes and goat cheese); Roasted Japanese Eggplant (page 114) and Artichoke Hearts with Crab & Tomato Sauce (page 17) make wonderful fillings, too.

4	ounces goat cheese, softened
1	tablespoon olive oil, plus more for drizzling
1	teaspoon sherry vinegar
24	very thin slices round zucchini or summer squash
	Fresh lemon juice
	White balsamic vinegar
	Salt and pepper
1	cup lima beans, blanched
6	halves Oven-Dried Plum Tomatoes (page 299), quartered lengthwise
6	zucchini blossoms, base trimmed, pistils removed, and halved lengthwise

Mash together the cheese, 1 tablespoon oil, and sherry vinegar in a small bowl.

Lay the summer squash slices on a cutting board and sprinkle both sides with oil, lemon juice, balsamic vinegar, salt, and pepper. Let marinate for a few minutes so they soften a bit. On half of the zucchini slices, layer the cheese mixture, limas, tomatoes, and zucchini blossoms, then top with the remaining zucchini slices.

ACKNOWLEDGMENTS

FIRST I'D LIKE TO THANK our team who cooked, photographed, ate (and debated) our way through producing this book: To Dorothy Kalins, my partner on this project, for her guidance, humor, expertise, and love of food. To the diligent eyes of Maura McEvoy, who's always looking to tell a wonderful story through her pictures. To Don Morris and his unrelenting search for clarity and beauty, to our recipe editor, Kathy Brennan, for standing up for practical home cooks everywhere, and to Sue Li, our acting sous chef, who embraced my approach to cooking and remained loyally connected. To Mindy Dubin who, as our illustrator, animated practically every page of this book with her fine vegetable drawings, and who, as my wife, brings to life all of my hopes and dreams for our family.

To Danny Meyer and Jeff Flug, my partners at Union Square Hospitality Group: Thanks for your heartfelt support of this book and, as a matter of fact, of everything else that I do.

To David Black, our most extraordinary agent. And friend.

At Little, Brown, we're grateful to Michael Sand, now at Abrams, for sharing our passion for this book. And great big thanks to executive editor Michael Szczerban for staying true to our vision and stewarding the book through to publication. We're grateful as well to Garrett McGrath, production editor Ben Allen, copyeditor Valerie Cimino, production manager Lisa Ferris, and art director Julianna Lee.

To Zaid and Haifa Kurdieh of Norwich Meadows Farm for letting us into their world: for planting, growing, and harvesting the most wonderful-tasting vegetables, and for planning the timing of each season's bounty to coincide with our photography sessions. Thanks, too, to Rod Lamborn, for celebrating his father Calvin's work on pea research and for hand carrying the delicate specimens to us. To the Union Square Greenmarket managers and farmers,

organized by GrowNYC, who tend our most precious resource in New York City and provide vision for the future of fresh food. Especially Cayuga Organics, Wild Hive Farm, and Alex Paffenroth, Tim Stark, and Bill Maxwell. Also Tony Gibbons of Radical Farm, Jeffrey Frank, Steve Yoo, Tama Matsuoka, Franca Tantillo, Rick Bishop, and John Schmidt.

To Patty Gentry of Early Girl Farm and all the other Long Island farmers who inspire our team every day.

To the potter Nancy Horwich, whose beautiful and soulful American plates, bowls, and platters we used throughout in the photography of this book; find her at nancyhorwich@me.com. To Saori Kawano of Korin (korin.com) for Japanese kitchenwares.

At Gramercy Tavern, special thanks to Jenny Jones (you know what you did!), Catherine Hines, and Beth Wisniewski, as well as chef de cuisine Howard Kalachnikoff and sous chefs Suzanne Cupps, Duncan Grant, Tracy Malechek, Rafiq Salim, and Paul Wetzel.

Dorothy and I both send our gratitude and admiration to our kindred spirits, the writers whose good words appear on each chapter opener. We are grateful, too, to Betsey Buddy for her ferocious research in Paris. And to the loyal and diligent Peter Rohowsky of Art Resource in New York, and Jennifer Belt, too. Thanks to Randy Smith at the Peter H. Raven Library, Missouri Botanical Garden; Stephen Sinon and Marie Long at the New York Botanical Garden; and Sandra Powlette at The British Library.

ILLUSTRATION CREDITS

The illustrations that open each chapter are reproduced from nineteenth-century lithographs made principally for the Vilmorin-Andrieux seed company based in Paris. Vilmorin is still in business today. Other images are sourced from botanical illustrations of the same period. Permission to reproduce these images is graciously given by the sources credited below:

Artichoke, © The British Library Board, N.Tab.2004/k, Plate 16
Beet, © The British Library Board, N.Tab.2004/11, Plate 6
Cabbage, © The British Library Board, N.Tab.2004/11, Plate 21
Daikon, © The British Library Board, N.Tab.2004/11, Plate 6
Eggplant, © The British Library Board, N.Tab.2004/11, Plate 23
Fennel, © RMN-Grand Palais/Art Resource, NY
Garlic, © The British Library Board, N.Tab.2004/k, Plate 19
Herbs, Peter H. Raven Library, Missouri Botanical Garden
Jerusalem Artichoke, Peter H. Raven Library, Missouri Botanical Garden
Kohlrabi, © The British Library Board, N.Tab.2004/k, Plate 4
Leek, © The British Library Board, N.Tab.2004/k, Plate 5
Mushroom, Peter H. Raven Library, Missouri Botanical Garden
Nuts, © RMN-Grand Palais/Art Resource, NY
Okra, © The British Library Board, N.Tab.2004/11, Plate 23
Pepper, © RMN-Grand Palais/Art Resource, NY
Quince, The LuEsther T. Mertz Library, NYBG/Art Resource, NY
Rutabaga, © The British Library Board, N.Tab.2004/11, Plate 10
Swiss Chard, © The British Library Board, N.Tab.2004/11, Plate 13
Tomato, © RMN-Grand Palais/Art Resource, NY
Upland Cress, © RMN-Grand Palais/Art Resource, NY
Vidalia Onion, © RMN-Grand Palais/Art Resource, NY
Winter Squash, © The British Library Board, N.Tab.2004/11, Plate 23
Extra-Virgin Olive Oil, Peter H. Raven Library, Missouri Botanical Garden
Yam, © The British Library Board, N.Tab.2004/k, Plate 19
Zucchini, © The British Library Board, N.Tab.2004/k, Plate 9

Index

A

Adler, Tamar, *138–39*

Adrià, Ferran, *73*

almonds

    roasted carrots with spiced, *70*

    in snow pea, cherry & baby chard salad, *232–33*

    toasted & spiced, *198*

anchovies, *7*

    braised leeks & yellow lentils with dressing of, *176–77*

    in broccoli bruschetta, *49*

    in stuffed baked artichokes, *13, 14*

Anthony, Grandmother and Grandfather, *32, 112, 116*

Anthony, Michael, *251*

apple puree, celery root and, *83*

arancini, sautéed chard, *288–89*

artichoke hearts

    in braised vegetables, *336–37*

    with crab & tomato sauce, *17, 352*

    prepping, *16*

artichokes, *10–19*

    about, *10*

    oyster mushrooms with braised baby, *18–19*

    prepping, *11, 18*

    stuffing, *13*

    "turning," *16*

    whole stuffed baked, *14–15*

    See also Jerusalem artichokes

asparagus, *20–25*

    about, *20*

    beluga lentils & salad of shaved, *24–25*

    blanching, *25*

    eggs with pan-roasted, *22–23*

    with ginger relish, *21*

avocado, *26–29*

    about, *3, 26*

    blood orange salad with quinoa and, *28–29*

    cutting, *27*

    in Jerusalem artichoke salad, *158–59*

    in yogurt with lime mash, *26–27*

B

bacon, cranberry beans & collards with, *34–35*

basil

    corn on cob with, *94–95*

    in herb salad with couscous, *142–43*

beans, *32–37*

    about, *32*

    cranberry, with bacon & collards, *34–35*

    dried, *32, 34, 36*

    salad of corn, tomato and, *96*

    with sesame sauce, *33*

    in shrimp & cipollini stew, *216–17*

    in summer squash "ravioli," *352, 353*

    in tomatillo & pepper salsa, *294*

    with tomatoes & mussels, *36–37*

    Vidalia onions with peas and, *318–19*

    in zucchini salad, *345*

    See also fava beans

Beard, James, *218*

beef, mushroom hot pot with daikon and, *191, 192–93, 302*

beef broth, horseradish, root vegetable stew in, *148–49*

beets, *38–45*
    about, *38*
    borscht, *42–43*
    pickled eggs & mustard seeds with roasted, *40–41*
    roasting, *39*
    rose ricotta with roasted, *41*
    tartare, *44–45*
Behr, Edward, *332*
beluga lentils, salad of shaved asparagus and, *24–25*
Benton, Allan, *328*
Besh, John, *202–3*
black bass, salted radish salad with, *257*
black beans, tomatoes & mussels with, *36–37*
black pepper, braised radishes with honey and,
    260–61
blanching
    asparagus, *25*
    garlic, *282*
    herbs, *147*
    spinach, *282, 283*
blood orange, salad of avocado, quinoa and, *28–29*
bok choy
    about, *46*
    in mushroom hot pot, *192–93*
    stir-fried, *46–47*
    summer squash & zucchini blossoms with,
        348–49
borscht, Michael's, *42–43, 56*
Boulud, Daniel, *82*
bowls, meals in, *6*
    cauliflower curry, *74–75*
    peas, rice & pickled onion, *215, 227*
braising
    artichokes, *18–19*
    fennel, *126–27*
    greens, *186–87*
    leeks, *176–77*
    mushrooms, *231*
    radishes, *260–61*
    vegetables in olive oil, *336*

brassicas, *48*
Bribery Pasta, *50–51*
broccoli, *48–51*
    in Bribery Pasta, *50–51*
    on bruschetta, *49*
    in caramelized cauliflower with Romanesco, *76*
    using stems, *50*
broth
    liquids for, *302*
    mushroom, *188, 190–91, 212, 231*
    in root vegetable stew in horseradish beef, *148–49*
    See also soups
bruschetta, broccoli, *49*
Brussels sprouts, *52–53*
    maple syrup with roasted, *53*
    roasted Jerusalem artichokes & leaves of, *160–61*
    using leaves of, *53*
bunching onions. See scallions
burdock root, in daikon kinpura, *106–7*
butter, horseradish compound, *150–51*
butternut squash, cauliflower curry with, *74–75*

C

cabbage, *56–63*
    about, *56–57*
    in borscht, *42–43*
    in cole slaw, *58–59*
    cooked quickly, *56–57*
    kimchi-style fermented, *45, 61*
    pork dumplings with dipping sauce and, *62–63*
    shredding red, *60*
    sweet potatoes with warm red, *60*
    See also bok choy

Index

Caponata, *113*

caramelizing
    cauliflower, *76*
    onions, *208, 211, 242, 318*

carrot dressing, cooked, *314–15*

carrot juice
    in carrots & farro, *72*
    cocktail, *66–67*

carrots, *64–72*
    about, *64*
    baby artichokes with, *18*
    in borscht, *42–43*
    braised vegetables with, *336–37*
    in chicken soup, *80–81*
    in chowchow, *77*
    in cole slaw, *58*
    in daikon kinpura, *106–7*
    farro and, *72*
    fermented turnips with, *310*
    glazed salsify and, *272–73*
    Japanese varieties, *307*
    pickled baby, *66, 228–29*
    in potato dumplings, *246–47*
    roasted with spiced nuts, *70–71*
    shaving, *69*
    in soup with coconut milk, *68–69*
    in stew in horseradish beef broth, *148–49*
    in upland cress salad, *314–15*

casserole, baked eggplant, *118–19*

cauliflower, *73–77*
    about, *3, 73*
    chowchow, *77*
    curry, *74–75*
    peppers & onions with caramelized, *76*

celery, *78–81*
    in chicken soup, *80–81*
    in chowchow, *77*
    in salad, *78–79*

celery root, *82–85*
    apple puree and, *83*

    chestnut soup and, *84–85*
    in daikon kinpura, *106–7*
    in salad, *78–79*
    trimming, *82*

chard. *See* Swiss chard

chawanmushi (custard), *197*

cheese
    potato croquettes and, *244–45*
    in quince mostarda, *252–53*

chestnuts, *198*
    peel & eat, *199*
    soup of celery root and, *84–85*

chicken, turnip & squash stew with, *7, 306–7*

chicken soup with celery & dill, *80–81*

chickpeas
    about, *86*
    cauliflower curry, *74–75*
    pureed, *86–87*

chicories, *120*

chiles (chillis). *See* hot peppers

Chimichurri on Steak, *144–45*

Chinese Red Meat (watermelon) radish, *256, 322–23*

chips
    kale, *166–67*
    parsnip, *220–21*

chives
    herb salad with couscous, *142–43*
    matzoh brei, *146–47*
    potato salad, *248–49*
    slicing, *209*
    stuffed peppers, *238–39*

chorizo, stuffed peppers with, *238–39*

Chowchow Relish, *77*

chowder, Jerusalem artichoke with monkfish, *161, 162–63*

citrus fruit, segmenting, *28*

clams, scallion & tarragon sauce with steamed, *276–77*

cocktails
    carrot juice, *66–67*
    tomato water, *297*

coconut milk
    in carrot soup, 68–69
    in chilled corn soup, 93
cole slaw, Goldie's, 58–59
collard greens
    about, 88
    cranberry beans with bacon and, 34–35
    in frittata, 88–89
Colwin, Laurie, 110–11
condiments
    chimichurri, 144–45
    garlic confit, 133, 292
    lemon zest confit, 154, 155
    quince mostarda, 252–53
    sweet & sour shallots, 278–79
    See also sauces
Corkendahl, John, 32
corn, 90–96
    about, 90–91
    chilled soup with coconut milk, 93
    on cob with basil, 94–95
    okra stew with, 207
    pancakes, 97
    salad with tomato, cranberry bean and, 96
    slicing off cob, 91
    stock, 92, 93
cornmeal, 90
    in fried okra, 205
    in pancakes, 97
couscous
    herb salad with, 143
    Israeli, 128
cowpea, Whippoorwill, 32
crab, artichoke hearts with, 17, 352
cranberry beans
    with bacon & collards, 34–35
    salad with corn, tomato and, 96
crème du Barry (creamed cauliflower soup), 73
crepes
    mushroom, 188–89
    spinach egg, 211, 284–85

cress, upland, 314–15
croquettes, potato & cheese, 244–45
croutons, parsley with brown butter, 140–41
cucumbers, 98–101
    in chilled soup, 98–99
    in herb salad with couscous, 143
    Japanese-style salt-cured, 45, 100–101
    sauce of yogurt and, 101
Cunningham, Marion, 152–53
curry, cauliflower, 74–75
custard, nettle, 197
cutting
    avocado, 27
    leeks, 179
    matchsticks, 108
    winter squash, 325
cutting boards, 65

D

daikon, 104–9
    about, 104, 256
    cutting matchsticks of, 108
    in fermented turnips, 310
    grated, on pan-roasted fish, 104–5
    kinpura, 106–7
    mushroom hot pot with beef and, 191,
        192–93, 302
dashi
    in daikon kinpura, 106–7
    in Jerusalem artichoke chowder, 162
    making, 109
    in mushroom hot pot, 192–93
    in turnip, squash & chicken stew, 306–7

Index

dates, rutabaga gratin, *268, 269*
dehydrators, *236*
dill
    in chicken soup, *80–81*
    in herb salad with couscous, *142–43*
dough
    pâte à choux (soft), *240*
    tart, *180, 182–83*
dressings
    anchovy, braised leeks & yellow lentils with,
        176–77
    carrot, upland cress salad with, *314–15*
    mayonnaise, *58, 154, 248–49*
    soy, kale salad with, *166–67*
    See also vinaigrette
dried beans, *32, 34, 36*
drying
    plum tomatoes, *299*
    seasoning peppers, *236*
Dubin, Dan, *147*
dumplings
    Granmaw Hartle's potato, *246–47*
    pork, cabbage and, *63*

E

échalote grise (shallot), *278*
eggplant, *112–19*
    about, *112, 307*
    baked casserole of, *118–19*
    in caponata, *113*
    grilled with miso glaze, *114*
    pickled, *116–17, 215*

    in ratatouille, *347*
    roasted Japanese, *114–15, 352*
eggs
    asparagus with, *22–23*
    in chard shakshouka, *286–87*
    roasted beets with pickled, *40–41*
    in spinach crepes, *211, 284–85*
escarole
    about, *120*
    in salad with fennel & pears, *120–21*

F

farming, *2, 32, 64, 90, 112*
farro, carrots and, *72*
fava beans, *124–25*
    braised vegetables with, *336–37*
    in salad, *125*
    with sea salt & olive oil, *124*
    Vidalia onions with peas and, *318–19*
    in zucchini salad, *345*
Fearnley-Whittingstall, Hugh, *164–65*
fennel, *126–29*
    about, *126*
    braised, with saffron & orange juice, *126–27*
    in braised vegetables, *336–37*
    in carrot soup, *68–69*
    in escarole salad, *120–21*
    in tabbouleh, *128–29*
fermented vegetables
    cabbage, *45, 61*
    Japanese turnips, *310–11*

fish, *2*
    grated daikon on pan-roasted, *104–5*
    Jerusalem artichoke chowder with, *161, 162–63*
    olive oil–poached, *334–35*
    salmon with sorrel, *266*
    salted radish salad with, *257*
    See also anchovies
Fisher, M.F.K., *v*
flatbread
    onion & bacon tart, *210–11*
    sautéed mushrooms on, *186–87*
Florentine, à la (spinach dish), *280*
foglie d'ulivo (olive leaf–shaped pasta), *304–5*
food processors, *209*
fries, baked sweet potato, *340–41*
frittata, collard greens, *88–89*
fruits, *3*
frying
    bok choy, *46–47*
    oysters, *279*

G

garlic, *132–35*
    about, *132*
    artichoke hearts with pureed, *17*
    blanching, *282*
    in chimichurri on steak, *144*
    confit of, *133, 292*
    in fermented cabbage, *61*
    in garlic scapes omelet, *134–35*
    green & black, *134*
    mincing, *133*

    in onion soup, *212*
    in oven-dried tomatoes, *299*
    in poached squid, *334–35*
    in ratatouille, *347*
    spinach & scallops with pureed, *282–83*
garlic scapes, *134*
    omelet of, *134–35*
    poached squid with, *334–35*
Gentry, Patty, *64*
ginger, *136–37*
    asparagus with relish of, *21*
    in fermented cabbage, *61*
    in Jerusalem artichoke chowder, *162*
    peeling, *137*
    pickled, *7, 21, 137*
    tea, *136*
    watermelon radish salad with vinaigrette of, *322*
globe artichokes. *See* artichokes
Goldie's Cole Slaw, *58–59*
Gramma Anthony's Pickled Eggplant, *116–17, 215*
Granmaw Hartle's Potato Dumplings, *246–47*
grapeseed oil, *84*
gratin
    parsnip & kale, *222–23*
    rutabaga, *268, 269*
grating
    daikon, *104, 105*
    horseradish, *148*
grecque, à la (Mediterranean style), *336*
green onions. *See* scallions
greens
    cooking, *88, 169*
    crepes, *284*
    glazed hakurei turnips with, *272, 308–9*
    mushrooms on flatbread with braised, *186–87*
    substituting, *7*
    washing, *281*
    See also salads; *specific types*
Grigson, Jane, *8–9, 290–91*
griselle (shallot), *278*

Index

grits, *90*
Gutenbrunner, Kurt, *84*
gyoza (dumplings), *63*

H

hakurei turnips
    about, *306*
    turnip & mustard greens with glazed, *272,*
        308–9
Halweil, Brian, *54–55*
ham, roasted spaghetti squash with country, *328–29*
Hanks, Tom, *278*
Harris, Jessica, *340*
Hazan, Marcella, *130–31*
hazelnuts
    about, *198*
    roasted parsnips with pesto of, *224–25*
heirloom vegetables, *32, 296*
Henderson, Fergus, *256*
herbs, *140–47*
    about, *140*
    blanching, *147*
    in brown butter croutons, *140–41*
    in chimichurri on steak, *144–45*
    in chive matzoh brei, *146–47*
    in salad with couscous, *143*
    in steamed clams with scallion, *276–77*
    See also chives
honey, braised radishes with black pepper and,
    260–61
horseradish, *148–51*
    in compound butter with roasted
        sweet potatoes, *150–51*

grating, *148*
    in potato salad, *248–49*
    root vegetable stew in beef broth with, *148–49*
hot peppers, *234*
    drying, *236*
    oil of, *235, 237*
    pickled, *74, 144, 236*
    See also peppers
hummus, 86

I

iceberg lettuce
    about, *154*
    marinated tomatoes with grilled, *154–55*
    in mushroom crepes, *188–89*
Issa, Kobayashi, *256*

J

Japanese eggplant, roasted, *114–15, 352*
Jerusalem artichokes, *158–63*
    about, *2, 3, 158*
    in borscht, *42–43*
    Brussels sprout leaves & roasted, *160–61*
    in chowder with monkfish, *161, 162–63*
    prepping, *161*

salad of sliced raw, *158–59*
See also artichokes
juices
    carrot, *66–67, 72*
    orange, *126–27*
    tomato water, *297*

K

kabocha squash, *307, 324, 325*
kale, *166–69*
    about, *166*
    cooked quickly, *169, 186, 284*
    parsnip gratin and, *222–23*
    in salad with kale chips & soy dressing, *166–67*
    in soup with potatoes & leeks, *7, 168–69*
    in winter squash stuffing, *325*
Kimchi-Style Fermented Cabbage, *45, 61*
Kingsolver, Barbara, *342–43*
King Tut's Carrots, *70–71*
kinpura, daikon, *106–7*
knives, *133, 209, 268, 325*
kohlrabi, *170–73*
    about, *170*
    in kale salad, *166–67*
    roasted quartered, *45, 173*
    salad of toasted walnuts and, *170–71*
    in sugar snap salad, *228–29*
    unlocking, *172*
kombu (seaweed)
    dashi, *109*
    in mushroom broth, *191*
Kurdieh, Zaid, *32*
kyo-yasai (Kyoto vegetables), *306–7*

L

Lamborn, Calvin, *226*
Lamborn, Rod, *226*
leeks, *176–83*
    about, *176*
    corn soup, *93*
    cutting & washing, *179*
    kale soup with, *7, 168–69*
    in mushroom hot pot, *192–93*
    in potato dumplings, *246–47*
    in quiche, *176, 180–83*
    roasted whole, with tangerine vinaigrette, *178–79*
    in stew in horseradish beef broth, *148–49*
    wild, *262–64*
    yellow lentils & braised, *176–77*
lemon juice, spinach and, *284*
lemons, preserving, *143*
Lemon Vinaigrette, *14*
Lemon Zest Confit, *154, 155*
lentils, *7*
    braised leeks & yellow, *176–77*
    salad of pickled onions and, *214–15*
    salad of shaved asparagus & beluga, *24–25*
lettuce. *See* iceberg lettuce
Li, Sue, *274*
lima beans, summer squash "ravioli" and, *352, 353*
lime mash, avocado yogurt with, *26–27*
liquid, cooking with, *92, 302*
locally-grown foods, *2, 5, 90*
lupini beans, *32*

Index

M

Madison, Deborah, *174–75*, *320–21*

Mallmann, Francis, *38*

mandoline, *25*, *69*, *108*, *258*

maple syrup, roasted Brussels sprouts with, *53*

masa, *90*

matchsticks

    cutting, *108*

    leek, *179*

    radish, *292–93*

Matzoh Brei, Chive, *146–47*

mayonnaise, homemade, *58*, *154*, *248–49*

McGee, Harold, *194*

Michael's Borscht, *42–43*, *56*

Microplane graters, *148*

miso glaze, grilled eggplant with, *114*

monkfish, Jerusalem artichoke chowder with, *161*, *162–63*

morel mushrooms, peas with braised, *231*

mostarda, quince, *252–53*

m'smen (Moroccan flatbread), *211*

mushrooms, *186–93*

    about, *3*, *186*

    braised baby artichokes with oyster, *18–19*

    broth of, *188*, *190–91*, *212*, *231*

    in crepes, *188–89*

    on flatbread with braised greens, *186–87*

    in hot pot with beef & daikon, *191*, *192–93*, *302*

    in Jerusalem artichoke chowder, *162*

    peas with morel, *231*

    winter squash stuffing with shiitake, *325*

mussels, black beans with tomatoes and, *36–37*

mustard greens, glazed hakurei turnips with, *272*, *308–9*

mustard seeds, roasted beets with, *40–41*

N

nectarines, tomato & peach salad, *302*, *303*

nettles, *196–97*

    custard, *197*

    handling, *197*

    pureed, *196*, *197*

Nish, Wayne, *299*

nukazuke (Japanese pickle), *310*

nuts, *3*, *198–201*

    about, *198*

    almonds, *70*, *198*, *232–33*

    chestnuts, *84–85*, *198*, *199*

    hazelnuts, *198*, *224–25*

    roasted carrots with spiced, *70–71*

    walnuts, *170–71*, *198*, *200–201*, *252–53*

O

oil

    grapeseed, *84*

    hot pepper, *235*, *237*

    See also olive oil, extra-virgin

okra, 204–7
    cornmeal-fried, 205
    pickled, 204
    stew with tomatoes, 206–7
olive oil, extra-virgin, 334–37
    about, 3, 334
    in braised vegetables, 336–37
    favas with, 124
    in My Tomato Sauce, 300
    in poached squid, 334–35
    in ratatouille, 347
    sweet potato fries and, 340
    in tomato sashimi, 299
Oliver, Jamie, 156–57
Olney, Richard, 184–85
Omelet of Garlic Scapes, 134–35
onions, 208–17
    about, 208
    baby artichokes with cipollini, 18
    bacon tart and, 210–11
    in borscht, 42–43
    braised fennel and, 126–27
    braised vegetables and, 336–37
    caramelized, 208, 211, 242, 318
    caramelized cauliflower with, 76
    in chicken soup, 80–81
    in chimichurri on steak, 144
    lentil salad & pickled, 214–15
    peas, rice & pickled, 215, 227
    peas with braised morels and, 231
    in pickled eggplant, 116–17
    in potato pancakes, 242–43
    potato salad, 248–49
    pureed, 208, 216–17
    ratatouille, 347
    shallots, 222, 269, 278–79
    shrimp & cipollini stew, 211, 216–17
    slicing, 209
    in soup, 212–13
    sweating, 36
    Vidalia, 3, 318–19
    in winter squash tempura, 330–31
    See also chives; leeks; scallions
orange, salad of avocado, quinoa and, 28–29
orange juice, braised fennel with, 126–27
organic foods, 2
orzo, 50
oxalic acid, 284
oysters, frying, 279

P

pancakes
    corn, 97
    potato, 242–43
    scallion, 274–75
parchment paper, 16
parsley
    brown butter croutons with, 140–41
    herb salad with couscous, 142–43
parsnips, 220–25
    about, 220
    chips, 220–21
    kale gratin and, 222–23
    roasted, with hazelnut pesto, 224–25
    in stew in horseradish beef broth, 148–49
pasta
    Bribery, 50–51
    tomato & shrimp, 302, 304–5
pâte à choux (soft dough), 240
peaches, salad of tomato & roasted, 302, 303
pears, escarole salad with, 120–21

Index

peas, 226–33
about, 226
braised morels with, 231
chickpeas, 74–75, 86–87
pea shoots with, 230
peeling sugar snaps, 228
rice, pickled onions and, 215, 227
salad of cherries, baby chard and, 232–33
in salad with quinoa, 228–29
Vidalia onions with beans and, 318–19
pea shoots, warm wilted, 230
peeling, 65
ginger, 137
Jerusalem artichokes, 161
kohlrabi, 172
rutabaga, 268
sugar snaps, 228
peppers, 234–39
about, 234
caramelized cauliflower with, 76
in chard shakshouka, 286–87
in chimichurri on steak, 144
in chowchow relish, 77
in corn pancakes, 97
drying, 236
hot pepper oil, 235, 237
pickled, 74, 144, 236
pickled eggplant with, 116–17
roasted tomatillo & salsa of, 294–95, 348
in stew, 237
stuffed, with chorizo & wild rice, 238–39
in tomato & shrimp pasta, 304–5
Persian cucumbers, 98, 100–101
pesto, hazelnut, 224–25
pickled foods
baby carrots, 66, 228–29
Basic Pickling Recipe, 66, 204, 215, 236, 263
eggplant, 116–17, 215
eggs, roasted beets with, 40–41
ginger, 7, 21, 137

hot peppers, 74, 144, 236
Japanese turnips, 310–11
okra, 204
onions, 214–15, 227
ramps, 263
red pickling liquid, 40–41
salt-cured cucumbers, 100
Pierre, Jean, 240
plum tomatoes, oven-dried, 207, 299, 352
polenta, 90
Pollan, Michael, 316–17
pommes Darphin (potato pancake), 242
pork dumplings, cabbage and, 62–63
potatoes, 240–49
about, 240
in borscht, 42–43
cheese croquettes and, 244–45
in collard greens frittata, 88–89
dumplings, 246–47
kale soup with, 7, 168–69
pancakes, 242–43
pan-roasted fingerling, 241
salad, 248–49
in spinach egg crepes, 284–85
in stew in horseradish beef broth, 148–49
walnut mashed, 200–201
See also sweet potatoes
prepping
artichokes, 11, 16, 18
broccoli stems, 50
Jerusalem artichokes, 161
nettles, 197
rutabaga, 268
proteins, 2, 96
purees
apple, 83
broccoli, 48
chickpea, 86–87
garlic, 17, 282–83
nettle, 196, 197
onion, 208, 216–17

Q

quiche, leek, *176*, *180–83*
quince
    about, *3*, *252*
    mostarda, *252–53*
quinoa
    avocado & blood orange salad with, *28–29*
    sugar snap salad with, *228–29*
Quintal d'Alsace cabbage, *57*

R

radishes, *256–61*
    about, *256*
    braised leeks & yellow lentils with, *177*
    honey & black pepper with braised, *260–61*
    salad with black bass & salted, *257*
    in salad with ginger vinaigrette, *322*
    sautéed tatsoi with matchstick, *292–93*
    slicing, *258–59*
    in upland cress salad, *314–15*
    watermelon, *256*, *322–23*
    See also daikon; horseradish
ramps, *262–64*
    pickled, *263*
    spaghetti and, *263*, *264*

ratatouille, *113*, *302*, *346–47*
"ravioli," of summer squash, *352–53*
relishes
    chowchow, *77*
    ginger, *21*
rhubarb
    about, *265*
    sweet & sour sauce, *266–67*
rice
    in chard arancini, *288–89*
    peas, pickled onions and, *215*, *227*
    roasted squash with wild, *326–27*
    stuffed peppers with wild, *238–39*
ricotta, roasted beet with rose, *41*
roasting
    beets, *39*
    Brussels sprouts, *53*
    carrots, *70*
    chestnuts, *199*
    eggplant, *114*
    Jerusalem artichokes, *160–61*
    leeks, *179*
    parsnips, *224–25*
    spaghetti squash, *329*
    tomatillos, *294*
    winter squash, *326*
Romanesco broccoli, caramelized cauliflower, *76*
Romano beans, tomatillo & pepper salsa, *294*
root vegetables
    glazed, *272*
    stew in horseradish beef broth with, *148–49*
    substituting, *7*
    See also specific type
rosemary
    in chimichurri on steak, *144*
    in chive matzoh brei, *146–47*
rose petals, dried, *41*
rose ricotta, roasted beet with, *41*

rutabaga, 268–69
    gratin of, 268, 269
    in potato salad, 248–49
    prepping, 268
    in stew in horseradish beef broth, 148–49
    See also turnips

S

saffron, braised fennel with, 126–27
Sakamoto, Yukari, 102–3
salads
    asparagus & beluga lentil, 24–25
    avocado & blood orange with quinoa, 28–29
    celery, 78–79
    cole slaw, Goldie's, 58–59
    corn, tomato, & cranberry bean, 96
    escarole with fennel & pears, 120–21
    fava bean, 125
    Fennel Tabbouleh, 128–29
    foraging for, 140
    herb with couscous, 142–43
    iceberg lettuce with marinated tomato, 154–55
    Jerusalem artichoke, sliced raw, 158–59
    kale & soy dressing, 166–67
    kohlrabi & toasted walnut, 170–71
    pickled onions & lentil, 214–15
    potato, 248–49
    radish with black bass, 257
    red cabbage with sweet potatoes, warm, 60
    snow pea, cherry & baby chard, 232–33
    sugar snap with quinoa, 228–29
    tomato & roasted peach, 302, 303
    upland cress with carrot dressing, 314–15

watermelon radish with ginger vinaigrette, 322
    zucchini, warm, 345
salmon with sorrel, 266
salsas
    chopping onions for, 209
    pepper, roasted tomatillo and, 294–95, 348
salsify
    about, 272
    carrots & glazed, 272–73
    in daikon kinpura, 106–7
    in potato dumplings, 246–47
salt-cured cucumbers, Japanese-style, 45, 100–101
sashimi, tomato, 298–99, 302
sauces
    cabbage & pork dumplings, 63
    cucumber-yogurt, 101
    liquids in, 302
    sesame, string beans with, 33
    sweet & sour rhubarb, 266–67
    tarragon, clams with scallion and, 276–77
    See also condiments; tomato sauce
saumon à l'oseille (salmon with sorrel), 266
scallions, 274–77
    about, 274
    in daikon kinpura, 106–7
    in mushroom hot pot, 192–93
    in pancakes, 274–75
    in potato salad, 248–49
    steamed clams & tarragon sauce with, 276–77
scallops, spinach & garlic puree with, 282–83
Scarlet Nantes carrots, 64
sea salt, favas with, 124
Seed Savers Exchange, 32
sesame oil, 21
sesame sauce, string beans with, 33
shakshouka, chard, 286–87
shallots, 278–79
    Parsnip & Kale Gratin, 222
    rutabaga gratin, 269
    sweet & sour, 278–79

shrimp
 cipollini stew and, *211, 216–17*
 pasta of tomato and, *302, 304–5*
skillets, *224*
Slater, Nigel, *30–31, 284, 312–13*
slicing
 asparagus, *25*
 corn off cob, *91*
 onions, *209*
 radishes, *258–59*
 workstation for, *65*
snow peas
 pea shoots with, *230*
 salad of cherries, baby chard and, *232–33*
 Vidalia onions with beans and, *318–19*
sorrel, salmon with, *266*
soups
 borscht, *42–43, 56*
 carrot with coconut milk, *68–69*
 celery root & chestnut, *84–85*
 chicken with celery & dill, *80–81*
 chilled corn with coconut milk, *93*
 chilled cucumber, *98–99*
 creamed cauliflower, *73*
 Jerusalem artichoke with monkfish, *161, 162–63*
 kale with potatoes & leeks, *7, 168–69*
 onion, *212–13*
 See also broth; stews; stocks
soy dressing, kale salad with, *166–67*
spaghetti, ramps and, *263, 264*
spaghetti squash, country ham with roasted, *328–29*
spinach, *280–85*
 about, *280*
 in asparagus with eggs, *22–23*
 blanching, *282, 283*
 in egg crepes, *211, 284–85*
 in mushroom hot pot, *192–93*
 in ramps & spaghetti, *264*
 scallops & garlic puree with, *282–83*
 washing, *281*

squash, varieties
 See also summer squash; winter squash; zucchini
  squash, varieties of, *307, 324*
squid
 about, *7*
 olive oil–poached, *334–35*
steak, chimichurri on, *144–45*
stews
 liquids in, *302*
 okra with tomatoes, *206–7*
 pepper, *237*
 ratatouille, *302, 346–47*
 root vegetables in horseradish beef broth, *148–49*
 shrimp & cipollini, *211, 216–17*
 turnip & squash with chicken, *7, 306–7*
 See also soups
stir-fry, bok choy, *46–47*
stocks
 corn, *92, 93*
 dashi, *106–7, 109, 162, 192–93*
 shrimp, *216*
 See also broth; soups
string beans
 with sesame sauce, *33*
 Vidalia onions with peas and, *318–19*
stuffing
 artichokes, *13*
 winter squash, *325*
sugar snap peas, *226*
 peeling, *228*
 in salad with quinoa, *228–29*
 Vidalia onions with beans and, *318–19*
summer squash
 fried zucchini blossoms with sautéed, *348–49*
 open "ravioli" of, *352–53*
 varieties of, *344*
 See also zucchini
sunchokes. *See* Jerusalem artichokes
Sun Gold tomato sauce, stuffed zucchini blossoms
  with, *350–51*

Index

Swede. *See* rutabaga
sweet potatoes
 about, *3, 340*
 baked fries, *340–41*
 horseradish compound butter with roasted, *150–51*
 in potato salad, *248–49*
 red cabbage salad with, *60*
Swiss chard, *286–89*
 in Bribery Pasta, *50–51*
 in carrots & farro, *72*
 salad of snow peas, cherries and, *232–33*
 sautéed, arancini, *288–89*
 in shakshouka, *286–87*
syrup, simple
 in carrot juice cocktail, *66*
 in snow pea, cherry & baby chard salad, *232*
 in tomato water cocktail, *297*

T

tabbouleh, fennel, *128–29*
tangerine vinaigrette, roasted whole leeks with, *178–79*
Tanis, David, *123*
tarragon
 in herb salad with couscous, *142–43*
 steamed clams with scallion and, *276–77*
tart
 dough for, *180, 182–83*
 onion & bacon, *210–11*
tartare, beet, *44–45*

tatsoi, *292–93*
 braised leeks & yellow lentils with, *177*
 matchstick radishes with sautéed, *292–93*
tea, ginger, *136*
tempura, lacy winter squash, *330–31*
thyme, in chimichurri on steak, *144*
tomatillo
 about, *294*
 pepper salsa & roasted, *294–95, 348*
tomatoes, *296–305*
 about, *3, 296*
 in asparagus with ginger relish, *21*
 black beans & mussels with, *36–37*
 in chard shakshouka, *286–87*
 in corn pancakes, *97*
 in eggplant casserole, *118–19*
 in fennel tabbouleh, *128*
 grilled iceberg lettuce with marinated, *154–55*
 in herb salad with couscous, *143*
 liquid for transforming, *302*
 in okra stew, *206–7*
 oven-dried plum, *207, 299, 352*
 pasta of shrimp and, *302, 304–5*
 in ratatouille, *347*
 roasted peach salad and, *302, 303*
 salad of corn, cranberry bean and, *96*
 in sashimi, *298–99, 302*
 in shrimp & cipollini stew, *216–17*
 in sweet & sour rhubarb sauce, *266–67*
 in tomato water cocktail, *297*
tomato sauce
 artichoke hearts with, *17, 352*
 in eggplant casserole, *118–19*
 My, *300–301, 302, 351*
 in okra stew, *207*
 in ratatouille, *347*
 stuffed zucchini blossoms with Sun Gold, *350–51*
 in tomato & shrimp pasta, *304–5*
trimming
 artichokes, *11, 18*

celery root, 82

trofie (pasta), 50

Troisgros, Jean and Pierre, 266

turnip greens, glazed hakurei turnips with, 272,
    308–9

turnips, 306–11
    about, 306–7
    Japanese fermented, 310–11
    in mushroom hot pot, 192–93
    in stew in horseradish beef broth, 148–49
    stew with squash, chicken and, 7, 306–7
    turnip & mustard greens with glazed hakurei,
        272, 308–9
    See also rutabaga

U

umami (savory flavor), 109, 299

upland cress
    about, 314
    in salad with carrot dressing, 314–15

V

vegetables, 1
    alphabet of, 3
    cooking with water, 92, 302

    fermenting, 310
    heirloom, 32, 296
    identifying, 2–3
    locally-grown, 2, 5
    olive oil–braised, 336–37
    peeling, 65
    sweating, 36

vegetarianism, 1

Vidalia onions
    about, 3, 318
    peas & beans with charred, 318–19

vinaigrette
    braised vegetables with, 336
    ginger, watermelon radish salad with, 322
    lemon, 14
    on snow pea, cherry & baby chard salad, 232
    tangerine, roasted whole leeks with, 178–79
    walnut, 170
    See also dressings

W

walnuts, 198
    in mashed potatoes, 200–201
    in quince mostarda, 252–53
    salad of kohlrabi & toasted, 170–71

washing
    greens, 281
    leeks, 179

water, cooking with, 92, 302

watermelon radish, 322–23
    about, 256, 322
    in salad with ginger vinaigrette, 322

Index

Waters, Alice, *256*, *270–71*
Weaver, William Woys, *338–39*
Whippoorwill cowpea, *32*
wild rice
    roasted squash with, *326–27*
    stuffed peppers with, *238–39*
winter squash, *324–31*
    about, *324*
    cauliflower curry with butternut, *74–75*
    country ham with roasted spaghetti, *328–29*
    cutting, *325*
    stew with turnip, chicken and, *7*, *306–7*
    stuffing, *325*
    tempura of lacy, *330–31*
    wild rice with roasted, *326–27*
wonton skins, *62*, *63*
workstation, setting up, *65*
Wroble, Jim, *90*, *132*

X

See olive oil, extra-virgin

Y

yams, *3*, *340–41*
    See also sweet potatoes
yogurt
    avocado, with lime mash, *26–27*
    sauce of cucumber and, *101*

Z

Zappa, Frank, *254–55*
zucchini, *344–46*
    open "ravioli" of, *352–53*
    poached squid with, *334–35*
    in ratatouille, *347*
    in shrimp & cipollini stew, *216–17*
    in warm salad, *345*
    See also summer squash
zucchini blossoms
    "ravioli" of summer squash and, *352*, *353*
    sautéed summer squash with fried, *348–49*
    sun gold tomato sauce with stuffed, *350–51*